FREE Study Skills Videos/DVD Offer

Dear Customer,

Thank you for your purchase from Mometrix! We consider it an honor and a privilege that you have purchased our product and we want to ensure your satisfaction.

As part of our ongoing effort to meet the needs of test takers, we have developed a set of Study Skills Videos that we would like to give you for FREE. These videos cover our *best practices* for getting ready for your exam, from how to use our study materials to how to best prepare for the day of the test.

All that we ask is that you email us with feedback that would describe your experience so far with our product. Good, bad, or indifferent, we want to know what you think!

To get your FREE Study Skills Videos, you can use the **QR code** below, or send us an **email** at studyvideos@mometrix.com with *FREE VIDEOS* in the subject line and the following information in the body of the email:

- The name of the product you purchased.
- Your product rating on a scale of 1-5, with 5 being the highest rating.
- Your feedback. It can be long, short, or anything in between. We just want to know your impressions and experience so far with our product. (Good feedback might include how our study material met your needs and ways we might be able to make it even better. You could highlight features that you found helpful or features that you think we should add.)

If you have any questions or concerns, please don't hesitate to contact me directly.

Thanks again!

Sincerely,

Jay Willis
Vice President
jay.willis@mometrix.com
1-800-673-8175

CSCS®

Exam Prep 2023 and 2024

2 Full-Length Practice Tests

Secrets Study Guide Book for the NSCA® Certified Strength and Conditioning Specialist® Assessment, Detailed Answer Explanations

2nd Edition

Copyright © 2022 by Mometrix Media LLC

All rights reserved. This product, or parts thereof, may not be reproduced, stored in a retrieval system, or transmitted in any form or by any means—electronic, mechanical, photocopy, recording, scanning, or other—except for brief quotations in critical reviews or articles, without the prior written permission of the publisher.

Written and edited by the Mometrix Test Prep

Printed in the United States of America

This paper meets the requirements of ANSI/NISO Z39.48-1992 (Permanence of Paper).

Mometrix offers volume discount pricing to institutions. For more information or a price quote, please contact our sales department at sales@mometrix.com or 888-248-1219.

Mometrix Media LLC is not affiliated with or endorsed by any official testing organization. All organizational and test names are trademarks of their respective owners.

Paperback
ISBN 13: 978-1-5167-2244-0
ISBN 10: 1-5167-2244-2

DEAR FUTURE EXAM SUCCESS STORY

First of all, **THANK YOU** for purchasing Mometrix study materials!

Second, congratulations! You are one of the few determined test-takers who are committed to doing whatever it takes to excel on your exam. **You have come to the right place.** We developed these study materials with one goal in mind: to deliver you the information you need in a format that's concise and easy to use.

In addition to optimizing your guide for the content of the test, we've outlined our recommended steps for breaking down the preparation process into small, attainable goals so you can make sure you stay on track.

We've also analyzed the entire test-taking process, identifying the most common pitfalls and showing how you can overcome them and be ready for any curveball the test throws you.

Standardized testing is one of the biggest obstacles on your road to success, which only increases the importance of doing well in the high-pressure, high-stakes environment of test day. Your results on this test could have a significant impact on your future, and this guide provides the information and practical advice to help you achieve your full potential on test day.

Your success is our success

We would love to hear from you! If you would like to share the story of your exam success or if you have any questions or comments in regard to our products, please contact us at **800-673-8175** or **support@mometrix.com**.

Thanks again for your business and we wish you continued success!

Sincerely,
The Mometrix Test Preparation Team

Need more help? Check out our flashcards at:
http://mometrixflashcards.com/CSCS

Copyright © 2022 by Mometrix Media LLC. All rights reserved.
Written and edited by the Mometrix Exam Secrets Test Prep Team
Printed in the United States of America

TABLE OF CONTENTS

Introduction

Thank you for purchasing this resource! You have made the choice to prepare yourself for a test that could have a huge impact on your future, and this guide is designed to help you be fully ready for test day. Obviously, it's important to have a solid understanding of the test material, but you also need to be prepared for the unique environment and stressors of the test, so that you can perform to the best of your abilities.

For this purpose, the first section that appears in this guide is the **Secret Keys**. We've devoted countless hours to meticulously researching what works and what doesn't, and we've boiled down our findings to the five most impactful steps you can take to improve your performance on the test. We start at the beginning with study planning and move through the preparation process, all the way to the testing strategies that will help you get the most out of what you know when you're finally sitting in front of the test.

We recommend that you start preparing for your test as far in advance as possible. However, if you've bought this guide as a last-minute study resource and only have a few days before your test, we recommend that you skip over the first two Secret Keys since they address a long-term study plan.

If you struggle with **test anxiety**, we strongly encourage you to check out our recommendations for how you can overcome it. Test anxiety is a formidable foe, but it can be beaten, and we want to make sure you have the tools you need to defeat it.

Copyright © Mometrix Media. You have been licensed one copy of this document for personal use only. Any other reproduction or redistribution is strictly prohibited. All rights reserved.
This content is provided for test preparation purposes only and does not imply an endorsement by Mometrix of any particular political, scientific, or religious point of view.

Secret Key #1 – Plan Big, Study Small

There's a lot riding on your performance. If you want to ace this test, you're going to need to keep your skills sharp and the material fresh in your mind. You need a plan that lets you review everything you need to know while still fitting in your schedule. We'll break this strategy down into three categories.

Information Organization

Start with the information you already have: the official test outline. From this, you can make a complete list of all the concepts you need to cover before the test. Organize these concepts into groups that can be studied together, and create a list of any related vocabulary you need to learn so you can brush up on any difficult terms. You'll want to keep this vocabulary list handy once you actually start studying since you may need to add to it along the way.

Time Management

Once you have your set of study concepts, decide how to spread them out over the time you have left before the test. Break your study plan into small, clear goals so you have a manageable task for each day and know exactly what you're doing. Then just focus on one small step at a time. When you manage your time this way, you don't need to spend hours at a time studying. Studying a small block of content for a short period each day helps you retain information better and avoid stressing over how much you have left to do. You can relax knowing that you have a plan to cover everything in time. In order for this strategy to be effective though, you have to start studying early and stick to your schedule. Avoid the exhaustion and futility that comes from last-minute cramming!

Study Environment

The environment you study in has a big impact on your learning. Studying in a coffee shop, while probably more enjoyable, is not likely to be as fruitful as studying in a quiet room. It's important to keep distractions to a minimum. You're only planning to study for a short block of time, so make the most of it. Don't pause to check your phone or get up to find a snack. It's also important to **avoid multitasking**. Research has consistently shown that multitasking will make your studying dramatically less effective. Your study area should also be comfortable and well-lit so you don't have the distraction of straining your eyes or sitting on an uncomfortable chair.

The time of day you study is also important. You want to be rested and alert. Don't wait until just before bedtime. Study when you'll be most likely to comprehend and remember. Even better, if you know what time of day your test will be, set that time aside for study. That way your brain will be used to working on that subject at that specific time and you'll have a better chance of recalling information.

Finally, it can be helpful to team up with others who are studying for the same test. Your actual studying should be done in as isolated an environment as possible, but the work of organizing the information and setting up the study plan can be divided up. In between study sessions, you can discuss with your teammates the concepts that you're all studying and quiz each other on the details. Just be sure that your teammates are as serious about the test as you are. If you find that your study time is being replaced with social time, you might need to find a new team.

Copyright © Mometrix Media. You have been licensed one copy of this document for personal use only. Any other reproduction or redistribution is strictly prohibited. All rights reserved.
This content is provided for test preparation purposes only and does not imply an endorsement by Mometrix of any particular political, scientific, or religious point of view.

Secret Key #2 – Make Your Studying Count

You're devoting a lot of time and effort to preparing for this test, so you want to be absolutely certain it will pay off. This means doing more than just reading the content and hoping you can remember it on test day. It's important to make every minute of study count. There are two main areas you can focus on to make your studying count.

Retention

It doesn't matter how much time you study if you can't remember the material. You need to make sure you are retaining the concepts. To check your retention of the information you're learning, try recalling it at later times with minimal prompting. Try carrying around flashcards and glance at one or two from time to time or ask a friend who's also studying for the test to quiz you.

To enhance your retention, look for ways to put the information into practice so that you can apply it rather than simply recalling it. If you're using the information in practical ways, it will be much easier to remember. Similarly, it helps to solidify a concept in your mind if you're not only reading it to yourself but also explaining it to someone else. Ask a friend to let you teach them about a concept you're a little shaky on (or speak aloud to an imaginary audience if necessary). As you try to summarize, define, give examples, and answer your friend's questions, you'll understand the concepts better and they will stay with you longer. Finally, step back for a big picture view and ask yourself how each piece of information fits with the whole subject. When you link the different concepts together and see them working together as a whole, it's easier to remember the individual components.

Finally, practice showing your work on any multi-step problems, even if you're just studying. Writing out each step you take to solve a problem will help solidify the process in your mind, and you'll be more likely to remember it during the test.

Modality

Modality simply refers to the means or method by which you study. Choosing a study modality that fits your own individual learning style is crucial. No two people learn best in exactly the same way, so it's important to know your strengths and use them to your advantage.

For example, if you learn best by visualization, focus on visualizing a concept in your mind and draw an image or a diagram. Try color-coding your notes, illustrating them, or creating symbols that will trigger your mind to recall a learned concept. If you learn best by hearing or discussing information, find a study partner who learns the same way or read aloud to yourself. Think about how to put the information in your own words. Imagine that you are giving a lecture on the topic and record yourself so you can listen to it later.

For any learning style, flashcards can be helpful. Organize the information so you can take advantage of spare moments to review. Underline key words or phrases. Use different colors for different categories. Mnemonic devices (such as creating a short list in which every item starts with the same letter) can also help with retention. Find what works best for you and use it to store the information in your mind most effectively and easily.

Copyright © Mometrix Media. You have been licensed one copy of this document for personal use only. Any other reproduction or redistribution is strictly prohibited. All rights reserved.
This content is provided for test preparation purposes only and does not imply an endorsement by Mometrix of any particular political, scientific, or religious point of view.

Secret Key #3 – Practice the Right Way

Your success on test day depends not only on how many hours you put into preparing, but also on whether you prepared the right way. It's good to check along the way to see if your studying is paying off. One of the most effective ways to do this is by taking practice tests to evaluate your progress. Practice tests are useful because they show exactly where you need to improve. Every time you take a practice test, pay special attention to these three groups of questions:

- The questions you got wrong
- The questions you had to guess on, even if you guessed right
- The questions you found difficult or slow to work through

This will show you exactly what your weak areas are, and where you need to devote more study time. Ask yourself why each of these questions gave you trouble. Was it because you didn't understand the material? Was it because you didn't remember the vocabulary? Do you need more repetitions on this type of question to build speed and confidence? Dig into those questions and figure out how you can strengthen your weak areas as you go back to review the material.

Additionally, many practice tests have a section explaining the answer choices. It can be tempting to read the explanation and think that you now have a good understanding of the concept. However, an explanation likely only covers part of the question's broader context. Even if the explanation makes perfect sense, **go back and investigate** every concept related to the question until you're positive you have a thorough understanding.

As you go along, keep in mind that the practice test is just that: practice. Memorizing these questions and answers will not be very helpful on the actual test because it is unlikely to have any of the same exact questions. If you only know the right answers to the sample questions, you won't be prepared for the real thing. **Study the concepts** until you understand them fully, and then you'll be able to answer any question that shows up on the test.

It's important to wait on the practice tests until you're ready. If you take a test on your first day of study, you may be overwhelmed by the amount of material covered and how much you need to learn. Work up to it gradually.

On test day, you'll need to be prepared for answering questions, managing your time, and using the test-taking strategies you've learned. It's a lot to balance, like a mental marathon that will have a big impact on your future. Like training for a marathon, you'll need to start slowly and work your way up. When test day arrives, you'll be ready.

Start with the strategies you've read in the first two Secret Keys—plan your course and study in the way that works best for you. If you have time, consider using multiple study resources to get different approaches to the same concepts. It can be helpful to see difficult concepts from more than one angle. Then find a good source for practice tests. Many times, the test website will suggest potential study resources or provide sample tests.

Copyright © Mometrix Media. You have been licensed one copy of this document for personal use only. Any other reproduction or redistribution is strictly prohibited. All rights reserved.
This content is provided for test preparation purposes only and does not imply an endorsement by Mometrix of any particular political, scientific, or religious point of view.

Practice Test Strategy

If you're able to find at least three practice tests, we recommend this strategy:

Untimed and Open-Book Practice

Take the first test with no time constraints and with your notes and study guide handy. Take your time and focus on applying the strategies you've learned.

Timed and Open-Book Practice

Take the second practice test open-book as well, but set a timer and practice pacing yourself to finish in time.

Timed and Closed-Book Practice

Take any other practice tests as if it were test day. Set a timer and put away your study materials. Sit at a table or desk in a quiet room, imagine yourself at the testing center, and answer questions as quickly and accurately as possible.

Keep repeating timed and closed-book tests on a regular basis until you run out of practice tests or it's time for the actual test. Your mind will be ready for the schedule and stress of test day, and you'll be able to focus on recalling the material you've learned.

Copyright © Mometrix Media. You have been licensed one copy of this document for personal use only. Any other reproduction or redistribution is strictly prohibited. All rights reserved.
This content is provided for test preparation purposes only and does not imply an endorsement by Mometrix of any particular political, scientific, or religious point of view.

Secret Key #4 – Pace Yourself

Once you're fully prepared for the material on the test, your biggest challenge on test day will be managing your time. Just knowing that the clock is ticking can make you panic even if you have plenty of time left. Work on pacing yourself so you can build confidence against the time constraints of the exam. Pacing is a difficult skill to master, especially in a high-pressure environment, so **practice is vital**.

Set time expectations for your pace based on how much time is available. For example, if a section has 60 questions and the time limit is 30 minutes, you know you have to average 30 seconds or less per question in order to answer them all. Although 30 seconds is the hard limit, set 25 seconds per question as your goal, so you reserve extra time to spend on harder questions. When you budget extra time for the harder questions, you no longer have any reason to stress when those questions take longer to answer.

Don't let this time expectation distract you from working through the test at a calm, steady pace, but keep it in mind so you don't spend too much time on any one question. Recognize that taking extra time on one question you don't understand may keep you from answering two that you do understand later in the test. If your time limit for a question is up and you're still not sure of the answer, mark it and move on, and come back to it later if the time and the test format allow. If the testing format doesn't allow you to return to earlier questions, just make an educated guess; then put it out of your mind and move on.

On the easier questions, be careful not to rush. It may seem wise to hurry through them so you have more time for the challenging ones, but it's not worth missing one if you know the concept and just didn't take the time to read the question fully. Work efficiently but make sure you understand the question and have looked at all of the answer choices, since more than one may seem right at first.

Even if you're paying attention to the time, you may find yourself a little behind at some point. You should speed up to get back on track, but do so wisely. Don't panic; just take a few seconds less on each question until you're caught up. Don't guess without thinking, but do look through the answer choices and eliminate any you know are wrong. If you can get down to two choices, it is often worthwhile to guess from those. Once you've chosen an answer, move on and don't dwell on any that you skipped or had to hurry through. If a question was taking too long, chances are it was one of the harder ones, so you weren't as likely to get it right anyway.

On the other hand, if you find yourself getting ahead of schedule, it may be beneficial to slow down a little. The more quickly you work, the more likely you are to make a careless mistake that will affect your score. You've budgeted time for each question, so don't be afraid to spend that time. Practice an efficient but careful pace to get the most out of the time you have.

Copyright © Mometrix Media. You have been licensed one copy of this document for personal use only. Any other reproduction or redistribution is strictly prohibited. All rights reserved.
This content is provided for test preparation purposes only and does not imply an endorsement by Mometrix of any particular political, scientific, or religious point of view.

Secret Key #5 – Have a Plan for Guessing

When you're taking the test, you may find yourself stuck on a question. Some of the answer choices seem better than others, but you don't see the one answer choice that is obviously correct. What do you do?

The scenario described above is very common, yet most test takers have not effectively prepared for it. Developing and practicing a plan for guessing may be one of the single most effective uses of your time as you get ready for the exam.

In developing your plan for guessing, there are three questions to address:

- When should you start the guessing process?
- How should you narrow down the choices?
- Which answer should you choose?

When to Start the Guessing Process

Unless your plan for guessing is to select C every time (which, despite its merits, is not what we recommend), you need to leave yourself enough time to apply your answer elimination strategies. Since you have a limited amount of time for each question, that means that if you're going to give yourself the best shot at guessing correctly, you have to decide quickly whether or not you will guess.

Of course, the best-case scenario is that you don't have to guess at all, so first, see if you can answer the question based on your knowledge of the subject and basic reasoning skills. Focus on the key words in the question and try to jog your memory of related topics. Give yourself a chance to bring the knowledge to mind, but once you realize that you don't have (or you can't access) the knowledge you need to answer the question, it's time to start the guessing process.

It's almost always better to start the guessing process too early than too late. It only takes a few seconds to remember something and answer the question from knowledge. Carefully eliminating wrong answer choices takes longer. Plus, going through the process of eliminating answer choices can actually help jog your memory.

Summary: Start the guessing process as soon as you decide that you can't answer the question based on your knowledge.

Copyright © Mometrix Media. You have been licensed one copy of this document for personal use only. Any other reproduction or redistribution is strictly prohibited. All rights reserved.
This content is provided for test preparation purposes only and does not imply an endorsement by Mometrix of any particular political, scientific, or religious point of view.

How to Narrow Down the Choices

The next chapter in this book (**Test-Taking Strategies**) includes a wide range of strategies for how to approach questions and how to look for answer choices to eliminate. You will definitely want to read those carefully, practice them, and figure out which ones work best for you. Here though, we're going to address a mindset rather than a particular strategy.

Your odds of guessing an answer correctly depend on how many options you are choosing from.

Number of options left	5	4	3	2	1
Odds of guessing correctly	20%	25%	33%	50%	100%

You can see from this chart just how valuable it is to be able to eliminate incorrect answers and make an educated guess, but there are two things that many test takers do that cause them to miss out on the benefits of guessing:

- Accidentally eliminating the correct answer
- Selecting an answer based on an impression

We'll look at the first one here, and the second one in the next section.

To avoid accidentally eliminating the correct answer, we recommend a thought exercise called **the $5 challenge**. In this challenge, you only eliminate an answer choice from contention if you are willing to bet $5 on it being wrong. Why $5? Five dollars is a small but not insignificant amount of money. It's an amount you could afford to lose but wouldn't want to throw away. And while losing $5 once might not hurt too much, doing it twenty times will set you back $100. In the same way, each small decision you make—eliminating a choice here, guessing on a question there—won't by itself impact your score very much, but when you put them all together, they can make a big difference. By holding each answer choice elimination decision to a higher standard, you can reduce the risk of accidentally eliminating the correct answer.

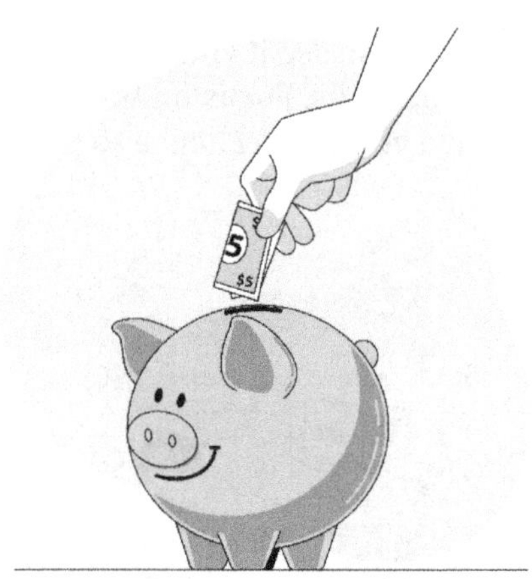

The $5 challenge can also be applied in a positive sense: If you are willing to bet $5 that an answer choice *is* correct, go ahead and mark it as correct.

Summary: Only eliminate an answer choice if you are willing to bet $5 that it is wrong.

Copyright © Mometrix Media. You have been licensed one copy of this document for personal use only. Any other reproduction or redistribution is strictly prohibited. All rights reserved.
This content is provided for test preparation purposes only and does not imply an endorsement by Mometrix of any particular political, scientific, or religious point of view.

Which Answer to Choose

You're taking the test. You've run into a hard question and decided you'll have to guess. You've eliminated all the answer choices you're willing to bet $5 on. Now you have to pick an answer. Why do we even need to talk about this? Why can't you just pick whichever one you feel like when the time comes?

The answer to these questions is that if you don't come into the test with a plan, you'll rely on your impression to select an answer choice, and if you do that, you risk falling into a trap. The test writers know that everyone who takes their test will be guessing on some of the questions, so they intentionally write wrong answer choices to seem plausible. You still have to pick an answer though, and if the wrong answer choices are designed to look right, how can you ever be sure that you're not falling for their trap? The best solution we've found to this dilemma is to take the decision out of your hands entirely. Here is the process we recommend:

Once you've eliminated any choices that you are confident (willing to bet $5) are wrong, select the first remaining choice as your answer.

Whether you choose to select the first remaining choice, the second, or the last, the important thing is that you use some preselected standard. Using this approach guarantees that you will not be enticed into selecting an answer choice that looks right, because you are not basing your decision on how the answer choices look.

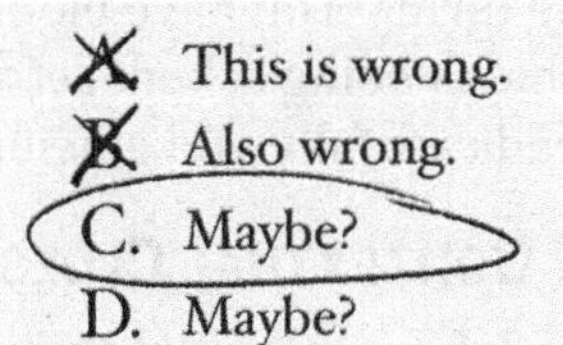

This is not meant to make you question your knowledge. Instead, it is to help you recognize the difference between your knowledge and your impressions. There's a huge difference between thinking an answer is right because of what you know, and thinking an answer is right because it looks or sounds like it should be right.

Summary: To ensure that your selection is appropriately random, make a predetermined selection from among all answer choices you have not eliminated.

Copyright © Mometrix Media. You have been licensed one copy of this document for personal use only. Any other reproduction or redistribution is strictly prohibited. All rights reserved.
This content is provided for test preparation purposes only and does not imply an endorsement by Mometrix of any particular political, scientific, or religious point of view.

Test-Taking Strategies

This section contains a list of test-taking strategies that you may find helpful as you work through the test. By taking what you know and applying logical thought, you can maximize your chances of answering any question correctly!

It is very important to realize that every question is different and every person is different: no single strategy will work on every question, and no single strategy will work for every person. That's why we've included all of them here, so you can try them out and determine which ones work best for different types of questions and which ones work best for you.

Question Strategies

⊘ Read Carefully

Read the question and the answer choices carefully. Don't miss the question because you misread the terms. You have plenty of time to read each question thoroughly and make sure you understand what is being asked. Yet a happy medium must be attained, so don't waste too much time. You must read carefully and efficiently.

⊘ Contextual Clues

Look for contextual clues. If the question includes a word you are not familiar with, look at the immediate context for some indication of what the word might mean. Contextual clues can often give you all the information you need to decipher the meaning of an unfamiliar word. Even if you can't determine the meaning, you may be able to narrow down the possibilities enough to make a solid guess at the answer to the question.

⊘ Prefixes

If you're having trouble with a word in the question or answer choices, try dissecting it. Take advantage of every clue that the word might include. Prefixes can be a huge help. Usually, they allow you to determine a basic meaning. *Pre-* means before, *post-* means after, *pro-* is positive, *de-* is negative. From prefixes, you can get an idea of the general meaning of the word and try to put it into context.

⊘ Hedge Words

Watch out for critical hedge words, such as *likely, may, can, sometimes, often, almost, mostly, usually, generally, rarely,* and *sometimes.* Question writers insert these hedge phrases to cover every possibility. Often an answer choice will be wrong simply because it leaves no room for exception. Be on guard for answer choices that have definitive words such as *exactly* and *always.*

⊘ Switchback Words

Stay alert for *switchbacks.* These are the words and phrases frequently used to alert you to shifts in thought. The most common switchback words are *but, although,* and *however.* Others include *nevertheless, on the other hand, even though, while, in spite of, despite,* and *regardless of.* Switchback words are important to catch because they can change the direction of the question or an answer choice.

Copyright © Mometrix Media. You have been licensed one copy of this document for personal use only. Any other reproduction or redistribution is strictly prohibited. All rights reserved.
This content is provided for test preparation purposes only and does not imply an endorsement by Mometrix of any particular political, scientific, or religious point of view.

☑ Face Value

When in doubt, use common sense. Accept the situation in the problem at face value. Don't read too much into it. These problems will not require you to make wild assumptions. If you have to go beyond creativity and warp time or space in order to have an answer choice fit the question, then you should move on and consider the other answer choices. These are normal problems rooted in reality. The applicable relationship or explanation may not be readily apparent, but it is there for you to figure out. Use your common sense to interpret anything that isn't clear.

Answer Choice Strategies

☑ Answer Selection

The most thorough way to pick an answer choice is to identify and eliminate wrong answers until only one is left, then confirm it is the correct answer. Sometimes an answer choice may immediately seem right, but be careful. The test writers will usually put more than one reasonable answer choice on each question, so take a second to read all of them and make sure that the other choices are not equally obvious. As long as you have time left, it is better to read every answer choice than to pick the first one that looks right without checking the others.

☑ Answer Choice Families

An answer choice family consists of two (in rare cases, three) answer choices that are very similar in construction and cannot all be true at the same time. If you see two answer choices that are direct opposites or parallels, one of them is usually the correct answer. For instance, if one answer choice says that quantity *x* increases and another either says that quantity *x* decreases (opposite) or says that quantity *y* increases (parallel), then those answer choices would fall into the same family. An answer choice that doesn't match the construction of the answer choice family is more likely to be incorrect. Most questions will not have answer choice families, but when they do appear, you should be prepared to recognize them.

☑ Eliminate Answers

Eliminate answer choices as soon as you realize they are wrong, but make sure you consider all possibilities. If you are eliminating answer choices and realize that the last one you are left with is also wrong, don't panic. Start over and consider each choice again. There may be something you missed the first time that you will realize on the second pass.

☑ Avoid Fact Traps

Don't be distracted by an answer choice that is factually true but doesn't answer the question. You are looking for the choice that answers the question. Stay focused on what the question is asking for so you don't accidentally pick an answer that is true but incorrect. Always go back to the question and make sure the answer choice you've selected actually answers the question and is not merely a true statement.

☑ Extreme Statements

In general, you should avoid answers that put forth extreme actions as standard practice or proclaim controversial ideas as established fact. An answer choice that states the "process should be used in certain situations, if..." is much more likely to be correct than one that states the "process should be discontinued completely." The first is a calm rational statement and doesn't even make a definitive, uncompromising stance, using a hedge word *if* to provide wiggle room, whereas the second choice is far more extreme.

Copyright © Mometrix Media. You have been licensed one copy of this document for personal use only. Any other reproduction or redistribution is strictly prohibited. All rights reserved.
This content is provided for test preparation purposes only and does not imply an endorsement by Mometrix of any particular political, scientific, or religious point of view.

☑ Benchmark

As you read through the answer choices and you come across one that seems to answer the question well, mentally select that answer choice. This is not your final answer, but it's the one that will help you evaluate the other answer choices. The one that you selected is your benchmark or standard for judging each of the other answer choices. Every other answer choice must be compared to your benchmark. That choice is correct until proven otherwise by another answer choice beating it. If you find a better answer, then that one becomes your new benchmark. Once you've decided that no other choice answers the question as well as your benchmark, you have your final answer.

☑ Predict the Answer

Before you even start looking at the answer choices, it is often best to try to predict the answer. When you come up with the answer on your own, it is easier to avoid distractions and traps because you will know exactly what to look for. The right answer choice is unlikely to be word-for-word what you came up with, but it should be a close match. Even if you are confident that you have the right answer, you should still take the time to read each option before moving on.

General Strategies

☑ Tough Questions

If you are stumped on a problem or it appears too hard or too difficult, don't waste time. Move on! Remember though, if you can quickly check for obviously incorrect answer choices, your chances of guessing correctly are greatly improved. Before you completely give up, at least try to knock out a couple of possible answers. Eliminate what you can and then guess at the remaining answer choices before moving on.

☑ Check Your Work

Since you will probably not know every term listed and the answer to every question, it is important that you get credit for the ones that you do know. Don't miss any questions through careless mistakes. If at all possible, try to take a second to look back over your answer selection and make sure you've selected the correct answer choice and haven't made a costly careless mistake (such as marking an answer choice that you didn't mean to mark). This quick double check should more than pay for itself in caught mistakes for the time it costs.

☑ Pace Yourself

It's easy to be overwhelmed when you're looking at a page full of questions; your mind is confused and full of random thoughts, and the clock is ticking down faster than you would like. Calm down and maintain the pace that you have set for yourself. Especially as you get down to the last few minutes of the test, don't let the small numbers on the clock make you panic. As long as you are on track by monitoring your pace, you are guaranteed to have time for each question.

☑ Don't Rush

It is very easy to make errors when you are in a hurry. Maintaining a fast pace in answering questions is pointless if it makes you miss questions that you would have gotten right otherwise. Test writers like to include distracting information and wrong answers that seem right. Taking a little extra time to avoid careless mistakes can make all the difference in your test score. Find a pace that allows you to be confident in the answers that you select.

Copyright © Mometrix Media. You have been licensed one copy of this document for personal use only. Any other reproduction or redistribution is strictly prohibited. All rights reserved.
This content is provided for test preparation purposes only and does not imply an endorsement by Mometrix of any particular political, scientific, or religious point of view.

✓ Keep Moving

Panicking will not help you pass the test, so do your best to stay calm and keep moving. Taking deep breaths and going through the answer elimination steps you practiced can help to break through a stress barrier and keep your pace.

Final Notes

The combination of a solid foundation of content knowledge and the confidence that comes from practicing your plan for applying that knowledge is the key to maximizing your performance on test day. As your foundation of content knowledge is built up and strengthened, you'll find that the strategies included in this chapter become more and more effective in helping you quickly sift through the distractions and traps of the test to isolate the correct answer.

Now that you're preparing to move forward into the test content chapters of this book, be sure to keep your goal in mind. As you read, think about how you will be able to apply this information on the test. If you've already seen sample questions for the test and you have an idea of the question format and style, try to come up with questions of your own that you can answer based on what you're reading. This will give you valuable practice applying your knowledge in the same ways you can expect to on test day.

Good luck and good studying!

Copyright © Mometrix Media. You have been licensed one copy of this document for personal use only. Any other reproduction or redistribution is strictly prohibited. All rights reserved.
This content is provided for test preparation purposes only and does not imply an endorsement by Mometrix of any particular political, scientific, or religious point of view.

Copyright © Mometrix Media. You have been licensed one copy of this document for personal use only. Any other reproduction or redistribution is strictly prohibited. All rights reserved.
This content is provided for test preparation purposes only and does not imply an endorsement by Mometrix of any particular political, scientific, or religious point of view.

Exercise Science

Tendon

A tendon is fibrous connective tissue made primarily of collagen that connects muscle to bone via the bone periosteum. The tendon bridges the muscle and bone together in order to produce movement.

Muscle Fiber

Muscle fibers are generally long, multi-nucleated and striated myocytes that are bundled together to form fasciculi. These bundles may consist of up to 150 individual strands that are covered by connective tissue (perimysium). There are numerous muscle fiber types that have been identified in the human body. Most important to the strength and conditioning coach are the type I, type IIa, and type IIb fibers. The type I fibers are slow oxidative fibers, are "slow-twitch," are primarily engaged during long duration activities as these fibers produce low levels of force, and are fatigue resistant. Type IIa fibers are considered fast oxidative and glycolytic, are "fast twitch," produce medium amounts of force, and are highly fatigue resistant. Type IIb are considered fast glycolytic, are "fast twitch," produce large amounts of force, and are rapidly fatigued.

Sarcoplasm

The sarcoplasm of a muscle fiber is analogous to the cytoplasm of other organisms, as this is where essential elements of muscular contraction are located such as glycogen, fat, various enzymes, mitochondria, and the sarcoplasmic reticulum.

Myofibrils

Myofibrils are the internal structure of the muscle fiber (myocyte), and contain the long, thin chains of protein responsible for contraction of the muscle fiber. Myofibrils are composed of long strands of the proteins actin, myosin, and titin. These proteins are arranged along the myofibril into thick and thin filaments, which are arranged into compartments known as sarcomeres. Muscle contraction takes place all along the myofibril as the actin filaments (also referred to as thin filaments) slide along the length of the myosin (also referred to as thick filaments) generating muscular contractions.

Myofilament

Myofilaments are the long, thin chains of protein that comprise the myofibril. The three different kinds of muscle are smooth muscle, obliquely striated muscle and striated muscle. Striated muscle tissue contains two types of myofilaments, actin and myosin.

Sarcomere

The sarcomere is the basic unit of a muscle fiber and is the area in which the contractile proteins actin and myosin are can be found. The sarcomere provides the striated appearance of skeletal and cardiac muscle, and is defined as the area occurring between two z-lines. Sarcomeres occur throughout the entire length of a muscle fiber, and can be thought of as the location of where all muscular contractions take place.

A sarcomere can be divided into four different segments: the A-band, H-zone, I-band, and Z-line. The A-band is the segment where both actin and myosin filaments are located. The H-zone is a part of the A-band located in the center of the sarcomere where only myosin filaments occur. The I-band

Copyright © Mometrix Media. You have been licensed one copy of this document for personal use only. Any other reproduction or redistribution is strictly prohibited. All rights reserved.
This content is provided for test preparation purposes only and does not imply an endorsement by Mometrix of any particular political, scientific, or religious point of view.

is an area that only consists of thin filaments, and is made of two contiguous sarcomeres. The Z-line occurs in the middle of the I-band and appears as a line running lengthwise throughout.

Sarcoplasmic Reticulum

The sarcoplasmic reticulum is a system of tubules surrounding each myofibril, and is responsible for pumping Ca^{+} ions into the muscle when an action potential has been released onto the sarcomere. The sarcoplasmic reticulum is responsible for pumping calcium ions into the muscle in order to generate a contraction, but is also the site of calcium ion storage. Without these essential functions, muscular contraction would not occur.

Sarcolemma

The sarcolemma is the cell membrane of striated muscle tissue, and is responsible for the separation of each individual muscle fiber. The sarcolemma is essential in conducting and receiving stimuli from the connecting nerve fibers. The ability of the sarcolemma to transduce an electrical signal allows the t-tubules that run from side-to-side throughout the sarcolemma to release Ca^{2+} ions into the sarcoplasm.

Protein Myosin

Myosin is the thicker myofilament and is responsible for cross-linking to actin filaments to produce the shortening of the sarcomere, resulting in muscular contraction. The myosin fiber is also the site of ATP hydrolysis. Once the phosphate has been released onto the myosin fiber, the energy required for the cross-linking between actin and myosin is available and the power stroke of muscular contraction will occur. Once the energy substrate has caused a conformational change and contraction has occurred, the cycle has completed, and with continued contraction stimulus, along with the availability of additional ATP, the myosin will unbind from the current actin fiber and bind with the next available actin molecule, causing shortening of the sarcomere. This cycle will continue as long as contraction stimulus and energy substrate are available.

Actin

Actin is the thin filament, arranged in a double helix shape, and serves as the binding site for myosin that, with the hydrolysis of ATP, generates a power stroke where the actin will slide past the myosin filament.

Role in Muscular Contraction

Actin is one of two myofilaments involved in muscular contraction. Actin is the primary binding site for the motor filament myosin, and once this binding takes place, the actin fiber will slide over the myosin fiber.

Sliding Filament Theory

The sliding filament theory is a brief overview of muscular contraction that outlines a series of repetitive events that cause a thin filament (actin) to slide over a thick filament (myosin) that causes a muscle to generate tension and movement.

All-or-None Principle

The all-or-none principle refers to the complete muscular contraction that takes place after an action potential has been released onto the sarcolemma of a muscle. This principle states that, once there is no variation in the signal strength associated with an action potential, the resultant reaction will not vary. Either there is a stimulus and a response, or there is nothing.

Copyright © Mometrix Media. You have been licensed one copy of this document for personal use only. Any other reproduction or redistribution is strictly prohibited. All rights reserved.
This content is provided for test preparation purposes only and does not imply an endorsement by Mometrix of any particular political, scientific, or religious point of view.

Neuromuscular Junction

The neuromuscular junction is the central communication point for the nervous and musculoskeletal systems that leads to muscular contraction. This is the translation point where the nervous system signal (electrical) is converted into a biochemical reaction and then into movement (mechanical).

Motor Neuron

A motor neuron is located in the central nervous system and is responsible for transmitting signals from the spinal cord to the muscles in order to produce muscular contraction. The motor neuron is the site of the release of an action potential into the neuromuscular junction.

Action Potential

An action potential is an electrical impulse that is triggered by the rapid depolarization of the cell membrane of a neuron. The action potential sets in motion a specific series of events, such as the release of calcium ions onto the sarcomere of a muscle fiber, and ultimately ends with the contraction of a muscle.

Tropomyosin

During muscular contraction, a chemical cascade takes place that causes a conformational change in tropomyosin that allows for the myosin filament to bind with the actin filament. In a relaxed state, the head of the tropomyosin wraps helically around troponin on the actin filament, thereby preventing the formation of the myosin cross bridge.

Troponin

Troponin is continuous throughout an actin fiber. Troponin is responsible for initiating the movement of tropomyosin from the myosin binding site after Ca+ has initiated a conformational change. Once this occurs, the myosin cross bridge can be carried out and muscular contraction can occur.

Acetylcholine

Acetylcholine is the primary neurotransmitter involved in muscular contraction. Once an action potential is released and arrives at a nerve terminal, acetylcholine is released from the nerve terminal and diffuses across the neuromuscular junction, causing excitation of the sarcolemma. After enough acetylcholine has been released, an action potential is released across the sarcolemma and a muscular contraction occurs.

Golgi Tendon Organs

Golgi tendon organs (GTO) are responsible for inhibiting tension overload in muscle and tendons when placed under stretch. The GTO achieves this by emitting electrical signals from its sensory neuron to an inhibitory neuron in the spinal cord, which inhibits the motor neuron in the same muscle. This signaling process is very rapid and leads to an immediate reduction in tension within the muscle, preventing excessive loading injuries and even reactive stress injuries.

Sympathetic Nervous System

The sympathetic nervous system is one of three separate branches of the autonomic nervous system, which includes the parasympathetic and the enteric systems. The sympathetic nervous system is responsible for the "fight or flight" response in humans, as this response causes a release of adrenaline and norepinephrine which causes increased rate of respiration, elevates heart rate, raises mental focus, increases body temperature, etc. This system is of key importance in the

Copyright © Mometrix Media. You have been licensed one copy of this document for personal use only. Any other reproduction or redistribution is strictly prohibited. All rights reserved.
This content is provided for test preparation purposes only and does not imply an endorsement by Mometrix of any particular political, scientific, or religious point of view.

preparation for competition as strength and conditioning coaches must maintain a high level of activity, increase performance, and develop specific work capacities for competition without overworking the sympathetic and central nervous systems.

Parasympathetic Nervous System

The parasympathetic nervous system is responsible for relaxation, or periods of decreased activity levels which governs various passive activities such as digestion. A high activity level in this division of the autonomic nervous system would be detrimental to competition because this system regulates mental acuity, focus, heart rate, and other physiological processes that need to be at heightened activity levels in order to respond to the competitive environment.

Antagonist Muscle Action

A muscle that is acting as an antagonist during a movement is performing a protective action, as the antagonist muscle groups are working to decelerate a force acting on the body, while also stabilizing the working joints. An example of an antagonist muscle action during movement is the resistive action of the hamstring during any squatting movement.

Agonist Muscle Action

A muscle, or multiple muscle groups, that is primarily responsible for generating the force to produce a movement is called the agonist. In sprinting the primary muscles that propel the body forward include the hip flexors, quadriceps, glutes, and hamstrings.

Synergist Muscles

A muscle that is acting as a synergist during a movement is acting to either stabilize the agonists as force is produced or indirectly assist in force production. In a barbell curl, there are multiple synergists engaged in the movement, assisting in the muscular contraction are the brachialis and brachioradialis muscles, but there are stabilizing muscles along the scapula that work to maintain structural and force integrity at the humerus and the scapula.

Lever

A lever is a machine that allows for a force to be produced about a fixed point, or pivot, and will increase the amount of force that is produced through this arrangement (leverage). A first class lever in human mechanics requires the muscle and resistive forces to be applied on opposite sides of the fulcrum. A second class lever in human mechanics requires muscular and resistive forces to occur on the same side of the fulcrum. A third class lever in human mechanics requires that the muscular and resistive forces act on the same side of the fulcrum through a distance shorter than the distance through which the resistive force is acting.

Fulcrum

A fulcrum is a simple point of rotation for a lever. In human mechanics, the fulcrum is more significant with regards to total force production than determining the levers involved. Consider that placement of the fulcrum will dictate the length of the moment arm, which dictates the total force required to overcome the resistive force. Fulcrum position determines the mechanical advantage.

Moment Arm

A moment arm is the distance from a muscle's line of action to the joint's center of rotation, and is oriented in the direction of the force being produced. An example of a moment arm in movement would be the humerus and biceps acting on the resistive force of a dumbbell during a biceps curl.

Copyright © Mometrix Media. You have been licensed one copy of this document for personal use only. Any other reproduction or redistribution is strictly prohibited. All rights reserved.
This content is provided for test preparation purposes only and does not imply an endorsement by Mometrix of any particular political, scientific, or religious point of view.

Torque

Torque is the capacity of a force to generate rotation on a fulcrum. Increasing the rate of torque produced during specific activities is dependent on rate of force production and this will require a range of training interventions including speed/acceleration training segments along with higher loading intensities in order to maximize torque production

Muscular Force

Muscular force is a mechanical reaction to biochemical stimuli or the response of an uncontrolled reaction in noncontractile tissues, i.e., excessive ligament or tendon stretching. Muscular force is the means in producing adequate forces required to produce a wide range of locomotion which includes low-velocity activities such as walking or typing on a keyboard to high-velocity movements such as sprinting or jumping.

Resistive Force

Resistive force refers to an external resistance acting on the body that is acting in opposition to the muscle forces. Resistive forces acting on the body are negative forces, as this includes the force of gravity ($-9.8\ m/s^2$) as well as static and kinetic frictions during activities such as running, swimming, or jumping.

Sagittal Plane

The sagittal plane is the plane that passes through the posterior and anterior aspects of the body, and divides the body into left and right halves. Leg extensions and biceps curls are examples of movements that occur in the sagittal plane.

Transverse Plane

The transverse plane is the plane that divides the body into superior and inferior aspects. Movements that occur in this plane can occur in front of or in the rear of an athlete, and include traditional and reverse lunges for the lower body as well as a dumbbell fly for the upper body.

Frontal Plane

The frontal plane, also called the coronal plane, divides the body into ventral (front) and dorsal (back) aspects. Movements that can occur in this plane include pull-ups, dips, and squats.

Mechanical Advantage

A mechanical advantage is simply a type of leverage that allows for greater work to be performed. Mechanical advantages for an athlete can assist in developing the athlete maximally by increasing the rate of progress. This can also be detrimental to a degree as an athlete or coach may overlook the development of weaknesses by overemphasizing development of the mechanical advantage.

Power

Power is defined as the average amount of work done per unit time ($P = W/T$). With regards to weight training, power and strength differentiate in one key area: time. Power is the ability to produce as much force as possible as quickly as possible. Strength is the ability to produce as much force as possible without regard for the amount of time needed to produce that force. Total force is the product of force and velocity at a specific speed, while strength is the capacity to produce force at any given speed.

Copyright © Mometrix Media. You have been licensed one copy of this document for personal use only. Any other reproduction or redistribution is strictly prohibited. All rights reserved.
This content is provided for test preparation purposes only and does not imply an endorsement by Mometrix of any particular political, scientific, or religious point of view.

Work

In physical terms, work is defined as the product of the application of force on an object and the distance the object is displaced in the direction the force is applied. Quantifying the training volume, in terms of physical work, an athlete engages in daily, weekly, or over the course of an entire training program provides significant insight into how the athlete handles varying levels of volume, loading intensity, and specific movement patterns. Quantifying work for conditioning periods is useful in the same manner, and is very helpful when working with larger athletes as the amount of work performed may be considerably higher for a larger athlete than a smaller athlete simply because of the size differential.

Force-Velocity Curve

The force-velocity curve is a reference to the representative curve of force and velocity along an x- and y-axis. This representation depicts an athlete's ability to contract with a range of qualities, including high total force and low velocity (maximal strength) and high velocity and low total force (speed). The force-velocity curve can be used to develop specific sport-related characteristics that will augment individual performance and correct characteristic weaknesses.

Strength-to-Mass Ratio

The strength-to-mass ratio refers to an athlete's ability to accelerate his or her own body mass. One of the primary points of emphasis in strength and conditioning is on preserving, or increasing, an athlete's ability to produce force, i.e., increasing vertical jump ability or decrease sprint distance times. The strength-to-mass ratio can help determine if an athlete is appropriately strong at a current body weight, or if increasing muscular size will be detrimental to acceleration and athletic performance. This ratio is significant for athletes that compete in sports that use weight classifications, as this type of athlete would attempt to reach maximum strength levels without going over the weight limit in order to have a competitive advantage.

Bracketing Technique

The bracketing technique is a training method that utilizes a sport-specific movement with less than or greater than standard resistance in order to generate greater acceleration during the sport-specific activity. The primary emphasis for the athlete is to develop acceleration and deceleration capacities to boost sport performance. An overload can be achieved using parachutes during sprinting, or a coach can reduce resistance and increase acceleration for a shot putter by having the athlete throw a lighter shot putt.

Valsalva Maneuver

The Valsalva maneuver involves performing a force exhalation against a closed glottis, which prevents air from leaving the lungs, causes the abdominal and ribcage muscles to contract, and causes air pressure to increase in the upper torso. Using the Valsalva maneuver when working with near maximal or maximal training loads can be beneficial as the increase in torso rigidity is helpful when the body is supporting heavy loads.

Movement Analysis

A movement analysis is significant in assessing an athlete's movement capacities prior to training, but is also very useful in assessing possible limitations to the sport-specific activities they will engage in during competition. Assessing an athlete's movement capacities will allow the strength and conditioning coach to make an informed decision based on the individual movement capacities for a particular athlete, which will lead to a more beneficial program being assimilated, but this

Copyright © Mometrix Media. You have been licensed one copy of this document for personal use only. Any other reproduction or redistribution is strictly prohibited. All rights reserved.
This content is provided for test preparation purposes only and does not imply an endorsement by Mometrix of any particular political, scientific, or religious point of view.

analysis will also alert the strength and conditioning coach to areas of limitation or possible pain that could ultimately lead to injury or long-term degenerative issues if not corrected.

Anaerobic Training/Conditioning

Anaerobic training refers to brief high-intensity bouts of exercise that includes lifting weights, sprinting, agility drills, plyometric activities, interval training, and speed training. In contrast with aerobic training, which consists of lower-intensity and longer duration training sessions while relying on oxygen for energy, anaerobic training relies on high rates of speed, power, neural recruitment, and the primary energy sources derived from the glycolytic or phosphagen systems.

Size Principle

The size principle refers to the recruitment patterns of the nervous system during muscular contraction. This recruitment pattern is established based on the relationship of the twitch force, size of the motor unit, and the recruitment threshold for each motor unit. This means that smaller, lower-force, fatigue-resistant units will contract first when movement is initiated and once threshold for the larger units is reached, they will then contract.

Neuromuscular Junction

The neuromuscular junction is a key element in muscular contraction, as this is the location of acetylcholine release that initiates muscular contraction. Studies comparing evaluating anaerobic training adaptations determined that higher intensity activities increased the surface area of the neuromuscular junction, the length of nerve terminal branching increased, and available synapse locations were increased and dispersed more widely. These alterations in morphology indicate that, with anaerobic training, neural transmission can be improved.

Bilateral Deficit

The bilateral deficit refers to a neural deficiency when performing bilateral movements that causes a reduction in total force produced bilaterally when compared to the sum total of force from a comparable unilateral movement. If bilateral deficits are left uncorrected, an athlete may develop imbalanced force relationships in certain movement patterns or in specific muscle groups, leading to poor length-tension relationships and possible injury over time.

Joints

There are three distinct types of joints in the human body: fibrous, cartilaginous, and synovial. Fibrous joints are joints that connect two bones via the fibrous connective tissue collagen, possess no joint cavity, and do not allow for movement. Cartilaginous joints are joints between two bones via cartilage and allow movement that is primarily intended to allow the body flexibility and elasticity, i.e., during growth or respiration. Synovial are joints that connect two bones via a joint cavity (articular capsule), contain a synovial membrane, are covered in cartilage (hyaline), and contain additional structures such as bursae, articular discs, etc. Fibrous: sutures of the skull. Cartilaginous: pubic symphysis. Synovial: knee.

Classes of Joints

There are three types of joints in the body: uniaxial, biaxial, and multiaxial. Uniaxial joints are hinge joints that allow flexion and extension in one plane of movement, i.e., the elbow. Biaxial joints are joints that have an odd arrangement between the articulating surfaces, with one being concave and the other convex and allow movement about two perpendicular planes, i.e., the ankle or wrist. Multiaxial joints are joints that are generally considered "ball and socket" joints that allow movement through all perpendicular axes, i.e., the shoulder or hip.

Copyright © Mometrix Media. You have been licensed one copy of this document for personal use only. Any other reproduction or redistribution is strictly prohibited. All rights reserved.
This content is provided for test preparation purposes only and does not imply an endorsement by Mometrix of any particular political, scientific, or religious point of view.

Bioenergetics

Bioenergetics is a biological science that is primarily concerned with the manner in which organisms convert macronutrients from food ingestion into useable energy substrates that allow the organism and organism's systems to perform work.

Catabolism

Catabolism is defined as the breakdown of larger, more complex molecules into smaller, less complex molecules that can be utilized as energy sources. Catabolism refers to processes that are involved in the digestion of food and metabolism of carbohydrates, fats, and proteins, but is also involved in the breakdown of muscle tissue in times of heavy training volumes, reduced caloric intake, and times of high life stress.

Anabolism

Anabolism is the process of restructuring, or building up of materials that have been reduced from catabolic processes in order to meet the organism's homeostatic needs. This process is primarily involved in the formation of new amino acids from previously catabolized amino acids in order to generate new muscle tissue.

Exergonic Reactions

Exergonic reactions are chemical reactions that cause the release of energy from a cell or molecule in order for an organism to utilize the released energy for the purpose of performing some form of work.

Endergonic Reactions

An endergonic reaction is a chemical reaction that is initiated by previously released energy being absorbed by reactants in order to initiate a status change. In the human physiology, anabolic processes are considered endergonic reactions because anabolism requires the release of energy to begin the process of amino acid assimilation and tissue rebuilding. Muscular contraction is also considered an endergonic reaction because the release of energy substrate is required to initiate the biochemical cascade that causes muscular contraction.

Metabolism

Metabolism is the totality of all chemical reactions, both endergonic and exergonic, in human physiology. Metabolism is essential to human physiology with regards to physiological processes such as muscle growth, hormonal balance, fat-loss, and essentially any process that is being undertaken in order to maintain homeostasis. The metabolism is a result of all activities, or lack thereof, taken part in by an athlete. The metabolic rate can be assessed using indirect calorimetry and other assorted tests in order to determine health and training status of an athlete.

ATP

Biological systems require energy to produce various types of work. Adenosine triphosphate (ATP) is the energy source that these systems utilize in order to carry out endergonic reactions, i.e., muscular contraction. ATP is composed of an adenine group, a ribose group, and three molecules of inorganic phosphates.

Hydrolysis of ATP

Hydrolysis of adenosine triphosphate (ATP) is a process of breaking apart the high energy bonds of the ATP molecule in order to utilize the energy from these bonds. Hydrolysis requires one molecule of water and several enzymes to break apart the high energy bonds for energy, which reduces the

Copyright © Mometrix Media. You have been licensed one copy of this document for personal use only. Any other reproduction or redistribution is strictly prohibited. All rights reserved.
This content is provided for test preparation purposes only and does not imply an endorsement by Mometrix of any particular political, scientific, or religious point of view.

ATP molecule from the original energy state to adenosine diphosphate (ADP) and ending with adenosine monophosphate (AMP).

ATPase

Adenosine triphosphatase (ATPase) is the enzyme responsible for catalyzing the decomposition of ATP to ADP. The dephosphorylation reaction releases energy into a system in order to carry out additional chemical reactions. Enzymes are utilized by all organisms to catalyze reactions, but each enzyme has a very specific effect and generally is only responsible for carrying out a single reaction, i.e. ATPase, or lipase.

Myosin ATPase

Myosin ATPase, like other enzymes, is involved in a specific chemical reaction. Myosin ATPase is responsible for catalyzing the actomyosin cross-bridging response in muscular contraction. This reaction creates the free energy needed for the contraction.

Calcium ATPase

Calcium ATPase is the enzymatic regulator of calcium movement into and out of the sarcoplasmic reticulum, which causes muscular relaxation. In muscular contractions, calcium pumps are of great importance because the removal of the CA^{+2} from the cell reduces the number of fibers that can cross bridge for muscular contraction and thus leads to muscular relaxation.

Sodium-Potassium ATPase

Sodium-potassium ATPase is responsible for maintaining cellular sodium potassium balance by pumping sodium out of a cell and potassium into the cell. For every two K^+ ions that are pumped into the cell, there are three Na^+ ions pumped out of the cell. This sodium-potassium pumping activity is necessary in order to maintain proper cellular resting potential and proper fluid balance in the cells.

ADP

Adenosine diphosphate (ADP) is composed of adenine, ribose, and two molecules of inorganic phosphate. From this energy state, ADP can be converted into ATP with the addition of an inorganic phosphate group, which can be achieved through the creatine phosphate energy system.

Phosphagen System

The phosphagen system relies on the hydrolysis of ATP from local muscle stores, as well as on the breakdown of creatine phosphate. This system is active during bouts of intense, brief exercise that includes heavy resistance exercises and short but intense sprints. This system is active during all activities at the outset, but is active for a short time before other systems become the predominant energy resource, depending on duration of exercise.

CP

Creatine phosphate (CP), also known as phosphocreatine (PCr), is used as a rapid energy resource for high-intensity muscular contractions. This system is able to resynthesize ATP by adding an inorganic phosphate group (creatine) to an existing ADP molecule via an enzymatic process involving creatine kinase.

Creatine Kinase

Creatine kinase is an enzyme that potentiates the activity of the replenishment of ATP molecules for energy utilization in the phosphagen system. Creatine kinase elevation in serum blood tests is indicative of muscle damage, whether from heart attack, kidney failure, or rhabdomyolysis. In

Copyright © Mometrix Media. You have been licensed one copy of this document for personal use only. Any other reproduction or redistribution is strictly prohibited. All rights reserved.
This content is provided for test preparation purposes only and does not imply an endorsement by Mometrix of any particular political, scientific, or religious point of view.

athletes, rhabdomyolysis is caused by the rapid breakdown of muscle tissue, generally caused by performing too much work in a training session either acutely or over the course of a training week.

Adenylate Kinase Reaction

Adenylate kinase is another enzyme that is responsible for the rapid replenishment of ATP. Adenylate kinase converts two ADP molecules into ATP + AMP. This reaction is significant in maintenance of cellular energy homeostasis, but is also crucial in stimulating glycolysis via increased AMP.

Law of Mass Action/Mass Action Effect

The law of mass action/mass action effect is specific to the concentrations of reactants or products in solution. The concentration of a reactant or a product is wholly dependent on establishing equilibrium within the system. With regards to energy production in human physiology during exercise, specifically enzyme driven reactions, the establishment of equilibrium is specific to maintaining a threshold of ATP in order to perform the necessary work that is being undertaken, which means the various enzymatic activities must continue throughout the exercise session in order to maintain threshold ATP levels, and once stimulus is reduced or ceased, then these processes will discontinue.

Glycolysis

Glycolysis is the process of breaking down carbohydrates, either in the form of glycogen or from glucose in the blood, to replenish ATP. Glycolysis is an enzymatically driven process, similar to PCr, but is not as rapid in resynthesizing ATP due to the multiple steps involved in the process. Glycolysis is able to supply a greater amount of ATP over time because of the larger amount of available energy generating resources from stored glycogen or free floating glucose in the blood stream.

Anaerobic Glycolysis

Anaerobic glycolysis specifically refers to the production of ATP through the breakdown of glucose in a state of reduced oxygen availability. This is generally referred to as "fast" glycolysis because this system is not dependent on oxygen to break down glucose, but is driven by the pyruvate, which is then converted to lactate, in order to replenish ATP stores during high intensity activities. This system will only operate until lactate threshold is reached, which will cause a slowing of muscular contractions even to the point of cessation of movement, at which point lactate can be cleared and homeostasis is restored.

Pyruvate

Pyruvate is a product of anaerobic glycolysis. In glycolysis, one molecule of glucose is reduced to two pyruvate molecules. The two pyruvate molecules can then be used through two separate mechanisms to further produce energy. The first is via conversion into acetyl-coenzyme A, which is the primary means of entering into the series of reactions known as the Krebs cycle. The second process for producing energy is via conversion to oxaloacetate in order to produce intermediaries involved in the Krebs cycle.

Aerobic Glycolysis

Aerobic glycolysis requires pyruvate to enter into the mitochondrion of a cell and then, when oxygen is present, is oxidized and enters into the Krebs cycle. The differentiation between the two types of glycolysis is governed by what takes place in the mitochondrion of the cell. If oxygen is present, then aerobic glycolysis will take place through oxidative phosphorylation, and if oxygen is

Copyright © Mometrix Media. You have been licensed one copy of this document for personal use only. Any other reproduction or redistribution is strictly prohibited. All rights reserved.
This content is provided for test preparation purposes only and does not imply an endorsement by Mometrix of any particular political, scientific, or religious point of view.

not readily available, then the pyruvate molecule will undergo fermentation in order to produce sufficient ATP.

Lactate

Lactate is a byproduct of anaerobic glycolysis. Lactate is considered to be a "waste" product and responsible for the "burning" sensation in muscle tissue during intense bouts of exercise. However, this may not be the case, as recent findings suggest the increased H^+ concentration in the blood is not caused by increased circulation of lactate in the blood, but that other mechanisms are involved. Lactate is also used as a fuel source in specific tissues which include the heart and the brain.

Lactate Dehydrogenase

Lactate dehydrogenase is the catalyst for conversion of pyruvate to lactate and back, while also being involved in the conversion of NADH to NAD^+. Lactase dehydrogenase is of great significance during anaerobic glycolysis, as without this conversion capability, the system would be strictly oxygen dependent, which would limit the intensity of physical activities that could be undertaken.

Metabolic Acidosis

Metabolic acidosis refers to a condition that occurs when the body produces too much acid. This condition in athletes is, generally, induced by intense bouts of exercise that causes a rapid decrease in blood pH due to increased H^+ ions in the blood. This response can be indicative of current training capacities of an athlete or group of athletes, but can also be used to determine proper training intensity levels.

Cori Cycle

The Cori cycle refers to the metabolic pathway in which lactate, produced from anaerobic glycolysis, is moved to the liver, converted to glucose, and returned to working muscles to be used as energy and again converted to lactate via gluconeogenesis. This process is utilized to prevent lactic acidosis, a specific form of metabolic acidosis.

Mitochondria

Mitochondria are the specialized organelles found in the nucleus of a cell that are responsible for aerobic metabolism. These specialized cells are the site where pyruvate is converted to acetyl-CoA via pyruvate dehydrogenase and can then enter into the Krebs cycle in order to produce ATP.

Phosphorylation

Phosphorylation refers to the process of adding an inorganic phosphate group to a molecule. Phosphorylation is of key significance to energy production in humans as ATP is the energy substrate required to produce all forms of work. Being able to restore ATP from various resources is of key significance when considering all the various activities that humans are capable of endeavoring into, which requires various processes to engage at different times in order to produce sufficient ATP.

Oxidative Phosphorylation

Oxidative phosphorylation is a metabolic pathway used to resynthesize ATP in the mitochondria of the muscle cell using various enzymes and energy-releasing reactions, primarily the electron transport chain, which drive the process. The electron transport chain, essentially, is the process of electrons being moved from electron donors to electron acceptors. This process generates energy by the formation of a pH gradient along with the electron potential that can move across the inner mitochondrial membrane. Energy is resynthesized through the activity of ATP synthase, which converts the electrical activity into mechanical energy, and results in the phosphorylation of

Copyright © Mometrix Media. You have been licensed one copy of this document for personal use only. Any other reproduction or redistribution is strictly prohibited. All rights reserved.
This content is provided for test preparation purposes only and does not imply an endorsement by Mometrix of any particular political, scientific, or religious point of view.

adenosine diphosphate into ATP. This process of energy production is predominant during long distance endurance-related activities, but as with all energy contributions, will provide some ATP during other activities, but will vary depending on systemic needs.

Substrate Level Phosphorylation

Substrate level phosphorylation refers to reactions that are enzymatically driven and lead to the generation of ATP. This type of phosphorylation is also known as anaerobic glycolysis, or fast phosphorylation. Substrate level phosphorylation operates via the transfer and direct donation of a phosphoryl (PO_3) group to adenosine diphosphate to form ATP. This process occurs in the cytoplasm of the cell as part of glycolysis, but can also be active in mitochondria as part of the Krebs cycle. This method of energy production can be active during anaerobic and aerobic activities.

Oxidative System

The oxidative system is the primary energy production system at rest and during low intensity exercise. This system can utilize all three macronutrients as substrate, but is predominantly oriented to using fats while at rest (about 70 percent) and carbohydrates during low-moderate exercise intensities. Proteins can be broken down into amino acids and then converted to glucose via gluconeogenesis, but this is not a common occurrence and generally will only be seen in periods of starvation and exercise bouts greater than 90 minutes. Oxidative phosphorylation will generate 40 molecules of ATP after two rotations through the Krebs cycle utilizing one molecule of glucose.

Lactate Threshold

Lactate threshold is the point of excess lactate accumulation in the blood stream during exercise. The lactate threshold is generally considered to occur at a level of 4 mL per dL of blood. Determining an athlete's lactate threshold is significant for determining the proper intensity for training intensities and, for competitive distance athletes, is very important for determining pacing strategies for competition.

Blood Lactate

The onset of blood lactate accumulation is the point in which exercise intensity causes lactate to accumulate in the blood of the participant or athlete at a rate faster than can be buffered. This is caused by two separate activities with the first being the release of H^+ ions into the blood as a result of the hydrolysis of ATP, and also the reduction of available bicarbonate in the blood due to increased physical activity.

Krebs Cycle

The Krebs cycle, or citric acid cycle, is a complex metabolic pathway that utilizes a series of chemical reactions to generate energy through the oxidation of acetyl-CoA that is derived from the three macronutrient classes: carbohydrates, proteins, and fats.

ETC

The electron transport chain (ETC) is a component of the oxidative system that uses redox reactions that transfer electrons from donors to acceptors via an electrochemical gradient. This system produces ATP via two different chemicals, NADH and $FADH_2$. NADH produces three molecules of ATP and $FADH_2$ produces two molecules of ATP. The ETC is extremely important for maintaining the necessary ATP stores available for energy utilization during aerobic exercise.

Oxygen Uptake

Oxygen uptake is the amount of oxygen that an athlete can take in and use during bouts of exercise or training. Being able to measure an athlete's ability to take in and effectively use oxygen will

Copyright © Mometrix Media. You have been licensed one copy of this document for personal use only. Any other reproduction or redistribution is strictly prohibited. All rights reserved.
This content is provided for test preparation purposes only and does not imply an endorsement by Mometrix of any particular political, scientific, or religious point of view.

provide insight into their overall work capacity and rate of fatigue, while also providing insight into their aerobic and anaerobic thresholds.

Oxygen Deficit

The oxygen deficit refers to the early initial contributions of the anaerobic energy systems during a bout of exercise until a steady state of oxygen consumption is achieved. The oxygen deficit provides insight into the contributions of the anaerobic energy systems during intense bouts of exercise, and can highlight weaknesses in individual athletes that can be improved via training.

Proteolytic Enzymes

Proteolytic enzymes (proteases) hydrolyze and break down peptide bonds that link proteins and amino acid groups together in order for these proteins to be assimilated into other amino acids or proteins. Protease activity allows for the body to break down existing proteins and amino acids in order for the broken amine groups to be repackaged and utilized in other cells and tissues.

Catecholamines

Catecholamines are released from the adrenal medulla, and are heavily involved in a wide array of physiological responses including neural upregulation, vasodilation, vasoconstriction, and enhancing enzyme activity in skeletal muscle. Catecholamines increase rate of muscle contraction, elevate blood pressure, increase blood flow, and improve testosterone secretion rates in response to resistance training.

Excess Post-Exercise Oxygen Consumption

Excess post-exercise oxygen consumption refers to the increased rate of oxygen above resting rates after an intense bout of exercise. This increased oxygen needed after a training session causes an increased metabolic demand that causes a significant increase in the resting metabolic rate for six to 12 hours after a training session. This phenomenon can be utilized for athletes that need to change body composition or reduce body fat for competitive considerations, i.e., making weight for a competition, or leaning out for a competitive season.

MHC

Myosin-heavy chain (MHC) protein is heavily involved in the remodeling and regeneration of muscle tissue after heavy resistance training. Myosin-heavy chain proteins can effectively alter fiber typing by impacting gene expression, increasing protein synthesis, and retarding protein loss/degradation, which is caused by increased MHC activity within the muscle cell.

Endocrine System

The endocrine system is the system responsible for maintaining physiological homeostasis in the human body in response to environmental stress or stimuli. The endocrine system responds to the stress of training by secreting specific hormone types, adrenal, steroid, thyroid, etc. in order to assist with tissue growth, neurological restoration, blood glucose regulation, and muscular recovery.

Review Video: Endocrine System
Visit mometrix.com/academy and enter code: 678939

Classes of Hormones

Hormones serve as the messengers of the endocrine system. There are numerous hormones in the body, but they generally can be categorized as steroid or peptide hormones. Steroid hormones are primarily responsible for primary and secondary sexual characteristics, and are highly involved in

Copyright © Mometrix Media. You have been licensed one copy of this document for personal use only. Any other reproduction or redistribution is strictly prohibited. All rights reserved.
This content is provided for test preparation purposes only and does not imply an endorsement by Mometrix of any particular political, scientific, or religious point of view.

water balance, inflammatory responses, metabolic control, and immunity. Peptide hormones are hormones that are synthesized in the nucleus of the cell from various proteins and are utilized as signal or template precursors for other hormones or hormonal cascades. This categorization envelops a majority of hormones in the body but can be further broken into anabolic or catabolic hormones.

Lock and Key Theory

The lock and key theory of endocrinology suggests that specific hormones and enzymes bind to specific receptor sites because of a designated structural composition that allows for a hormone to bind to a single binding site while preventing this hormone from binding at other sites, similar to a "lock in key" arrangement. This theory is limited, and has been shown to have considerable weaknesses, as this view of hormone interaction with the binding site cannot take into account allosteric binding and cross reactivity.

Allosteric Binding Sites

Allosteric binding sites in the endocrine system are non-primary binding sites that allow for other non-hormonal substances to bind on a receptor and either increase or decrease activity at the site. Allosteric binding sites are heavily involved in feedback loops within the endocrine system and are capable of encouraging or discouraging binding based on homeostatic feedback.

Cortisol

Cortisol is part of the glucocorticoids class of hormones, and is responsible for converting amino acids to carbohydrates. Cortisol is primarily thought of as a catabolic hormone, but it is heavily involved as a signaling hormone in carbohydrate metabolism and is related, specifically, to the storage of glycogen in muscle tissue. Cortisol, in acute responses, is linked to increases in growth hormone response to exercise during anaerobic training protocols that include resistance training. Chronically high levels of cortisol can be an indication of systemic overtraining, which can be exhibited through loss of strength, lowered lean muscle mass, and increased fat mass.

Testosterone

Testosterone is the primary androgenic hormone in human physiology, which impacts women and men both, although in different proportions. Testosterone impacts muscular physiology via increased protein synthesis and increased growth hormone production in the pituitary glands. Testosterone can also impact central nervous system adaptations to resistance training by increasing neuronal receptor activity, increasing neurotransmitter activity and availability, and altering structural proteins that facilitate muscular contraction.

Steroid and Polypeptide Hormones

Steroid hormones are hormones that are secreted from the adrenal cortex and gonads, they are fat soluble, and are passively transported across the sarcolemma of a muscle fiber. Polypeptide hormones are composed of amino acids, are not fat soluble, rely on secondary messengers to deliver their message to the cell and bind to receptors located in a cell membrane of a targeted tissue.

Growth Hormone

Growth hormone, also known as somatotropin, is primarily responsible for an increase in cellular amino acid uptake, as well as increasing protein synthesis in skeletal muscle leading to muscle growth of type I and type II muscle fibers. Generally, growth hormone is responsible for a wide array of responses, including increased lipolysis, increased availability of glucose and amino acids in circulation, and can strengthen the immune response.

Copyright © Mometrix Media. You have been licensed one copy of this document for personal use only. Any other reproduction or redistribution is strictly prohibited. All rights reserved.
This content is provided for test preparation purposes only and does not imply an endorsement by Mometrix of any particular political, scientific, or religious point of view.

Diastole

Diastole is the period of time in the cardiac cycle that the heart fills with blood. This phase of the cardiac cycle is the lowest measured pressure taken during blood pressure measurement, and is represented as the final or lower number in the annotation, i.e., the 80 in 120/80.

Systole

Systole is the contractile phase of the cardiac cycle. This phase of the cardiac cycle causes the forceful ejection of blood out into the rest of the body, either delivering oxygen-rich blood to working tissues or sending blood into the lungs to be oxygenated. With regards to blood pressure, systole is the highest pressure value measured, and is denoted as the top or first number in reporting, i.e., the 120 in 120/80.

Sinoatrial Node

In cardiovascular anatomy, there are key elements that serve significant purpose during the cardiac cycle and provide insight into the electrical performance of the heart. One of these anatomical structures is the sinoatrial node. The sinoatrial node serves as the electrical impulse-generating tissue of the heart, is commonly referred to as the pace-maker, and is located in the right atrium. The sinoatrial node establishes the normal heart rhythm, which is referred to as the sinus rhythm.

Atrioventricular Node

The atrioventricular node is responsible for delaying the initial signal from the sinoatrial node. This delay allows for the complete ejection of blood from the atria into the ventricles prior to the contraction of the ventricles that sends the blood from the heart to either the rest of the body or the lungs.

Atrioventricular Bundle

The atrioventricular bundle conducts an electrical signal initially sent from the atrioventricular node. Once the atrioventricular bundle has received the signal from the atrioventricular node, the signal is then transmitted to the left and right bundle branches. This signal is significant as this is a point in conduction that occurs between the atria and ventricles, and is crucial in maintaining constant cardiac rhythm.

Left and Right Bundle Branches

The left and right bundle branches move away from the atrioventricular (AV) bundle and towards the ventricles. These fibers have significantly different characteristics from the AV fibers, as these fibers transmit electrical impulses at a much faster rate. This increase in signal velocity is out of necessity as the left and right bundles communicate directly with the Purkinje fibers, and these electrical signals are directly responsible for the contraction of the left and right ventricles, which eject the blood into the rest of the body or to the lungs.

Purkinje Fibers

Purkinje fibers are essential for the maintenance of constant cardiac rhythm. Located in the subendocardium, within the ventricular walls, Purkinje fibers are able to conduct action potentials more quickly than any other cells in the heart because of their specialized muscle cells, cardiomyocytes. These specialized cells allow for cardiac signals to be conducted quickly and consistently, which allows the heart to maintain a constant rhythm.

Copyright © Mometrix Media. You have been licensed one copy of this document for personal use only. Any other reproduction or redistribution is strictly prohibited. All rights reserved.
This content is provided for test preparation purposes only and does not imply an endorsement by Mometrix of any particular political, scientific, or religious point of view.

Electrocardiogram

An electrocardiogram (ECG or EKG) is used to assess the electrical signals generated during polarization and depolarization of cardiac tissue, which provides insight into the overall function and health of an athlete's heart. This testing procedure is used to assess the rate and frequency of the heartbeats while also assessing the size and position of the heart's chambers, which for assessing cardiovascular health in athletes is of extreme importance when considering issues like left ventricular hypertrophy, congenital heart defects, or other cardiac rhythm distortions that may cause health complications or even sudden death.

P-Wave

The P-wave represents atrial depolarization, which involves the electrical signal from the sinoatrial node to the atrioventricular node and spreading from the right to the left atrium. This can lead to atrial contraction.

QRS Complex

The QRS complex represents the rapid depolarization of the left and right ventricles. This signal segment is much larger in amplitude than the P-wave because of the larger mass of the ventricles of the hearts in comparison to the atria.

T-Wave

The T-wave represents the repolarization of the left and right ventricles of the heart. When EKG tests are completed, analysis of the various sections can indicate possible abnormalities in cardiac rhythm and indicate pathological abnormalities. The T-wave is of primary interest because the electrical impulses, both positive and negative, that occur in this phase and can be used as leading indicators for early detection. For example, a hyper acute T-wave is possibly the first manifestation of an acute myocardial infarction (heart attack). Another possible indicator for coronary ischemia is an inverted T-wave.

Arterial System

The arterial system serves to deliver blood from the heart to the rest of the tissues in the body. The arterial system consists of two divisions, the pulmonary and systemic arteries. The pulmonary division is responsible for delivering deoxygenated blood from the heart to the lungs and returning oxygenated blood back to the heart. The systemic arteries are responsible for carrying oxygenated blood away from the heart and returning deoxygenated blood back to the heart.

Venous System

In human circulation, the venous system serves to bring blood toward the heart. There are two separate categories of venous activity: pulmonary and systemic veins. Pulmonary veins carry oxygenated blood from the lungs to the heart, and the systemic veins are responsible for carrying deoxygenated blood from the various tissues of the body to the heart.

Arteries

Arteries are thick, muscular blood vessels that function to take blood away from the heart or to the lungs, which are delineated into systemic and pulmonary arteries, respectively. Arteries operate under varying rates of pressure due to the cardiac cycle of systole (high pressure) and diastole (low pressure). Arteries are significant for determining blood pressure and pulse rate because of their proximity to the contractions of the heart.

Copyright © Mometrix Media. You have been licensed one copy of this document for personal use only. Any other reproduction or redistribution is strictly prohibited. All rights reserved.
This content is provided for test preparation purposes only and does not imply an endorsement by Mometrix of any particular political, scientific, or religious point of view.

Arterioles

Arterioles serve as the controlling factor of blood flow into and out of capillary beds. The muscular walls have the capacity to reduce blood flow (vasoconstriction), or they have the capacity to increase their diameter in order to allow greater blood flow into the capillary beds (vasodilation).

Capillaries

Capillaries play a primary role in several essential aspects of human physiology. Capillaries are the smallest division of the blood vessel and serve as part of the microvasculature. The role of the capillary is to exchange fluids, gases, nutrients, hormones, electrolytes, and other substances with the interstitial fluids from various tissues throughout the body.

Bronchi

The primary bronchi are part of the conducting zone in the respiratory system. The primary bronchi are formed from the trachea and are divided into left and right branches. No gas exchange takes place in the primary bronchi as they serve as the primary conductor for air passage into the bronchioles.

Bronchioles

Bronchioles serve in both the conduction and respiratory zones of respiration. The bronchioles are formed from the tertiary bronchi, and have three distinct divisions: the lesser bronchioles, the terminal bronchioles, and the respiratory bronchioles. The lesser bronchioles, initially, are formed from the tertiary bronchi and as the diameter of the bronchioles decreases, the terminal bronchioles begin. The division of the terminal bronchioles represents the end of the conduction zone in human respiration and can be identified with the occurrence of alveoli, which represents the beginning of the respiration zone. The respiratory bronchioles are responsible for approximately 10 percent of gas exchange during respiration.

Alveoli

Alveoli are the terminal ends of the respiratory tree. They are located in alveolar sacs and alveolar ducts, and are the primary sites for gas exchange. The alveolar membrane serves as the gas exchange surface. The systemic circulation returns deoxygenated blood from the rest of the body, via the alveolar blood vessels, and through passive diffusion, the carbon dioxide that has been carried from the body's tissue is unloaded. At the same time that the unloading of carbon dioxide is taking place, the oxygen is being diffused into the red blood cells, and will be carried to the working tissues via pulmonary circulation.

Alveolar Pressure

Alveolar pressure is the pressure when the glottis is open and there is no air movement into or out of the lungs. This pressure is the same throughout the respiratory system at this moment. For this to change, the pressure must drop below atmospheric pressure during inspiration and above atmospheric pressure during expiration.

Pleura

There are multiple layers of tissue that make up the functional elements of lung anatomy. One such element is the pleura. The pleura is an essential structure in lung anatomy, as this structure is heavily involved in reducing surface tension, via a small amount of pleural fluid, which assists with making breathing easier, but also helps to inflate alveoli to potentiate gas exchange by improving the appositional proximity of the lungs to the chest wall. This arrangement provides flexibility in all

Copyright © Mometrix Media. You have been licensed one copy of this document for personal use only. Any other reproduction or redistribution is strictly prohibited. All rights reserved.
This content is provided for test preparation purposes only and does not imply an endorsement by Mometrix of any particular political, scientific, or religious point of view.

the various breathing patterns that can occur because of various activities, as well as assisting with gas exchange.

Pleural Pressure

Pleaural pressure is significant because it maintains the tension between the chest wall and the pleura of the lungs, allowing for inspiration and expiration. This pressure is slightly negative in order to compensate for the expansion capacities of the lungs, while also allowing the lungs to maintain pressures below atmospheric levels. If the pleural pressure becomes equal or exceeds atmospheric pressure, the lungs will collapse, which is also referred to as a pneumothorax.

Diffusion

Respiratory exchange of gases occurs through a simple process of diffusion. The diffusion of CO_2 and O_2 through the alveoli in the lungs occurs according to a concentration gradient. The concentration gradient is formed by molecules from a higher concentration region into a region with a lower concentration of molecules, which is dictated by the partial pressure of the gases as well as the concentrations in the capillaries and alveoli. This is a passive process that is driven by the motion of the molecules as they transition from regions of higher and lower concentration.

Chronic Adaptations to Heavy Resistance Exercise

Chronic adaptations to heavy resistance exercise are considerable and extensive. These adaptations include hypertrophy of high-threshold motor units, increased importation and affinity for nutrients in muscle tissue, increased insulin sensitivity, increased number of androgen receptors, etc.

Muscular Adaptations to Resistance Training

Muscular adaptations to resistance exercise are extensive, and are primarily oriented to muscular hypertrophy. For hypertrophy to take place, there must be a net increase in protein-related activities, i.e., protein synthesis, reduced degradation, etc., along with an increase in myofilaments. The structural changes that take place within the muscle are directly related to the increased available surface area. These changes include increased myofibrillar volume, increased density of the cytoplasm, increased sarcoplasmic and t-tubule density, and increased enzyme activity. There are other adaptations that occur because of muscular growth, which include reduced mitochondria density, reduced capillary density, and increased lactate buffering capacity.

Connective Tissue Adaptations

The primary alterations that occur in connective tissue are related specifically to increasing the functional capabilities of these tissues in response to increased muscular strength and growth. These changes occur because of an increased demand placed on these tissues via external loading. The areas that change the most significantly are the tendon junctions that occur between two bony surfaces, the body of the tendon and ligament, along with the fascia covering a hypertrophied muscle thickening and stiffening.

Mechanical Loading

Mechanical loading causes osteoblasts to move towards the surface of a bone in order to begin modeling a new bone matrix along the spaces between bone cells, which occurs primarily on the surface of the bone to increase bone density and overall strength.

Specificity of Loading

Specificity of loading refers to the use of specific movement patterns to load a specific region of an athlete's body. Using external stimuli to increase bone density in specific joints that are more likely to experience bone loss or mineral thinning can prevent this occurrence but can also increase bone

Copyright © Mometrix Media. You have been licensed one copy of this document for personal use only. Any other reproduction or redistribution is strictly prohibited. All rights reserved.
This content is provided for test preparation purposes only and does not imply an endorsement by Mometrix of any particular political, scientific, or religious point of view.

density at these specific sites, i.e., the hip and spine. Maintenance of bone mass follows very similar rules to maintaining muscle mass, as progressive overloading must be applied via compound movements that involve performing work through the specific joints that are being targeted.

Peak Bone Mass

Peak bone mass is the maximum achieved bone mass density that a person has been able to reach. Reaching peak bone mass allows for natural bone loss to occur during the aging process without becoming detrimental over the long term, as there is a higher percentage of bone loss that can be lost before a harmful threshold is reached. Another aspect for consideration is maintaining activity levels in order to maintain bone levels at near-peak levels across the aging cycle, as this will contribute to the rate of decline slowing substantially and allow structural integrity to remain intact for many years.

Collagen

Collagen is a major component to morphological changes that occur in the soft tissues due to anaerobic training protocols. There are two primary types of collagen in the human body: type I, which occurs in bone, tendon, and ligaments; and type II, which occurs in cartilage. Procollagen is the primary protein composing both types of collagen, and interacts with specific enzymes to form long filaments that are then formed into microfibrils. Similar to myofibrils, the microfibrils of collagen are laid out in parallel to one another and form single fibers that are then bundled together. The proximity of the collagen bundles to one another leads to a chemical bonding process known as cross-linking, which is the primary source for the strength and durability of collagen as a connective tissue. The primary response of collagen to anaerobic training is the increased enzyme activity that causes the increased formation of new long filaments.

Tendon Stiffness

The intensity of training load (less than 80 percent) during anaerobic training will have a significant impact on increasing tendon stiffness. Tendon stiffness, the ability to transmit force under strain, is directly correlated to muscular recoil and power production. This simply means that the greater the tendon stiffness, the greater the force that is required for transmission to a muscle in order to produce a recoil response. This is useful for power athletes as improving the athlete's ability to transmit forces through the tendons and into the muscles at a high rate when under strain, either from high velocity or from an opponent resisting forward progress, is essential in improving their overall performance in their selected sport.

Rate Pressure Product

Rate pressure product is a reference point for workload of the heart during exercise. The rate pressure product is the number of beats per minute multiplied by the systolic pressure that the heart is working against. This provides direct insight into how hard the heart is working via the hemodynamic response. When performing high-intensity workloads, being able to quantify performance is essential for evaluating athlete effort during training sessions, but also provides a means of assessing cardiovascular responses and progression over time.

Ventilation Equivalent

The ventilation equivalent is a method of indexing an athlete's ability to utilize oxygen. The ventilation equivalent delineates the rate of oxygen being inhaled in comparison to the amount of oxygen that is being exhaled (V_E/VO_2). This equivalency provides the coach with insight into how effectively the athlete unloads the oxygen being brought into the body and into the working muscle tissue. This measurement will indicate whether an athlete is in condition for the competitive

Copyright © Mometrix Media. You have been licensed one copy of this document for personal use only. Any other reproduction or redistribution is strictly prohibited. All rights reserved.
This content is provided for test preparation purposes only and does not imply an endorsement by Mometrix of any particular political, scientific, or religious point of view.

season, as the ventilator equivalency will decrease in an athlete that effectively unloads oxygen into the active tissues.

Cardiac Output

Cardiac output is the volume of blood pumped through the heart specifically by a right or left ventricle in the time period of one minute. The volume of blood being pumped is a factor of the heart's stroke volume (mL/min) and the heart rate (BPM).

End-Diastolic Volume

End-diastolic volume is the volume of blood available to be pumped by the left and right ventricles after diastole. End-diastolic volume is very significant with regards to stroke volume, as this volume of blood is what will be pumped from the heart to the rest of the body and during exercise, thereby working muscle. Over time, the muscle fibers of the heart become stretched, which allows for a greater end-diastolic volume, and increases the volume of blood ejected during systole.

Venous Return

Venous return refers to the volume of blood that is returning to the heart from the periphery. Venous return increases as an adaptation to aerobic conditioning. Over time, the volume of the left ventricle will increase to accommodate the increased blood flow from the right atrium. This leads to greater volumes of blood being ejected from the left ventricle, enhancing aerobic performance.

Frank-Starling Mechanism

The Frank-Starling mechanism refers to the more forceful contraction of the heart in response to increased stroke volume that, over time, has caused a stretching of the left ventricle. This mechanism is primarily responsible for the increased ejection fraction, which means a greater volume of blood is being ejected because of this mechanism.

Oxygen Uptake

Oxygen uptake is the amount of oxygen being transported and unloaded into working tissues. Oxygen uptake is a reflection of the training intensity, selected exercise method, and duration of the session. Exercise selection impacts the rate of oxygen uptake because a chosen method may involve smaller muscle groups, i.e., arm ergometer, or larger muscle groups, i.e., treadmill running, that will require varying amounts of oxygen to supply the working tissues.

Maximal Oxygen Uptake

Maximal oxygen uptake (VO_2 max) refers to the maximal amount of oxygen that can be consumed by an athlete. The VO_2 max is evaluated using a graded exercise test where the amount of work performed is gradually increased over time until a maximum oxygen value is reached, and is generally indicated once O_2 consumption plateaus. Maximal oxygen uptake is the best measure of cardiovascular fitness because it indicates the upper limit capacities for the endurance athlete across varying heart rates and workloads, and in anaerobic athletes, VO_2 max is indicative of the anaerobic lactate threshold and aerobic potential.

METS

Metabolic equivalent of tasks (METS) can be used to assess energy expenditure of various physical activities. METS for a broad range of tasks have been established in *The Compendium of Physical Activities* and allow for generalizations regarding energy expenditure to be made with a fair level of accuracy. The central limiting factor of the METS assessment is the general assumptions that are made regarding a specific individual, as this measure cannot account for individual differences which include fat mass, fat free mass, exercise intensity, and overall conditioning of the person.

Copyright © Mometrix Media. You have been licensed one copy of this document for personal use only. Any other reproduction or redistribution is strictly prohibited. All rights reserved.
This content is provided for test preparation purposes only and does not imply an endorsement by Mometrix of any particular political, scientific, or religious point of view.

Fick Equation

The Fick equation is the equation for assessing maximal oxygen uptake. The Fick equation utilizes three essential pieces of information: the cardiac output (Q), the arterial oxygen content (a), and the venous oxygen content (vO_2). To properly assess maximal oxygen content, you must be able to calculate the difference in the arterial oxygen and venous oxygen content because the difference is the volume being unloaded into the working tissues. You must also know how hard the heart is working to pump the oxygen to the working tissues, which is why cardiac output is essential.

Arteriovenous Oxygen Difference

The arteriovenous oxygen difference is the differentiation between the amount of oxygen being transported through the arterial and venous divisions of the circulatory system. The arteriovenous oxygen difference is the primary means of evaluating the amount of oxygen being unloaded into active tissues during exercise, and is crucial to determining aerobic fitness as this difference is an elemental component in the Fick equation.

Mean Arterial Pressure

Mean arterial pressure, often represented as MAP, is the average arterial blood pressure in the cardiovascular system. Mean arterial pressure can be used as an indicator for the rate of perfusion throughout the cardiac cycle, either at rest or during activity, as this will indicate if there are any issues with an athlete's ability to move blood into working tissues which can be used to alert to possible disease if a perfusion issue is identified. Mean arterial pressure can be assessed using the equation MAP = [(SBP-DBP)/3] + DBP.

Total Peripheral Resistance

Total peripheral resistance is the measure of the vascular resistance in the systemic circulation. Total peripheral resistance in the systemic circulation is caused by the opening and closing of vessels throughout the systemic circulation. These circulation-controlling mechanisms are referred to as vasoconstriction, which constricts blood flow, and vasodilation, which increases blood flow. Total peripheral resistance and pulmonary vascular resistance differentiate from one another via the aspect of the vascular system that is responsible for generating the resistive forces that must be overcome in order to move blood through the system. The peripheral resistance is concerned with the resistance in the systemic vasculature, while the pulmonary vascular resistance is concerned with the resistance from the vasculature of the lungs. Total peripheral resistance can be determined via the equation total peripheral resistance = (mean arterial pressure - mean vascular pressure) / Q (cardiac output).

Vasoconstriction

Vasoconstriction is the primary means of reducing blood flow in specific tissues both at rest and during exercise. During exercise, specific organ systems and certain functions are limited because of increased blood flow to other organs and tissues. The reason for constricting blood flow to certain tissues during exercise is to maximize the available blood volume for the active tissue sites that need oxygen, but also to reduce the functions of certain systems during exercise, i.e., digestion.

Vasodilation

Vasodilation is the process of blood vessels and arteries dilating to allow for maximum blood flow into an organ or body tissue. This response is invaluable with regards to aerobic and anaerobic exercise. In both forms of exercise, the vasodilation response transports oxygenated blood, nutrients, and electrolytes to working tissues. Vasodilation also plays a significant role in allowing

Copyright © Mometrix Media. You have been licensed one copy of this document for personal use only. Any other reproduction or redistribution is strictly prohibited. All rights reserved.
This content is provided for test preparation purposes only and does not imply an endorsement by Mometrix of any particular political, scientific, or religious point of view.

for the maximum transport of CO_2 for clearance in the lungs, or for transporting lactate and other assorted waste materials from working tissues for buffering.

Minute Ventilation

Minute ventilation refers to the volume of gas a person inhales per minute. Minute ventilation is a significant factor in exercise and sport performance. Minute ventilation is primarily responsible for increasing or decreasing the rate of ventilation based on the amount of carbon dioxide in the blood when exercising. In order to clear excess carbon dioxide from the blood, respiration must increase and, once levels have been normalized or exercise has ceased, the rate of ventilation will decrease.

Tidal Volume

Tidal volume is the total volume of air inhaled and exhaled during each breath in a resting state. This volume is established without mechanical assistance from the accessory muscles for respiration, which limits the application of tidal volume as a measure during exercise. This term is often used as reference for increased oxygen volumes during exercise, but this is incorrect, as the correct references would be specific to increased minute volume or the ventilatory equivalence.

Ventilatory Equivalent

The ventilatory equivalent is the ratio of minute ventilation and oxygen uptake during exercise, which is expressed V_E/VO_2 for oxygen consumption and V_E/VCO_2 when evaluating carbon dioxide output. At the onset of lactate accumulating in the blood more rapidly than can be effectively buffered, ventilation rate increases at a rate disproportionate to the rate of oxygen uptake in the tissues. The lactate threshold and the ventilatory equivalence are very closely connected because of the necessity of clearing excess lactate and CO_2 from the body.

Physiological Dead Space

The term "physiological dead space" refers to alveoli that do not receive necessary blood flow, experience poor ventilation, or have other restrictive issues along the alveolar surface that reduce functional gas exchange capacity. Physiological dead space is most commonly seen in diseased populations that include various chronic obstructive pulmonary diseases such as emphysema.

Impact of Exercise on Diffusion Rates

Diffusion refers to the movement of gases from areas of high concentration to areas of lower concentration. The movement of the gases along the gradient is due to the partial pressure exerted by each molecule of gas. During exercise, the partial pressures of the gases are altered depending on their location in the circulatory system. At the alveolus level the pressures are $PO_2 = 100$ mm Hg and $PCO_2 = 40$ mm Hg, while in the venous blood, after unloading into muscle tissue, the partial pressures are $PO_2 = 40$ mm Hg and $PCO_2 = 46$ mm Hg. The changes in pressures will determine whether or not the gases move into or out of the circulation during exercise.

Blood Transport of Gases and Metabolic Byproducts During Exercise

Oxygen is carried through circulation via hemoglobin at a level of approximately 3 mL per liter of plasma. Carbon dioxide is transported out of the cell via diffusion and into the plasma for transport to the lungs for clearance. This process is a bit more involved as buffering CO_2 relies on bicarbonate and water, which requires catalyzation by carbonic anhydrase, in order to buffer the hydrogen ions accumulating in the blood. This process is supported through the natural acid-base buffering capacity of hemoglobin in order to maintain blood pH balance. Once exercise intensity reaches a level where aerobic metabolism is not sufficient to maintain pH balance, then lactic acid begins to accumulate quickly, and is referred to as the onset of blood lactate, or OBLA.

Copyright © Mometrix Media. You have been licensed one copy of this document for personal use only. Any other reproduction or redistribution is strictly prohibited. All rights reserved.
This content is provided for test preparation purposes only and does not imply an endorsement by Mometrix of any particular political, scientific, or religious point of view.

Cardiovascular Adaptations to Aerobic Exercise

Responses to aerobic exercise are related to unloading oxygen into working muscles as effectively as possible. Adaptations to aerobic exercise include increased cardiac output, reduced heart rate at rest and during submaximal exercise intensities, increased stroke volume per heartbeat, and a significant increase in density in the microvasculature. These adaptations occur over time with the most significant changes occurring with the hypertrophy of the left ventricle and the increased contractile strength of that chamber.

Bradycardia

Bradycardia is a reduction in the resting heart rate due to chronic aerobic exercise. Bradycardia is a physiological adaptation to aerobic exercise and is directly related to the hypertrophy of the left ventricle that increases the stroke volume capacity of the heart. At rest, this increased stroke volume will result in a lower resting heart rate (BPM) because the excess stroke volume reduces the need to beat as frequently as would be considered normal (80-100 BPM). Bradycardia in untrained or elderly populations may be indications of decreased electrical activity in the sinoatrial node and someone experiencing symptoms not related to exercising should be directed to a physician for evaluation.

Muscular Adaptations to Aerobic Training

Muscular adaptations to aerobic training center on enhancing the muscular capacity for sustained work, which include hypertrophy of type I fibers, increased mitochondria, and increased myoglobin activity. The hypertrophy of type I fibers is caused by the increased recruitment during aerobic activities, and the cross-sectional increase is not as great as that of type II fibers. The increased mitochondrial density in the muscle leads to greater ATP production, and is significant in enhancing aerobic capacity. The other significant adaptation in muscle is the increased activity of myoglobin, which is the protein responsible for transporting oxygen into the muscle cell. The greater concentration of myoglobin increases the amount of oxygen available for energy production within the working muscle.

Altitude Training

Altitude training causes several adaptations both acutely and chronically. Acute adaptations are necessary to stabilize respiration and heart rate, while chronic adaptations primarily impact cellular function. The acute adaptations are an increase in pulmonary ventilation and cardiac output in both resting and exercising states. The chronic adaptations are oriented towards delivering sufficient oxygen into the working tissues, which requires increased myoglobin concentrations (five to 15 percent), greater diffusion capacity through the pulmonary membranes, increased capillary density in trained muscle, and increased buffering capacity of lactate through hyperventilation and greater availability of bicarbonate. The drawbacks to altitude training center around the length of time the chronic adaptations persist, as generally these adaptations normalize after a month

Overtraining

The term overtraining refers to the combination of physiological and psychological status of an athlete that persists for weeks or months. This state is caused by training too often, excessive training in volume and intensity, poor nutrition/reduced calorie intake, or inadequate rest provisions in the programming. This training state generally presents with symptoms such as extreme fatigue, frequent illness, and minor injuries that do not seem to resolve over time.

Overtraining syndrome can lead to decreased performance, sleeplessness, and possible injury. Overtraining syndrome is a chronic state, and requires varying degrees of intervention. There is

Copyright © Mometrix Media. You have been licensed one copy of this document for personal use only. Any other reproduction or redistribution is strictly prohibited. All rights reserved.
This content is provided for test preparation purposes only and does not imply an endorsement by Mometrix of any particular political, scientific, or religious point of view.

much discussion regarding possible interventions to resolve this issue. The most common recommendations range from reduction in training intensity and volume to taking substantial time off from training (up to six months or longer) in order to recover.

There are two types of overtraining syndrome, parasympathetic and sympathetic. Parasympathetic overtraining is marked by an increase in parasympathetic activity at rest, which would be highlighted by a reduction in heart rate at specific workloads. The sympathetic form, most commonly seen in athletes performing in power sports, is highlighted by an increased heart rate at rest and general inability to relax and achieve a rested state. In both cases the most often recommended resolution is either a reduction in training volume or a cessation of training-related activities for a significant period of time, or until symptoms have been resolved.

Overreaching vs. Overtraining

Overreaching is an abbreviated period of time that is characterized by excessive training, and can be resolved with rest and recovery. The primary differences between overreaching and overtraining are the duration of the time period that the training state persists, as overtraining is a chronic state and overtraining phases can be a structured part of an athlete's competitive preparation. Overreaching can function to force an athlete to go beyond his or her ability to adapt and recover, which produces an overstressing on all physiological systems, and with planned rest and recovery allowing the body to supercompensate. Planned overreaching phases can be significantly beneficial to an athlete, while overtraining is detrimental.

Phases of Aging and Human Development

Preadolescence is the phase in development during early childhood that is prior to the development of secondary sex characteristics and is highlighted by significant physical and psychological growth. Adolescence is the developmental segment that is predominated by the development of secondary sexual characteristics, rapid physical growth, and significant cognitive developments with increased capacity for reasoning and communication. The third definitive phase of development is adulthood. This phase is characterized by a cessation in physical growth, maturity of cognitive function, and reaching sexual maturity.

Chronological and Biological Age

Chronological age is simply a measure of how long, in months and years, a person has lived. Biological age is an assessment of the physiological development of a person. The problem with using chronological age as a means of determining athletic capabilities is the problem with physiological development rates as there is no set rate of development. Biological age provides accurate insight into rate of sexual development, structural musculoskeletal age, and neurological maturity through movement assessments.

Training Age

Training age is an assessment of an athlete's training experience. Determining experience level will help direct the course of action a strength coach is able to effectively take in order to ensure maximal progression but also safeguarding against overuse or disuse injuries, and ensuring maximal safety for the athlete. Training age can impact the rate of acclimation to a program, i.e., greater initial gains for the inexperienced versus reduced strength progress in an experienced trainee, which will require a strength coach to individualize the training programs for an athlete based on physical maturity, training age, and work capacities.

Copyright © Mometrix Media. You have been licensed one copy of this document for personal use only. Any other reproduction or redistribution is strictly prohibited. All rights reserved.
This content is provided for test preparation purposes only and does not imply an endorsement by Mometrix of any particular political, scientific, or religious point of view.

Peak Height Velocity

Peak height velocity refers to the increased growth rate during puberty that causes bones to weaken, muscular imbalances, and a tightening of muscle tendon relationships at the connecting points between rapidly growing bones. During peak height velocity, an athlete is at higher risk for an epiphyseal plate fracture than at any other time due to overuse/repetitive injury, and is the primary reason a strength and conditioning coach must monitor training volumes, intensities, and session duration in order to minimize the possibility of damage to the growing athlete.

Skeletal Structure Changes During the Growth and Development Cycle

During the adolescent growth phase, there are substantial changes in the length and general anatomy of the skeletal system. During the growth phase, there are two primary sites of growth: along the diaphysis of a long bone and in the growth cartilage. The growth cartilage occurs in three sites along the long bone: at the joint surfaces, the apophyseal insertions of muscle tendons, and along the epiphyseal plates. After the epiphyseal plates have ossified, bone growth will cease.

Youth Training Program

In youth resistance training programs, the key is to emphasize proper movement skill and technique over loading intensity and training volume. Training an adult is significantly different from training a young athlete. An adult will have a higher capacity to handle stress, will generally have a higher training age, and can sustain efforts of higher intensity and volume more frequently. Young athletes need to be taught how to perform a variety of movement skills, develop work capacity, and guard against overtraining or overuse injuries that can occur during periods of significant physical growth.

Differences in Males and Females During Preadolescence and Adolescence

During preadolescence in boys and girls, there are no statistical differences in body size, composition, or psychological response to training between the two genders. This begins to change during adolescence. Due to increases in circulation of the primary sex hormones, estrogen and testosterone, body composition and bone formation changes begin to take place and impact physical capacities significantly. These changes result in women being shorter than men due to reduced growth cycles, while also being lighter in body weight with less muscle and higher body fat than their male counterparts.

Sex-Related Differences to Be Considered When Training Female Athletes

A fully mature female athlete will not require a special program to be implemented in order for her to achieve parity with her male counterparts, as studies have indicated that, with corrections for body mass differences, total power output and strength is very similar in trained men and women. From a muscular perspective, the training program for strength and power will be very similar, if not identical, to that of a male athlete.

Possible Programming Modifications or Considerations for Female Athletes

Program considerations can be made with regards to structural differences for a female athlete, primarily with regards to injury prevention for the knee and improving upper body strength. Female athletes are at greater risk for knee injuries because of the angle of the femur formed from the hip to the knee, as this creates natural sheer forces at the knee and can lead to a variety of injuries. To guard against this possibility, a strength and conditioning coach can emphasize different lower body movements to improve muscle strength and neural control of the knee joint. A female athlete also has natural upper body weakness, when compared to lower body strength,

Copyright © Mometrix Media. You have been licensed one copy of this document for personal use only. Any other reproduction or redistribution is strictly prohibited. All rights reserved.
This content is provided for test preparation purposes only and does not imply an endorsement by Mometrix of any particular political, scientific, or religious point of view.

which can be heavily affected by performing additional training volume for the upper body while also utilizing varying loading intensities to improve strength and work capacity.

Modifications for Older Adults

Resistance training has become a popular approach to maintaining fitness, health, and longevity in older adults. Older adults should complete a full health history and medical questionnaire prior to initiating a training program. Any questions or concerns that arise from the health history and questionnaire should be referred to a physician for exercise clearance. Physical assessments should occur after clearance is obtained in order to determine body composition and anthropometrics, along with cardiovascular, flexibility, and strength testing to evaluate these specific work capacities. Older adults may train at a reduced frequency in order to ensure adequate recovery from resistance training, but with appropriate programming that develops movement skill, strength, and work capacities, there are generally no limitations as to the exercise movement selection and loading parameters selected when working with a healthy older adult. A strength coach must always be aware of contraindications in older adults.

Modifications for Trainees with Osteopenia

Osteopenia is a skeletal disease that presents with symptoms of thinning bones. Osteopenia is not a limiting factor when considering possible movements a client is able to perform, as weight-bearing exercise will help to reduce the rate of bone loss and has been seen to reverse the process. Following the standard pre-screening practices, which include completing the health history and questionnaire, and implementing developmentally appropriate movements, loading intensities, training frequency, and volume for an older adult, will produce the desired effect on the trainee without engaging in any risky behaviors that may lead to injury due to thinning joints or falls.

Sarcopenia

Sarcopenia is the natural occurrence in a reduction in cross-sectional muscle fiber mass as a result of aging, and most significantly impacts older adult women. Sarcopenia is a result of reduced or complete inactivity, which results in a loss of neural drive to the type II fast twitch motor units. The primary factors that impact the age-related decline in muscle loss are activity levels over time, reduced neural capacity, poor nutrition, and alterations in hormone levels.

Health and Risk Assessment Portion of Evaluations for Older Adults

Physical fitness is a very important pursuit across the span of human development. The risk assessment establishes the historical health background with which the strength and conditioning coach can work. Having a well-rounded and thorough view of a trainee's background allows the strength and conditioning coach to choose a developmentally appropriate training program, while also determining possible contraindications, training limitations, and whether or not medical clearance is necessary prior to initiating the training program. Most importantly, the risk assessment is a guide with which the strength coach must pay attention to in order to develop a safe and low-risk training program.

Ideal Performance State

The ideal performance state represents the pinnacle of performance, where the individual skill, focus, and overall capacities of an athlete are functioning at the highest level and competition seems almost "easy." The ideal performance state, or "zone," occurs when an athlete is able to relax, focus, and engage with the competitive activity with joy and confidence, as this allows for the body to respond rapidly and without hesitation. The ideal performance state is a very interesting crossover point between psychology of sport and the physiology of sport, and there is substantive research being performed in this area in order to more fully understand the relationship between the two.

Copyright © Mometrix Media. You have been licensed one copy of this document for personal use only. Any other reproduction or redistribution is strictly prohibited. All rights reserved.
This content is provided for test preparation purposes only and does not imply an endorsement by Mometrix of any particular political, scientific, or religious point of view.

Cognitive Anxiety

Cognitive anxiety is characterized by negative thoughts or memories associated with negative outcomes, i.e., memories of missing an important free throw in high school arising when attempting an important free throw in college. This sort of anxiety can have physical manifestations that limit performance because the negative mental influence will cause a negative physical outcome and performance.

Somatic Anxiety

Somatic anxiety is a form of anxiety that causes physical manifestations that the person cannot determine the cause of, i.e., butterflies in the stomach prior to a soccer match. Somatic anxiety can have either positive or a negative impact on performance, as this is dependent on the mental capacity of the person experiencing this type of anxiety. Some athletes are able to perform under high levels of somatic stress, and others are unable to overcome the stress responses and perform poorly. The relationship between psychological arousal and performance are very important in understanding how an athlete may overcome certain types of stress in order to utilize that stress to their advantage.

Selective Attention

Selective attention refers to a person's ability to engage with the correct source of input while ignoring other forms of input simultaneously. For an athlete, this means focusing on the performance tasks required during a competitive event while ignoring other inputs such as fans, loud noises, cheerleaders, players from the opposing team, etc. An athlete that has high capacity to focus on the important aspects of performance will perform at a higher level than an athlete that struggles to handle excessive sensory inputs.

Cue Utilization Theory

Cue utilization theory refers to the changing of focus a person will undergo during periods of arousal. Cue utilization theory is an attempt at explaining the impact that stress and psychological arousal will have on an individual with regards to how this person processes attentional information, i.e., focus capacity and relevancy. Cue utilization theory suggests that moderate levels of arousal, coupled with a moderate narrowing of focus, is the area where optimal performance is possible, as too little arousal causes focus to be too broad, while too much arousal focus is too narrow, with both yielding poor performance results. Finding the right balance between psychological and physiological arousal are essential to excellent performance.

Preparatory Routine

A preparatory routine can be utilized by an athlete to bring the focus and attention to a specific task instead of focusing on an upcoming moment in a sporting event, past sporting events, or negative self-talk. This singular focus acts to functionally limit the brain's ability to consider other issues that would be problematic or negatively impact performance. Establishing a preparatory routine forms a consistent approach to stressful situations, which will lead to consistent performance.

Mental-Psychological Efficiency

Mental-psychological efficiency refers to an athlete's ability to process the cues and cognitive functions necessary for athletic performance. This particular form of mental discipline allows an athlete to perform at his or her physical peak without conscious thought directing their movements. This is seen with superior performers that are able to "glide" effortlessly during competition and exemplifies the symbiotic relationship between the mind and the body.

Copyright © Mometrix Media. You have been licensed one copy of this document for personal use only. Any other reproduction or redistribution is strictly prohibited. All rights reserved.
This content is provided for test-preparation purposes only and does not imply an endorsement by Mometrix of any particular political, scientific, or religious point of view.

Intrinsic Motivation

Intrinsic motivation is a type of motivation that occurs internally and is specific to the individual athlete. Intrinsic motivation is a form of motivation that is driven by a personal interest or enjoyment in performing a specific task. The primary reason intrinsic motivation is superior to other forms is because the athlete is engaging in the process of his or her own volition and personal enjoyment, which leads to more consistent effort during practices and competition. Over the short term, goals can be set in order to keep the athlete focused on a specific task, and over the long term, understanding the process involved in obtaining and sustaining success will be significant in maintaining a high level of performance.

Achievement Motivation Construct

The achievement motivation construct refers to an athlete's desire and determination to achieve a standard of performance, master a skill, or win a sporting event. The two types of achievement motivation are the motive to achieve success (MAS) and the motive to avoid failure (MAF). The motive to achieve success is an aspect of the achievement construct that is driven by a desire to succeed even if the challenge is substantial and failure is a possibility. The motive to avoid failure is predominated by a desire to avoid failure and is generally driven by the ego of an athlete, which means the athlete will avoid full effort in attempting to meet a goal or overcome a challenge that is perceived as being too difficult or if the athlete calculates the percentage chances of failure to be too high.

Positive Reinforcement

Positive reinforcement refers to the type of reinforcement engaged when a favorable or preferred behavior, movement, or performance occurs. Positive reinforcement is used to increase positive behaviors by providing a positive incentive to an athlete or a team, i.e., a reward. Positive reinforcement can take a variety of forms that can include increased playing time or a position in the starting line-up. Essentially anything that a player places significant value in can be used to reinforce positive behaviors.

Negative Reinforcement

Negative reinforcement is used to increase positive behaviors by removing an adverse stimulus which serves as the "reward." Negative reinforcement can also take a variety of forms, which could include reducing practice time because of superior efforts over a series of practices or a big team victory.

Positive Punishment

Positive punishment is the presentation of an adverse stimulus in order to reduce the occurrence of a specific undesirable behavior. An example of positive punishment in an athletic setting would be to have a player run additional sprints after practice, or increased time with a tutor for missing class time.

Negative Punishment

Negative punishment is the antithesis of positive reinforcement, as it requires the removal of something that is highly valued in order to deter negative behavior. A strength and conditioning coach can utilize this tactic by removing some aspect of training that the athlete really enjoys. This approach could have several different avenues for application that could include the removal of a preferred movement pattern for an individual athlete or the removal of music playing during training sessions as a result of poor group training efforts.

Copyright © Mometrix Media. You have been licensed one copy of this document for personal use only. Any other reproduction or redistribution is strictly prohibited. All rights reserved.
This content is provided for test preparation purposes only and does not imply an endorsement by Mometrix of any particular political, scientific, or religious point of view.

Inverted U Theory

The inverted U theory states that arousal will function as a facilitator of performance up to an optimal level, but if arousal continues past this point, performance will decrease. Arousal is the increased activity of specific physiological responses based on internal and external stimuli. If the physiological function is optimized at a certain level of arousal for an individual athlete, then performance will be enhanced. For instance, the heart rate will be fast but not so rapid as to impact how the heart will be capable to respond later in competition once fatigue has set in. If an athlete becomes overly aroused during a match, this can lead to increase physiological activities that will lead to premature fatigue and decreased performance. Athletes have varying tolerance levels for arousal, which means awareness of differences between athletes is very important during preparation for training and competitive events.

Optimal Functioning Theory

Optimal functioning theory suggests that individuals will have different levels of anxiety and arousal that will allow them to perform at their optimal abilities. This theory utilizes a standardized mood state evaluation, such as the state anxiety inventory, in order to quantify the arousal state and correlate this information to the actual physical performance of the athlete. An average score for an athlete is derived from the assessments of an athlete's best performances

Catastrophe Theory

Catastrophe theory suggests that over-arousal leads to a rapid and precipitous decline in performance, and once this occurs, the previous level of performance will not be reached even with a reduction in arousal. The catastrophe theory is, essentially, proposing a relationship between the level of arousal and the manifestation of cognitive anxieties once the arousal threshold has been exceeded. This leads to a change in an athlete's thought processes, causing focus to be shifted towards what he is no longer capable of executing during a competition, which leads to a catastrophic decline in performance.

Self-Efficacy

Self-efficacy refers to athletes' individual belief in their abilities and capacities to reach their goals. Self-efficacy can be very beneficial in a team sport, even though this is an individual belief system. An athlete that believes in himself can positively impact his team by providing a positive influence in difficult circumstances and put an emphasis on positive possibilities instead of the negative. This internal belief also allows the individual to remain positive when failure is experienced, which can be helpful if a team experiences a losing streak.

Association

Association refers to the process of connecting or relating between two different states that are connected through proximity to one another or through time. Association with regards to sport psychology refers to the process of being aware of the body's physical status during competition or training. Association of this type involves engaging with the discomfort of competition, maintaining focus on the task at hand, and not becoming focused on nonessential elements of the competition.

Dissociation

Dissociation during physical activity or competition refers to an athlete disconnecting from the physical tasks in order to block out fatigue, discomfort, and pain. This type of mental management leads to decreased physical performance because of an increase in anxiety about task performance and completion due to increased fatigue or pain.

Copyright © Mometrix Media. You have been licensed one copy of this document for personal use only. Any other reproduction or redistribution is strictly prohibited. All rights reserved.
This content is provided for test preparation purposes only and does not imply an endorsement by Mometrix of any particular political, scientific, or religious point of view.

Goal Setting

Goal setting is the process of setting performance standards in order to increase focus on task performance, improve consistency of effort, and instill a sense of accomplishment in athletes as they achieve and surpass their performance goals. Goal setting establishes fixed criteria in which athletes must perform to achieve their short-, mid-, and long-term goals which can consist of skill acquisition, improved physical conditioning, or enhanced mental discipline through physical effort. Establishing goals for an athlete, or athletes setting goals of their own, will produce a higher level of focus on the areas that need improvement, while also continuing to produce a challenge after each goal is successfully achieved.

Process Goal

A process goal is a goal that an athlete has direct control over achieving. A process goal is generally a daily goal that is achieved simply by an athlete performing a certain activity, i.e., lifting weights to meet off-season training goals. This type of goal will cause an athlete to engage in the behaviors necessary day to day in order to achieve the long-term result without becoming too focused on accomplishing the final result.

Outcome Goal

An outcome goal setting approach is the establishment of a long-term end result goal or standard which an athlete has little or no control over. These goals are typically focused on achieving some clearly defined level of success that is the culmination of an effort, i.e., winning a championship. Combining a long-term vision for success with process oriented goals, which place the focus on what must be achieved daily, will lead to consistent efforts towards the successful completion of the outcome goal. This is an effective method of delineating goals, creating achievable daily goals with an eye on achieving the final outcome but avoiding being overwhelmed by the length of time or effort required to reach the final result.

Successive Approximation

Successive approximation is an approach to shaping an individual's behavior. Successive approximation is the process of reaching a desired behavior by establishing a series of related short-term goals that increase in difficulty and, as the athlete progresses, more closely resembles the desired final behavior. This type of behavior modification can be used to improve movement execution by breaking down the proper execution elements of a movement and then standardizing a scoring system that will indicate incremental improvement in the movement throughout the process. This system can be used to eliminate bad habits or dangerous motor patterns in athletes, but also improve adherence to proper lifting technique and develop results consistency through a training cycle.

Manipulating Breathing Patterns and Muscle Tension

Manipulating breathing patterns via diaphragmatic breathing and muscle tension via progressive muscle relaxation are processes that an athlete can undertake that involve increasing awareness of the body, levels of tension or stress, and engaging the mind to focus on specific elements occurring in response to these techniques. This approach to mental and physical preparedness can be harnessed by an athlete to gain a greater level of control over their mental and physical responses to stress and this can also positively impact recovery from training and competition by allowing an athlete to achieve relaxation quickly and seemingly at will.

Copyright © Mometrix Media. You have been licensed one copy of this document for personal use only. Any other reproduction or redistribution is strictly prohibited. All rights reserved.
This content is provided for test preparation purposes only and does not imply an endorsement by Mometrix of any particular political, scientific, or religious point of view.

Reciprocal Inhibition

Reciprocal inhibition is a neurological process that prevents contraction of antagonist muscle groups from occurring at the same time. This is an injury prevention mechanism in the body, but can be utilized to alter whole body tension prior to competition or training. Reciprocal inhibition allows for a maximal contraction to occur in an agonist muscle group while inhibiting and actually forcing relaxation to occur in the antagonist muscle group. Manipulating this phenomenon will allow an athlete to achieve relaxation and enhance mental focus by alternating between cycles of contraction and relaxation in different muscle groups throughout the body. This will increase awareness of whole body tension by making an athlete aware of areas that contain higher levels of tension and, over time, give an athlete greater control over his or her responses to stress.

Autogenic Training

Autogenic training can be used to reduce whole body tension without the use of muscular tension as a mechanism for achieving this state. Autogenic training is a visualization technique that requires an athlete to get into a relaxed sitting, lying, or other resting position and then begin to visualize and sensationalize the relaxation of individual muscles or limbs by emphasizing the warmth and increasing heaviness of the limbs. This approach may cause a shifting from sympathetic neural dominance and high arousal to parasympathetic dominance and reduced arousal levels, which can improve mental clarity and focus on task performance optimally. This particular relaxation technique can be used with older athletes that may not want to produce high levels of muscular tension but want to be able to achieve a state of relaxation in order to improve performance.

Mental Imagery

Mental imagery is a visualization technique that involves mentally creating a competitive situation and performance. Creating a vivid imaginary competitive situation can positively impact an athlete's ability to perform by increasing their exposure to specific situations, even on a subconscious level, which can improve an athlete's confidence and comfort in how they will respond in reality. In preparation for a competitive season, using visualization techniques can expose the athlete to a larger volume of competitive experiences, without physical effort, which can be beneficial to supporting response to actual in-game situations. An athlete can practice visualization during training sessions by envisioning the sights, sounds, smells, and physical exertions required to complete a physically demanding task in training and then perform the activity which will solidify the experience and further integrate mental imagery to physical outcomes.

Hypnosis

Hypnosis is the process of inducing a state of increased focus and awareness using instruction and suggestion. Once hypnosis has been induced and the athlete is in a state of hyper-suggestibility, the therapist can then use positive suggestion and instruction to increase performance via removal of mental blocks or improve confidence by illuminating an athlete's physical potential. This approach can be very useful with athletes that may be underperforming because of a lack of self-efficacy.

Counterconditioning

Counterconditioning uses a combination of somatic and cognitive responses in order to reduce an athlete's performance-related anxiety. This is achieved through systematic desensitization which requires an athlete to engage in visualization of a stressful competitive situation and, in order to counter the stress response, the athlete engages in progressive muscle relaxation to induce a relaxed mental and physical state. Over time, the consistent application of this technique to

Copyright © Mometrix Media. You have been licensed one copy of this document for personal use only. Any other reproduction or redistribution is strictly prohibited. All rights reserved.
This content is provided for test preparation purposes only and does not imply an endorsement by Mometrix of any particular political, scientific, or religious point of view.

competitive situations that cause mild anxiety in an athlete can be effective in eradicating the anxiety and improve physical performance in difficult situations.

Copyright © Mometrix Media. You have been licensed one copy of this document for personal use only. Any other reproduction or redistribution is strictly prohibited. All rights reserved.
This content is provided for test preparation purposes only and does not imply an endorsement by Mometrix of any particular political, scientific, or religious point of view.

Nutrition

DRI System

The Dietary Reference Intakes (DRI) are recommendations for specific nutrients intake, which include 18 macronutrients, 18 minerals, and 14 vitamins. This system provides nutritional guidelines based on research across different populations and includes average intakes needed for the needs of an average person, while also providing insights for assessment and planning for utilizing the DRI. Athletic populations need to be aware of their baseline needs, and have a plan in place that will meet those needs in order to perform at a high level in competition and training. This system provides a functional system that provides the process of creating and implementing a plan and for making adjustments to the plan over time as needs change.

Protein Intake Requirement Guidelines

The protein intake requirement is a reference for amino acids intake for general populations that are consuming adequate calories from high-quality protein sources, and the general recommendation is 0.8 g/kg of body weight for males and females. Athletes, depending on the selected sport, will require a higher protein intake than general population requirements because of the increased need to regenerate various tissues, maintain a positive nitrogen balance, or as a fuel source (endurance athletes). The range for athletic populations generally falls between 1.5 to 2.0 g/kg of bodyweight.

Carbohydrate Intake

Carbohydrates are a primary energy source for human physiological processes ranging from muscle recovery to bouts of heavy prolonged physical activity. The various forms of carbohydrates, mono-, di-, and polysaccharides are the resources from which glycogen is synthesized. Dietary recommendations for athletes should be based on the sport they participate in, but also their general response to carbohydrate intakes, as some athletes tolerate higher carbohydrate intake well and others do not. Generally, aerobic athletes will benefit from consuming 8 to 10 g/kg of body weight, while anaerobic athletes seemingly respond well to 5 to 6 g/kg of body weight.

Daily Fat Requirements and Recommendations

Dietary fat recommendation for the general population is set between 20 and 35 percent of total calories consumed daily. While structured recommendations for athletic populations do not exist, athletes will generally consume greater than 30 percent of calories from fat, and studies have indicated diets with 50 percent of caloric intake from dietary fats in athletes engaged in heavy aerobic training do not increase circulating plasma lipid levels. Dietary fats are of great importance as they are involved in carrying fat soluble vitamins (A, D, E, and K), provides essential fatty acids (omega-3, -6) which support cellular membrane health, maintains brain and central nervous system health, and are essential in the production of hormones (testosterone).

Hydration and Performance

Hydration status plays a substantive role in competitive performance because all physiological processes require water and electrolytes (chloride, magnesium, potassium) but especially thermoregulation, muscle contraction, and nerve signaling. If hydration status is not maintained during competition then performance will decline as nerve signaling speed may decline, rate of muscular contractions may be reduced, cardiovascular strain occurs, and reduced thermoregulatory control will take place, resulting in injury and possible death.

Copyright © Mometrix Media. You have been licensed one copy of this document for personal use only. Any other reproduction or redistribution is strictly prohibited. All rights reserved.
This content is provided for test preparation purposes only and does not imply an endorsement by Mometrix of any particular political, scientific, or religious point of view.

Voluntary Dehydration

Voluntary dehydration refers to an athlete not adequately replenishing fluids during exercise, as the athlete only replenishes roughly 75 percent of the amount sweated off during activity. The possible dangers of allowing this practice to occur is a gradual decrease in fluid balance prior to initiation of practice or training session, which could place an athlete in danger for experiencing reduced training capacity, or poor competitive performance, but they could also incur a heat-related injury, as thermoregulation capacities will be reduced. Maintaining hydration status is of great significance to performance and requires monitoring and a restorative plan for after training and competition.

Proper Fluid Balance for Athletes

Proper fluid balance is defined as the required level of fluid intake needed to replace lost fluids that occur during normal bodily processes such as urine excretion, loss from lungs and skin, and excretion of feces. An athlete will need significantly more than the general guideline recommendation of 3.7 L for men and 2.7 L for women, and this value is related specifically to the sweat rate and duration of an activity. Research has indicated continuous sweating during prolonged activities can require an extra 11-15 L to replenish fluids lost.

Electrolytes

Electrolytes are critical in maintaining proper osmotic balance inside and outside the cell, but are also absolutely important in the regulation of fluid balance and blood pressure. Electrolytes are crucial to the maintenance of proper osmotic balance, as this is the primary control mechanism of hydration and maintenance of blood pH levels. This system is tightly controlled because of the significant role of electrolyte balance in a wide range of physiological responses. Maintaining proper electrolyte balance will impact everything from nerve conduction to blood pressure. Recommended sodium replacement levels for general adult population is four to six grams, but an athlete who sweats profusely may need significantly more to replenish the balance. Potassium replacement needs are slightly lower at two to six grams per day, with some athletes requiring more if they sweat profusely.

Significant Periods to Replenish Fluid Balance

The first period for fluid replenishment is prior to activity, which is generally two hours prior to competition or training, and can include water or any other non-alcoholic beverage of at least half a liter. The second period of interest is during activity replacement, which will persist until the activity is completed, and is highlighted by free access to fluids throughout activity and should be initiated prior to the onset of thirst response. The during-activity rehydration window can include cool water and amounts can vary depending on tolerance. The post-activity window for fluid replacement extends from the cessation of the activity until the pre-activity window prior to the next training session or competitive event. Replacement levels of 0.5 L per 0.45 kg of body weight lost, and with consideration of urine loss would be greater than 0.5L / 0.45 kg lost, and similar to the pre- activity period can include any non-alcoholic fluids. An exception can occur in the case of multiple periods of activity or competitions in a single day, and in this case, fluids containing sodium chloride more quickly restore fluid balance.

EAA

Essential amino acids (EAA) are amino acids that are not synthesized in the body and must be obtained from food sources. These amino acids include isoleucine, leucine, valine, phenylalanine, tryptophan, methionine, lysine, and threonine. Research investigating EAAs have found that these

Copyright © Mometrix Media. You have been licensed one copy of this document for personal use only. Any other reproduction or redistribution is strictly prohibited. All rights reserved.
This content is provided for test preparation purposes only and does not imply an endorsement by Mometrix of any particular political, scientific, or religious point of view.

amino acids can significantly impact the rate of muscle anabolism as a result of ingesting EAAs prior to resistance training. Studies have not indicated any significant negative effects.

Increasing MBC in Anaerobic Athletes

Increasing the rate of muscle buffering capacity (MBC) in an anaerobic athlete will increase the physiological capacity to buffer H^+ ions from lactate in order to continue performing at a high intensity or rate of work. Increasing an athlete's capacity to buffer H^+ ions through training or ingestion of sodium bicarbonate, citrate, or beta-alanine will improve work capacity at higher intensity by reducing blood pH levels, which will allow an athlete to continue to recruit high threshold motor units to produce force and delay the onset of fatigue.

Increasing PWC_{FT}

Physical working capacity at fatigue threshold (PWC_{FT}) refers to the ability to sustain a high rate of effort without fatigue. This threshold is highly correlated with ventilatory threshold and the lactate threshold as measures of anaerobic capacity. Improving the athlete's ability to perform work at higher intensities without reaching fatigue will significantly improve an athlete's ability to perform in competition as they will reduce fatigue, be able to sustain mental focus more effectively, and sustain higher rates of activity and muscular contraction throughout competition.

Complimentary Proteins

Complimentary proteins, also referenced as essential amino acids, are significant for athletic performance because these amino acids are not synthesized in the body and must be ingested. Research has indicated that certain essential amino acids can be helpful for recovery and muscular growth. Recent studies have shown the essential amino acid leucine to be responsible for initializing protein synthesis.

Cell Turnover

Cell turnover is a general description of the process of breaking down and regenerating the body's cellular environments. This is significant for athletic populations, as cell turnover is heavily involved with the breakdown and regeneration of proteins. These proteins are used to rebuild muscle tissue and help with physical adaptations. Over time, the clearance of old or deteriorating body tissues and cells will slow, resulting in reduced recovery time and presenting with general symptoms of aging on facial structures, hands, reduced reaction times, decreased muscle mass, etc.

Glycogenesis

Glycogenesis is the process the body undertakes to replenish glycogen stores in muscle tissue and the liver, and is the primary source of energy for the glycolytic energy system. The glycolytic system is of great importance in energy production for athletes of all types and durations, and the replenishment of glycogen through good nutrition is of absolute importance.

Ketosis

Ketosis is a physiological process that utilizes broken-down fatty acids for energy substrate. Ketosis will serve as a primary resource for energy production if carbohydrate intake falls below 50 to100 g per day over a period of time, generally seven to 10 days are required for this process to predominate. Ketosis can be detrimental for an athlete as the body needs significantly higher levels of energy substrate to perform higher intensity or long duration activities, and the supply of energy from ketosis will not provide adequate energy substrate for optimal performance levels. Transitioning into this state due to a low carbohydrate diet can impact performance with regards to physical endurance, mental focus, reduced cognitive function, and an inability to produce maximal

Copyright © Mometrix Media. You have been licensed one copy of this document for personal use only. Any other reproduction or redistribution is strictly prohibited. All rights reserved.
This content is provided for test preparation purposes only and does not imply an endorsement by Mometrix of any particular political, scientific, or religious point of view.

muscular contractions for either absolute strength purposes or to produce high velocity muscle activities such as sprinting or jumping.

Pre-Competition Meals

The pre-competition meal is significant because it is the meal that will provide the fluid and energy needs of an athlete during competition. This meal should occur three to four hours prior to competition in order to avoid gastric discomfort. All athletes should consume a meal that contains all three macronutrients, as this will allow for proper energy and blood glucose levels throughout competition. Endurance athletes will require larger amounts of carbohydrates as a percentage of total calories consumed because of energy demands of their selected sport. All pre-competition meals should be suited to the athlete's preferences and individual differences and responses to various food types and meal composition.

Determining an Athlete's Daily Energy Needs

Determining an athlete's energy needs will determine how much food an athlete requires in order to recover from training and competition, but will also serve to assist with maintaining an optimal competitive body weight. Providing an athlete with a guideline for caloric intake will make food selection, number of meals, and consuming enough essential vitamins and minerals easier and less stressful. While equations for estimating caloric intake vary and can incur some error, this is still an effective and accurate approach to providing an essential value to athletic populations short of using indirect calorimetry for an exact measure.

Altering Body Composition

In athletic populations there is great importance placed on a light athlete gaining weight and a heavy athlete losing weight. Athletes may need to alter body composition, adding muscle mass or dropping excess body fat, in order to enhance performance in competition. Adding lean muscle mass can enhance an athlete's ability to challenge an opponent by being more imposing and more difficult to overcome. An athlete can add lean muscle mass safely and without significant fat gain by increasing caloric intake moderately by 350 to 700 kilocalories over maintenance per day. Reducing body fat may be necessary for an athlete to improve their strength-to-weight ratio, or to enhance physical work capacities. Consuming a well-balanced diet along with reduced caloric intake of 500 to 1,000 kilocalories will result in gradual body fat reduction at a 1.1 to 2.2-pound rate per week.

Diet-Induced Thermogenesis

Diet-induced thermogenesis refers to the increase of internal body temperatures due to the intake of calorie-dense foods. The increase in body temperature is caused by the breakdown and assimilation of the meal in order to meet recovery and regenerative demands placed on it from training or competition. This is representative of an increase in metabolic activities. This diet-induced thermogenesis is an opportunity for a heavier athlete to induce additional calorie expenditure through consumption of calorie-dense foods that will assist with meeting metabolic demands, which would include protein-rich foods, vegetables, and healthy fats.

Energy Density

Energy density refers to the total caloric value of the foods consumed in a meal. Foods that are considered high energy density foods that yield significant calories per ounce individually or in combinations are animal-based proteins, nuts, and oils. Foods that are considered low energy density foods alone or in combination are vegetables, various salad greens, and fruits. The energy densities of meals need to be structured according to the body composition and performance goals of an athlete. Over time, over-consuming high energy density foods will lead to excess fat gain, and

Copyright © Mometrix Media. You have been licensed one copy of this document for personal use only. Any other reproduction or redistribution is strictly prohibited. All rights reserved.
This content is provided for test preparation purposes only and does not imply an endorsement by Mometrix of any particular political, scientific, or religious point of view.

consuming too few high density foods can lead to excess muscle loss and poor recovery for training. Striking a balance for most athletes is the best course of action for achieving body composition and performance goals.

Nutrient Density

Nutrient density refers to the ratio of nutrient content to total caloric content. Nutrient-dense foods are foods that provide a larger amount of vitamins and minerals while yielding lower calorie values. Foods that are considered nutrient-dense are primarily fruits and vegetables. Consuming a proper amount of nutrient-dense foods will provide the athlete with the essential vitamins and minerals needed to maintain proper hormonal balance and function at optimal levels throughout the training and competitive seasons.

BMI

The primary function of the body mass index (BMI) is to provide an assessment tool for determining an athlete's optimal body mass relative to their height. The BMI essentially provides a method to assess the significance an obese individual's body weight is from the normal range for someone of the same height. The primary limitation of the BMI is the overemphasis on total body weight without consideration for the body composition of the individual. BMI is limited to being a general measure of height-to-weight ratio and is used as a quick assessment tool for an athlete that is clearly obese and in need of weight reduction.

Muscle Dysmorphia

Body dysmorphia is a psychological disorder that manifests in an individual as an excessive preoccupation with overall body appearance or a specific aspect of their body. Muscle dysmorphia is an extreme preoccupation with a perceived small or thin body, even though these individuals will tend to be muscular or very muscular, and this will manifest behaviors such as obsessive working out, the use of anabolic steroids, or being overly concerned with dietary adherence. Body dysmorphia is not very common among competitive athletes, but is very common among bodybuilders, both male and female, and is considered a leading indicator of steroid abuse among bodybuilders in their pursuit of the "ideal" physique.

Anorexia Nervosa and Bulimia Nervosa

Anorexia nervosa is characterized by excessive caloric restriction, even self-imposed self starvation, in order to lose weight for fear of gaining weight. Bulimia nervosa is characterized by consuming large amounts of food and immediately purging the meal via forced vomiting and can include the use of diuretics, laxatives, and stimulants as well as excessive exercising habits because of obsessive concern over body weight. The primary difference in the disorders is that anorexia centers on excessive food restriction and bulimia is characterized by excessive food consumption and purging in close proximity thereafter. The essential keys to recognizing an athlete suffering with an eating disorder include lack of menstrual cycle, conflicting accounts between athletes on concerning behaviors, refusal to adapt nutritional changes, and significant weight loss and refusal to gain weight. An athlete dealing with these disorders needs clinical assistance and counseling as these are psychologically-governed disorders and are not based in rational thought and behaviors.

Binge Eating

An athlete with a binge eating disorder significantly overeats on a frequent basis but does not present with the purging behavior seen in bulimia nervosa. Binge eating over time will lead to significant weight gain from increased body fat stores. Increased body weight from additional body fat stores will negatively impact sport performance by requiring more energy to be used to move a larger mass during training and competition, but will also reduce work capacity, decrease total

Copyright © Mometrix Media. You have been licensed one copy of this document for personal use only. Any other reproduction or redistribution is strictly prohibited. All rights reserved.
This content is provided for test preparation purposes only and does not imply an endorsement by Mometrix of any particular political, scientific, or religious point of view.

velocity in high force movements, and can also lead to bone or soft tissue injury from increased structural loading. The long-term health risks associated with excessive fat gain include increased risk for diabetes, heart disease, high blood pressure, high cholesterol, stroke, and elevated triglyceride levels.

Ergogenic Aids

Ergogenic aids are pharmacological substances that are utilized to enhance physiological processes in order to improve athletic performance. These substances can be used to enhance physiological responses to exercise and training, such as muscular recovery, metabolism, or increasing circulating hormone levels. These substances are used by athletes to improve athletic performance and can become a focal point in preparations to the exclusion of whole foods, or in the case of steroid or amphetamine use, can become addictive due to the feelings associated with the use of these substances.

Creatine

Creatine is one of the most heavily researched ergogenic aids available on the market. Creatine supplementation is most effective in athletes that perform high intensity, but very brief, bouts of activity during competition. Increasing intramuscular levels of creatine increases the body's ability to sustain higher intensity muscular contractions by having additional resources to utilize for energy. The primary benefits found across several studies center on increasing strength levels, and generally indicate improved recovery from training as well as reduced fatigue during training sessions. The primary adverse effect to creatine supplementation is an increase in body mass, which may be undesirable in certain sports. Studies have not found significant deleterious effects of creatine supplementation, but have found mild acute effects that include gastrointestinal issues such as gas or mild bloating.

EPO

Erythropoietin (EPO) is notorious for being a performance-enhancing substance used by professional cyclists. Erythropoietin (EPO) is a protein-based hormone that is produced in the kidneys and is responsible for the production of new red blood cells. Increasing the availability of EPO in the body will increase the volume of red blood cells available for carrying and delivering oxygen to working tissues. Endurance athletes use EPO in order to improve aerobic capacity, which studies have indicated can be improved on average by 17 percent. The downside to EPO use is a significant increase in hematocrit levels and a substantive reduction in plasma volume. This change in hemodynamic increases blood viscosity, causing systolic blood pressure to be higher, this also increases the rate of blood clotting, and significant problems with maintaining body temperature during exercise.

Caffeine

Caffeine is a heavily studied ergogenic aid that stimulates the central nervous system and has been found to be of low risk to healthy individuals. There are issues that can arise when an athlete becomes overly reliant on stimulants and these issues are general restlessness, trouble sleeping/insomnia, hyperactivity, heart palpitations or arrhythmias, and frequent urination. An athlete that uses caffeine or other stimulants in order to improve performance prior to a workout may lead to a reduction in performance over time due to overstimulation of the central nervous system.

Beta-Adrenergic Agonists to Enhance Lipolysis

Lipolysis is a natural physiologic process that results in the breakdown of fats. Beta-adrenergic agonists will increase the rate of energy expenditure by increasing heart rate, blood pressure, rate

Copyright © Mometrix Media. You have been licensed one copy of this document for personal use only. Any other reproduction or redistribution is strictly prohibited. All rights reserved.
This content is provided for test preparation purposes only and does not imply an endorsement by Mometrix of any particular political, scientific, or religious point of view.

of respiration, and the increased activity of cyclic-AMP. These factors will increase metabolic rate and induce additional calorie expenditure, which will lead to increased fat loss over time. An athlete that wants to improve leanness due to being overweight, or a lean athlete wanting to drop additional fat in order to enhance performance, may use these substances to enhance metabolism when under significant caloric restrictions. These substances may be problematic for an athlete due to the increased heart rate and blood pressure, and are contraindicated in individuals that have heart conditions or abnormal cardiac rhythm.

HGH

Human growth hormone (HGH) is a protein hormone that originates from the anterior pituitary gland and has several physiological effects which include stimulating muscle and bone growth, increasing the release of fatty acids from adipose tissue, increasing uptake of amino acids, and has a role in maintaining blood glucose levels. Studies investigating the efficacy of exogenous HGH have found improvements in body composition in deficient populations, but very little strength-related research has been performed. The most significant deleterious effect of HGH usage is the occurrence of acromegaly, which is a disease that causes bone growth, increases in the size of organs, metabolic abnormalities, and the onset of arthritis.

Copyright © Mometrix Media. You have been licensed one copy of this document for personal use only. Any other reproduction or redistribution is strictly prohibited. All rights reserved.
This content is provided for test preparation purposes only and does not imply an endorsement by Mometrix of any particular political, scientific, or religious point of view.

Exercise Technique

Autogenic Inhibition

Autogenic inhibition is part of a negative feedback loop that is governed by the Golgi tendon organ and the central nervous system. Autogenic inhibition is a rapid relaxation of muscle tissue that prevents a muscle from tearing or otherwise being injured in the presence of sudden overload or when attempting to produce too much force in response to an external stimulus. This type of neural inhibition is a protective mechanism that is necessary to prevent injuries from occurring during sudden changes of direction, sudden distortions of a joint, or when attempting to perform a maximal muscle contraction beyond the current neural and mechanical capacities. Autogenic inhibition is generally governed by the Golgi tendon organ, and is essentially the opposite response to the myotatic stretch reflex.

Reciprocal Inhibition

Reciprocal inhibition allows for a maximal contraction of a particular muscle group or groups while preventing the antagonist muscle group from contracting simultaneously. This type of neural signaling essentially paralyzes the antagonist muscle group, which allows for the muscle to be stretched with little resistance, facilitating the agonist muscle group's complete contraction. Without this type of inhibition, muscles could not contract along the same joint articulation without interfering with one another, or without risking significant ligament, tendon, or muscle damage due to excessive forces accruing at the articulation site.

Range of Motion

Range of motion in a joint will either allow for maximum movement that will facilitate a complete muscular contraction during activity, or there may be limiting factors that will cause reduced contractile function, reduced force production, and possible injury due to compensatory movements creating odd forces in other joints. The primary limiting factor to range of motion is connective tissue quality and structure reducing movement around a joint. This is generally caused by age, activity levels, and gender.

Stretching

Stretching prior to physical activity is necessary in order to prepare the muscles, joints, and nervous system to perform at a high level. Stretching at initiation of a training session or a competitive event will reduce the risk of injury. Stretching will cause positive changes in the muscles and joints, but will also impact neural elements such as the Golgi tendon organ and will prepare the body to recruit the necessary motor units for optimal athletic performance regardless of sport.

Static Flexibility Movements

Including static flexibility in a training program is necessary when a change in muscle length or a reduction in tension is desired, as static flexibility can positively impact muscle tension and joint relationships over time. Static flexibility can be used post-training or competition, and can be effective for an athlete that is excessively stiff or has limitations due to past injuries. Static flexibility has been used prior to competition and training for many years, but has recently been challenged as an appropriate method for athletes to use prior to an event or training as there are indications that static stretching can negatively impact an athlete's explosive capabilities and increase joint laxity when stiffness is required, placing an athlete at higher risk for injury.

Copyright © Mometrix Media. You have been licensed one copy of this document for personal use only. Any other reproduction or redistribution is strictly prohibited. All rights reserved.
This content is provided for test preparation purposes only and does not imply an endorsement by Mometrix of any particular political, scientific, or religious point of view.

Dynamic Flexibility

Dynamic flexibility is a type of stretch that utilizes an athlete's movement, via minor shifts in momentum during a movement, to achieve a full range of motion. Dynamic flexibility can be performed from a standing, prone, supine, or kneeling position as there are a variety of movements that can be utilized to prepare the body for a competitive event or practice. Dynamic flexibility prior to an event will cause a cascade of physiological responses that include increased heart rate, increased neural activity from the central and peripheral nervous systems, increased blood flow to working tissues, systemically increased body temperature, etc. Dynamic flexibility is considered to be the superior approach to athletic event preparation because of the upregulation of the various body systems, but there are also no negative implications for dynamic flexibility due to joint or muscle laxity.

Elasticity

Elasticity is a specific muscular response to stretching. Elasticity is a significant component in the pursuit of increased flexibility and injury prevention because this capacity allows for a gradually or suddenly stretched muscle to return to a normal state quickly. The muscle's responsiveness to a rapid muscular stress, or a significant rapid change in joint angle in order to produce a large force, is of great importance as this is a key component in the myotatic stretch reflex that an athlete must utilize during sporting activities. If muscular elasticity is significantly reduced due to lack of neurological responsiveness or age, then total force production and proper tension length relationships between muscles and joints will lead to reduced performance and greater change for muscle strains and tears. Maintaining a high level of muscular flexibility over time will help prevent these reductions in elasticity, allowing an athlete to compete at a high level and with reduced injury risks.

Plasticity

Plasticity refers to a change in resting muscle tissue length. Altering the plasticity component in muscle tissue can improve muscle tension relationships between muscles and the articulating joint surfaces, which will reduce inflammation and possible injuries in athletes that present with excessive muscle shortening and tendon stiffness. The alteration of the resting state of a muscle will also increase the range of motion that can be achieved using static or dynamic movements. This change can be detrimental to an athlete that requires significant levels of muscle tension to stabilize the joints while producing force. Decreasing the tension capacity in the muscle tissue significantly will reduce an athlete's capacity to produce force suddenly. The importance of plasticity for athletes is that they possess an adequate amount of plasticity in order to move freely and with force when necessary. Assessing plasticity can be done by performing an athletic movement screening.

Mechanoreceptors

There are various types of mechanoreceptors located in muscles and around joints. Mechanoreceptors are primarily proprioceptors that respond to mechanical forces acting on the body while moving through space. These receptors provide constant feedback to the nervous system on body position, responses to external forces acting on the body, as well as providing mechanical feedback from internal force responses. Mechanoreceptors, generally the Golgi tendon organs and joint receptors, will govern the flexibility and extensibility responses the muscles and joints engage in when placed under stretching force, muscular contraction, or reactive forces. The role of governing muscular and joint responses to various types of stressors and forces is the primary means of preventing injury during training or competition when engaging in high force activities, and prevents a muscle or joint from going beyond the limit range of motion when under stretching forces.

Copyright © Mometrix Media. You have been licensed one copy of this document for personal use only. Any other reproduction or redistribution is strictly prohibited. All rights reserved.
This content is provided for test preparation purposes only and does not imply an endorsement by Mometrix of any particular political, scientific, or religious point of view.

Active Stretching

Active stretching requires the athlete to produce the necessary force to stretch the desired muscles. This form of stretching covers a significant spectrum of stretching methodologies, and includes dynamic and static variations. Active stretching is especially useful in the pre-training or pre-competition periods as the athlete will generally be moving through a full range of motion while moving through space, or performing light static stretching, moving through different positions in order to activate the joints, increase body temperature, and prepare for the proceeding activity.

Passive Stretch

A passive stretch requires a partner or other form of external force to produce the desired stretch. When preparing an athlete that presents with excessive stiffness, or struggles to perform stretching-related activities due to discomfort, using a passive stretching approach can be beneficial as this approach will reduce the strain on the individual, emphasize moving through a full range of motion through partner assistance, and will yield positive results over time. The passive stretching approach can be helpful with establishing an appropriate range of motion for an athlete to move through on their own by having a partner or coach assist the athlete through the range of motion they are capable of and comfortable with. This establishes a functional baseline range of motion that an athlete can use to build on over the course of a season.

Static Stretching

Static stretching is performed by moving slowly into a position that will gradually lengthen the desired muscle or muscle groups and then holding the final position, usually considered to be the point when discomfort is reached, for approximately 30-60 seconds. Static stretching prior to a competitive event is considered to be a normal procedure, but has recently fallen out of favor as research into this area has shown a decrease in muscle force production and an increased laxity in the joints, which are both detrimental to overall performance. The most beneficial period for an athlete to utilize static stretching would be post-training or post-competition in order to restore the highly tensed and fatigued muscles to a normal and possibly more relaxed resting state in order to facilitate recovery.

Ballistic Stretch

Ballistic stretches can be performed either statically or dynamically. To perform a ballistic stretch, an athlete needs to assume either a static or dynamic position and perform a rhythmic bouncing action in and out of the starting and ending positions of the stretch. This form of stretching forces the muscles and joints into a range of motion beyond the norm while under tension. The presence of tension during a stretched position is not abnormal, but moving into an extended range of motion while under tension can lead to significant muscle injury as a pull, strain, or possible tear can occur when engaging in ballistic stretching. This type of stretching does not need to be utilized in an athletic training program as there are safer warm-up and flexibility activities that are easily taught, corrected, and executed.

Dynamic Stretching

Dynamic stretching is a form of movement-based stretching that mimics many of the athletic movements required in competition or training. The essential differences between static, dynamic, and ballistic stretches are the types of movement required to achieve changes in range of motion. Dynamic stretches are a type of active stretches that are performed in a controlled manner while moving through a full range of motion. Static stretches are generally slow moving patterns that require an isometric hold in a stretched position for a set period of time. The ballistic stretch is

Copyright © Mometrix Media. You have been licensed one copy of this document for personal use only. Any other reproduction or redistribution is strictly prohibited. All rights reserved.
This content is provided for test preparation purposes only and does not imply an endorsement by Mometrix of any particular political, scientific, or religious point of view.

performed with rhythmic bounces to achieve changes in range of motion, and is generally not recommended as a stretching technique.

Mobility Drills

Mobility drills are a form of dynamic stretching that provides a stretch as an athlete moves through space. Mobility drills generally resemble sport-specific movements and are very useful for pre-training and pre-competition warm-up periods. Mobility drills similar to other methods of stretching will increase range of motion at the active muscle and joint sites, but the positive responses to this form of stretching include increased body temperature, increased circulation of synovial fluid in the joints, activation of the central nervous system, as well as increasing blood flow into the working muscles. These changes are all beneficial to an athlete prior to training or competition as this type of stretching provides all of the essential physiological changes from a resting state to a high-activity state. These physiological changes are not routinely found in traditional static methods and are much safer than ballistic stretching.

Proprioceptive Neuromuscular Facilitation

Proprioceptive neuromuscular facilitation (PNF) is a specific approach to increasing flexibility that utilizes neurological phenomena to overcome physical range of motion limitations that an athlete may have. PNF stretching was originally developed for use in clinical settings to assist with reclamation of proper range of motion post-surgery. PNF stretching utilizes the neuromuscular responses to specific feedback from various types of muscular actions, specifically isometric and concentric contractions, which result in changes in muscle tension relationships that allow for greater range of motion to be achieved. This method can be beneficial because of the greater range of motion that is achieved, but is also helpful in negating the impact of excessive discomfort and natural resistance that some individuals have when engaging in flexibility training.

Contract-Relax Partner Stretching Technique

The contract-relax stretching method is a form of proprioceptive neuromuscular facilitation (PNF) stretching that utilizes a brief isometric contraction during the initial stretching phase that, upon cessation of the contraction, the stretch is continued into a greater range of motion. This type of stretching is excellent for improving range of motion, preparing the joints for activity, and is very easy to execute. This specific type of PNF stretching is excellent pre-competition for athletes that have trouble stretching, or require longer warm-up periods in order to perform their best.

Hold-Relax Partner Stretching Technique

The hold-relax technique is a form of proprioceptive neuromuscular facilitation (PNF) stretching that begins by moving a partner's limb into a position that causes a very mild level of discomfort and is maintained for a set period of time. After the period of stretch has ended, the partner is allowed to relax and all tension is removed from the stretched limb, and the process is begun again using the same stretch-relax technique. The hold-relax technique is a very easy process to undertake and requires only mild levels of discomfort, which will allow an athlete that is resistant to stretching and flexibility training because of excessive stiffness or wants to avoid overwhelming levels of discomfort to increase range of motion without issue.

Hold-Relax with Agonist Contraction

The hold-relax with agonist contraction technique is a type of proprioceptive neuromuscular facilitation (PNF) stretching that requires an athlete to produce a contraction in the agonist muscle when stretched. Similar to the hold-relax method, the initial stretch position is held for 10-30 seconds and then a relaxation phase occurs. Once the relaxation phase ends, a contraction in the agonist must take place for three to five seconds and then the stretch and hold is initiated again.

Copyright © Mometrix Media. You have been licensed one copy of this document for personal use only. Any other reproduction or redistribution is strictly prohibited. All rights reserved.
This content is provided for test preparation purposes only and does not imply an endorsement by Mometrix of any particular political, scientific, or religious point of view.

The contraction phase in a relaxed muscle results in a decrease in the resting muscle tension, and allows for greater range of motion. This form of PNF stretching uses both reciprocal and autogenic inhibitions and is very helpful with overcoming range of motion limitations governed by neurogenic tone.

Copyright © Mometrix Media. You have been licensed one copy of this document for personal use only. Any other reproduction or redistribution is strictly prohibited. All rights reserved.
This content is provided for test preparation purposes only and does not imply an endorsement by Mometrix of any particular political, scientific, or religious point of view.

Program Design

SAID

The specificity adaptation to imposed demands principle (SAID) states the human body will adapt in a very specific manner in accordance with the demands that are placed on it. The adaptations to either physical or mental stress can occur across multiple systems, and will result in gradual resistance to the current level of demand, which will ultimately require change and manipulation of different variables over time. This principle is the foundation for training program progression, as an athlete must first acquire the necessary technique and movement skills required in a training program and then advancement can occur, either by increasing load, training speed or power qualities, adding intensification techniques, etc.

Needs Analysis

A needs analysis is a multi-faceted process that includes an analysis of the physical requirements and essential characteristics of the sport as well as a full spectrum assessment of the athlete. A movement analysis serves as an evaluation of body and limb movement along with assessment of muscles used, and serves as a starting point for movement selection for the resistance program. The physiological analysis is essential in determining the physical capacities that will be most heavily taxed during competition and practice and serves as a primary programming influence on the resistance and conditioning portions of the strength and conditioning program. To further tailor the resistance and conditioning program to the individual athlete's needs, an injury analysis is completed to determine possible limitations to performing certain movements or performing at higher intensity levels. All of these components together significantly improve the strength and conditioning coach's understanding of the needs of his athletes and will improve the quality of the program designed and implemented.

Assessing an Athlete's Training Status Prior to New Training Program

Assessing an athlete's current level of conditioning, or physical preparedness, is extremely important to program design as this will provide the coach with the necessary information to produce a training program that will improve the athlete's functional capacities without overtaxing the athletes if they are excessively deconditioned or undertaxing the athletes if they have maintained their conditioning levels. Assessing the training status of the athletes involves evaluation of their previous injury histories by a physician of sports medicine, as well as gathering information regarding previous training histories and training background information.

RPE

In many instances, simply asking an athlete, "How do you feel?" is not adequate when attempting to determine their current mental and physical status during a conditioning session. Using the ratings of perceived exertion (RPE) can effectively be implemented to monitor the athlete's effort during a training session, while also serving as an early alert system if an athlete is working too hard during a conditioning session. The Borg scale, from 6-20, is most commonly used to determine RPE and has been proven to be accurate, although environmental influences such as temperature can impact RPE reporting. Using this approach to athlete monitoring is an effective method, as it is easy to communicate the meaning of the assigned values, but is also cost effective for departments that may not be able to purchase heart rate monitors or other systems for athlete monitoring.

Copyright © Mometrix Media. You have been licensed one copy of this document for personal use only. Any other reproduction or redistribution is strictly prohibited. All rights reserved.
This content is provided for test preparation purposes only and does not imply an endorsement by Mometrix of any particular political, scientific, or religious point of view.

Long-Term Planning

Long-term planning for a group of athletes can be challenging, but assigning them into development categories can be very helpful in developing the athlete correctly according to their capabilities, skill level, and mental development. The key development phases are fundamental, novice, intermediate, advanced, and elite. During the fundamental phase (first two weeks) of training, the athletes should focus on playing their sport for enjoyment and developing basic skills needed to play the game. The novice phase (third and fourth weeks) is the beginning of structured practice, but is still emphasizing essential movement competency and mechanics. The intermediate phase (fifth and sixth weeks) signals the start of deliberate practice that is split between performance-based tasks and movement competency. The advanced training phase (seventh and eighth weeks) is the point which an athlete will begin to focus on specific techniques and abilities which are used in application with complex tactical planning and competitive circumstances. The elite phase (ninth and 10th weeks) is the phase in which mastery in specific strategies, skills, and abilities are the prime directive, along with maximal sport performance.

Exercise Selection

Exercise selection is the primary component of designing the resistance portion of a strength and conditioning program. Exercise selection is simply choosing the exercises for the resistance portion of the training program, which requires significant understanding of the types of exercises, i.e., structural, core, power, or assistance exercises; the physiological and movement requirements of the sport; an athlete's training history and movement capabilities; along with the amount of time available for training the athletes. A possible in-season training session for a collegiate basketball team could consist of two structural movements, with the first being a power movement, i.e., a power clean from blocks; and the second core exercise could be a squat or an overhead press. The final three movements could be single-joint movements performed in a circuit in order to condense the work into the remaining time. A circuit to finish the training session will stimulate metabolic fatigue and stress the muscles while reducing structural loading during the season.

Dynamic Correspondence

Dynamic correspondence refers to the exercise selection process determined by the specific activity that the training is intended to support. The criterion for selecting the correct movements for a training program according to the desired outcome is reliant on determining the desired rate and time for peak force production, dynamic of effort, region of force production, regimen of muscular work, amplitude and direction of movement, and accentuated region of force application. There are three elements for optimal transfer: identify target activity's mechanics through task specific needs analysis, choose movement patterns according to the needs analysis, and distinguish between specificity and simulating a task's outward appearance.

Lower Body Plyometrics

Lower body plyometrics can be included into a variety of athlete's training programs in order to improve athletic performance. Sports that benefit most significantly from lower body plyometrics generally require athletes to produce large amounts of force through sprinting, jumping, or changing direction repeatedly throughout the course of a game or match. Athletes in sports such as football, basketball, rugby, soccer, or volleyball must be able to produce substantial forces across multiple planes and in different body positions in order to excel. Lower body plyometrics can be utilized in brief periods of time in order to elicit the necessary training adaptations. Possible plyometric movements to choose for inclusion in a training program, in order from least to most demanding, are jumps in place, standing jumps, countermovement jumps, bounds, and depth jumps.

Copyright © Mometrix Media. You have been licensed one copy of this document for personal use only. Any other reproduction or redistribution is strictly prohibited. All rights reserved.
This content is provided for test preparation purposes only and does not imply an endorsement by Mometrix of any particular political, scientific, or religious point of view.

Upper Body Plyometrics

Upper body plyometric movements should be included in any athlete's training program to meet the physical demands of their sport, which will generally include any sport that relies on the upper body to throw, catch, tackle, or hold off an opponent. Upper body plyometrics are not used as often, or as heavily, as lower body plyometrics, but utilize the same neuromuscular responses to generate force. A training program for a football, basketball, lacrosse, baseball, or golf team should include upper body plyometrics such as medicine ball throws, medicine ball catches, or various push-up variations.

Modifications for Performing Trunk Plyometrics

Performing trunk plyometrics that specifically target the muscles of the trunk is very challenging as these muscles may not possess all of the necessary plyometric elements to elicit the potentiation response of other plyometric exercises. Research indicates that the stretch reflex may not be sufficiently involved during trunk exercises to increase the force of muscle contraction, and this lack of a response may be caused due to proximity of the muscles to the spinal cord. In order to achieve a similar effect to other plyometric exercises, traditional trunk movements' range of motion can be shortened and include the use of a medicine ball to generate rapid eccentric loading and potentiated muscular contraction.

Frequency of Plyometric Training Activities

Frequency of plyometric activity is governed primarily by the needs of the sport and the sport season. Typically, the number of plyometric training sessions can range from one to three per week. Plyometric activity, similar to resistance training and conditioning activities, must be evaluated based on the stress of the movements performed, i.e., jumps to a box (low stress) compared to depth jumping (high stress), number of repetitions required each session, and the training volume of all other activities in a single training session, throughout the training week, or training cycle. A strength and conditioning coach will need to develop frequency guidelines based on experience and some trial and error over time as research into this area specifically is very limited.

Recovery Between Plyometric Exercises

Recovery between sets of plyometric exercises must allow for complete recovery between sets to take place in order to ensure maximal performance during the working sets, as plyometric activities emphasize anaerobic power and technical skill development. Work-to-rest ratios ranging from 1:5 to 1:10 can be utilized to establish proper recovery periods during a training session. The proper recovery ratio will be dependent on the type of exercise, the number of repetitions, and the total number of sets to be performed. Recovery between training sessions follows similar guidelines to traditional resistance training and conditioning activities, as adequate recovery time must be allotted in order to avoid overtraining, which generally requires two to four days depending on the sport season.

Age Considerations and Possible Limitations for Plyometric Training Activities

Plyometric and plyometric-like activities can be included in training programs for a wide variety of age groups safely as long as general guidelines are followed in order to maximize safety and productivity. This is especially true when considering implementing a plyometric training program with younger athletes. Considerations for younger athletes include emphasizing development of proper technical movement patterns, neuromuscular control, and anaerobic skills necessary to participate in athletic endeavors. The key with younger athletes is gradual progression from simple movement tasks and drills to more complex drills. When designing and implementing a plyometric training program for a Masters-level athlete, considerations for their injury history, or pre-existing

Copyright © Mometrix Media. You have been licensed one copy of this document for personal use only. Any other reproduction or redistribution is strictly prohibited. All rights reserved.
This content is provided for test preparation purposes only and does not imply an endorsement by Mometrix of any particular political, scientific, or religious point of view.

orthopedic condition are necessary while also being sure to adhere to the overall goal or goals of the training program. The Masters' program should include no more than five low to moderate, a lower overall training volume, total foot contacts should be limited per session, and recovery from sessions should be at least three to four days.

Plyometric Training Volumes

Plyometric training volumes for lower body exercises are generally expressed as the total number of sets and repetitions performed during a specific training session, with total foot contacts or distance also being options for tracking training volumes. Training volumes for upper body plyometrics are generally tracked as total number of throws or catches per training session. The general recommendations for plyometric training volumes vary depending on the experience of the athlete with beginners needing between 80-100 total repetitions per session, intermediates 100-120 repetitions per session, and advanced trainees 120-140 repetitions per session.

Program Length and Progression Model for Plyometric Training Activities

The length of a plyometric training program can range from six to 10 weeks, as research has not determined an optimal plyometric training length, although vertical jumping has been found to improve in as little as four weeks of plyometric training. Progression during a plyometric training program is similar to traditional resistance training and must follow the progressive overload principle, which requires a strength and conditioning coach to manipulate training loads, frequency, and intensities in various combinations throughout a training program. Program length and progression are determined by the sport season, athlete experience performing plyometric exercises, and the needs of the sport.

Complex Training Model

A complex training model is an approach to using resistance training, sport-specific activities, and plyometrics in order to maximize athletic performance. The complex training model is very challenging to the nervous and musculoskeletal systems and is beneficial for athletes that require more advanced training methodologies. This training model utilizes heavy resistance-training exercises to activate the fast-twitch muscle fibers and the plyometric movement recruits these previously activated fibers to produce even greater force. This is a form of neural potentiation that occurs because of the combination of movements and threshold of activation that can be achieved through manipulating movement selection and contraction types in a training program. A possible combination of movements using this model include: A1: Back Squat at 85-90 percent, two or three reps. A2: Box jump to maximum height, three to five reps, or B1: bench press, 80-90 percent, three to five reps. B2: plyometric push-up, 3-5 reps.

Mobility Training

Mobility training is a component of a dynamic flexibility program. Mobility and flexibility are key elements to proper sprint and agility mechanics as optimal ranges of motion are required to perform specific tasks. The ability to move through the proper ranges of motion without significant tissue or joint resistance will increase the fluidity of the athlete's movement and improve the turnover rate from phase to phase of the sprint or agility actions. An athlete that is in need of improved range of motion due to restricted range of motion, muscular strength imbalances, or inactivity can be evaluated for these issues and have a mobility and flexibility regimen implemented to correct these issues and improve overall performance.

Tactical Metabolic Training

Tactical metabolic training is a systematic approach to modeling the speed-endurance needs of an athlete by sport. Using this approach allows a coach to optimize training economy by outlining the

Copyright © Mometrix Media. You have been licensed one copy of this document for personal use only. Any other reproduction or redistribution is strictly prohibited. All rights reserved.
This content is provided for test preparation purposes only and does not imply an endorsement by Mometrix of any particular political, scientific, or religious point of view.

amount of time needed per session, and enhances athlete performance by optimizing arousal, attention, and motivation through skill and sport-specific metabolic conditioning drills. This approach allows the strength and conditioning coach to prioritize movement patterns to include in the routine, while also allowing the coach to determine preset times for rest and activity, as well as the necessary distances to cover per repetition, all while emphasizing sport-based activities. The drawbacks to this approach are specific to quantifying the volume of work performed and intensity level.

Sequenced Training

The central concept guiding sequenced training is specific to the decaying rate of adaptation during a training phase, which occurs during sustained training blocks when adaptation to the training stress has occurred, and the capacity to maintain the progress made in the next training phase while training at lower volumes. Sequenced training is an approach to planning an athletic program that specifically selects characteristics for improvement during a training phase and then inverting the focus in the next training block, i.e., training for strength with lower volume of speed and agility during the accumulation phase and inverting this in the succeeding restitution phase. This approach allows the strength and conditioning coach to outline the training plan for a specific period of time in the sport season or an entire calendar year with a focus on multiple core areas based on needs of the athletes without overworking the athletes in the core areas and without limiting training in other areas that can serve as a focus during a restitution phase.

Pace/Tempo Training Method

The primary purpose of pace/tempo training is to train at an intensity slightly above normal competition race pacing, with the primary goal to enhance both aerobic and anaerobic energy systems' contributions during a race. The pace intensity corresponds to the lactate threshold and is commonly referred to by athletes as threshold training or aerobic/anaerobic interval training. There are two common approaches to pace/tempo training: steady and intermittent. Steady pace/tempo is a continuous training session where the intensity is equal to the lactate threshold for 20- to 30-minute segments. The intermittent approach is similar to steady pace/tempo training but the training session consists of shorter intervals with brief recovery periods in between. The key to pace/tempo training is staying within the prescribed intensity levels and increase the distance covered in a training session, as this will help the athlete develop a sense of race pace and improve the capacity to sustain effort at that pace.

Interval Training for Aerobic Athletes

Interval training for the aerobic athlete is similar to the interval training for the anaerobic athlete, as both are training at higher intensities relative to VO_2 max, but the duration of the intervals are significantly different, as are the rest periods. Interval training for the aerobic athlete consists of timed intervals lasting from three to five minutes, with a three to five minute rest period (1:1 work/rest ratio) in order to facilitate full recovery between bouts. The key to interval training—having a firm aerobic conditioning base—has been established in order to fully realize the benefits of interval training without overstressing the athlete's various systems. Interval training will increase the athlete's VO_2 max while also enhancing anaerobic metabolism.

Choosing Mode of Aerobic Exercise for Endurance Athlete

Selecting the correct mode of aerobic exercise for the endurance athlete is important, much in the way choosing movement patterns in resistance training programs are sport specific, as this needs to closely resemble the competitive activities and events of the endurance athlete. This is because, in order for the necessary adaptations to take place in the muscles and generate a positive physiological response, the specific muscles must be engaged in the sporting activity. Training

Copyright © Mometrix Media. You have been licensed one copy of this document for personal use only. Any other reproduction or redistribution is strictly prohibited. All rights reserved.
This content is provided for test preparation purposes only and does not imply an endorsement by Mometrix of any particular political, scientific, or religious point of view.

frequency must be selected according to the same general standards for all sports, but for the aerobic endurance athlete, training frequency is determined most specifically by the relative heart rate intensity of the training session and the duration of that session, as well as the sport season. High-intensity sessions will require greater recovery time and reduce overall training frequency, while low-intensity sessions and shorter duration sessions may occur more frequently as recovery time is not as substantial.

Repetition Training

Repetition training is a training approach that consists of multiple high-intensity sprint intervals performed, generally, at greater than VO_2 max, for bouts of 30 to 90 seconds at a time. When using this training method, work-to-rest ratios are significantly different than other methods, and generally suggested to be four to six times longer than the length of the interval. This work-to-rest ration is primarily due to the reliance on anaerobic metabolism for energy, as this system requires longer rest periods to facilitate complete or near complete metabolic recovery. The benefits of this training method include the athlete being able to run faster, enhanced running economy, an increased anaerobic capacity/resilience and metabolism, along with improving an athlete's ability to finish the race with a big push or final kick at the end.

Fartlek Training

Fartlek training is a combination method of aerobic endurance training, and can be used with cyclists, runners, and swimmers. A fartlek training session will combine lower intensity level pace work and short burst intervals or hill running for brief periods of time. This training format can help alleviate the boredom and arduous nature of daily training sessions of a single type, and allows an athlete to pursue daily challenges within the structure of the prescribed training session. This session is best used during periods of heavy training as a change of pace from the buildup to an event, but can also serve as a staple in a training program as a reward of sorts to allow the athletes the opportunity to challenge themselves on a weekly basis. This approach will enhance VO_2 max and increase lactate threshold, while also improving running economy and fuel utilization.

Stretch-Shortening Cycle

The stretch-shortening cycle is the rapid elongation of a muscle that is followed by a rapid countermovement resulting in muscular contraction that is generated through a series of neurological and muscular feedback systems that allows for the generation of tremendous amounts force during explosive muscle actions such as running, jumping, bounding, etc. This system is also active at lower levels to reduce the occurrence of muscle tears, i.e., stepping off a curb and twisting an ankle, in order to prevent injuries due to odd forces. The uses of plyometric exercises utilize this phenomenon to train the stretch-shortening cycle to respond more rapidly and produce greater forces to improve sport performance.

Series Elastic Component

The mechanical model of plyometric exercise is primarily focused on the role and responses of the series elastic component. The series elastic component (SEC) of the stretch-shortening cycle is the most important component of the stretch-shortening cycle response as this is the epicenter of activity in the muscles and tendons when a rapid eccentric muscle action occurs. The series elastic component acts as a spring in response to the stretch on the musculotendinous unit. When the musculotendinous unit is stretched, as in an eccentric contraction, the series elastic component is lengthened and stores this elastic energy until a concentric muscle contraction occurs. The more rapidly the contraction occurs, the greater the amount of stored energy is released; a more prolonged contraction will release a smaller amount of energy; and should a muscular contraction place too much motion around the joint, the stored energy will be lost as heat energy.

Copyright © Mometrix Media. You have been licensed one copy of this document for personal use only. Any other reproduction or redistribution is strictly prohibited. All rights reserved.
This content is provided for test preparation purposes only and does not imply an endorsement by Mometrix of any particular political, scientific, or religious point of view.

Eccentric Phase

The eccentric phase is the initial phase of the stretch-shortening cycle that involves the preloading force to occur in the agonist muscle group. In this phase, the series elastic component stores the elastic energy generated during the preloading of the muscle, which stimulates the muscle spindles. After the stimulation of the muscle spindles occur, they communicate the change in muscle length to the ventral root of the spinal cord via afferent nerve fibers (Type Ia), which is the beginning of phase II of the stretch-shortening cycle. A possible example of the eccentric phase is when an athlete lands during a depth jump, as the feet of the athlete contact the ground, the eccentric loading of the calves, quads, hips, and hamstrings will begin and end once the movement is completed.

Amortization Phase

Phase II, the amortization or transition phase, occurs at the cessation of the eccentric phase and before the initiation of the concentric phase. Continuing from the end point of the eccentric phase, the afferent neurons (type Ia) synapse with the motor neurons (alpha) that then transmit signals to the agonist muscle group. This portion of the stretch-shortening cycle is extremely important with regards to the magnitude of the muscular contraction and total force generated, as this phase must remain brief in order to potentiate the contraction phase maximally. If this phase is too long then the stored elastic energy will be lost as heat and the reflex response will not be able to generate a maximal response.

Concentric Phase

The concentric phase is the terminal phase of the stretch-shortening cycle, and serves as the oppositional response to the eccentric loading on the body that occurs during phase I. Continuing from phase II, the motor neurons (alpha) stimulate the agonist muscle group resulting in a reflexive muscle contraction. The reflexive contraction will be greatest when the amortization phase, phase II, is most brief as the stored elastic energy in the series elastic component can be released as rapidly generating the maximal potentiated contraction possible. During a depth jump, once the upward movement of the jump is initiated, the concentric phase has begun, resulting in the contraction of the calves, hips, glutes, and quadriceps.

Stretch Reflex

The stretch reflex is the primary element of focus in the neurophysiological model of plyometric exercise. The stretch reflex is a type of muscular contraction that is generated in response to a rapid stretching force within a muscle. The stretch reflex is primarily governed by the nervous system via a monosynaptic reflex that is responsible for maintaining constant muscle length. This response can be activated in a wide range of situations, from sprinting or jumping activities to slipping and nearly falling in the shower. Because the stretch reflex is activated when a rapid stretching force is applied to a muscle, a strength and conditioning coach can utilize movements that require rapid changes in direction such as bounding horizontally repeatedly to cover a set distance, jumping from side to side quickly over a low object, dropping from the top of a box and immediately jumping into the air, etc.

Muscle Spindles

Muscle spindles are proprioceptive structures that are located within the belly of muscle tissues throughout the human body and are sensitive to rate and magnitude of an eccentric muscle action. The muscle spindle is the primary proprioceptive feedback structure in the muscle and is the most important component in the stretch reflex response. The muscle spindle senses when a rapid stretch is applied to a muscle and reflexively contracts, which serves to potentiate the force-generating capacity of the muscle as well.

Copyright © Mometrix Media. You have been licensed one copy of this document for personal use only. Any other reproduction or redistribution is strictly prohibited. All rights reserved.
This content is provided for test preparation purposes only and does not imply an endorsement by Mometrix of any particular political, scientific, or religious point of view.

Speed Development

Speed development is essential for athletes in a wide variety of sports and consists of methods that involve teaching the proper technique and acquiring the necessary movement skills to run effectively and at high rates of speed. Speed development programming has two primary objectives, with the first emphasizing proper running technique and correcting technical errors, along with using various methods to increase an athlete's ability to produce force when sprinting. Technique and technical adjustments require significant time and effort, and are generally beyond the scope of the strength and conditioning coach's ability to correct with large groups. Running or sprinting at great speeds is a reflection of an athlete's physical strength, which the strength and conditioning coach can most directly impact. Various methods to addressing speed development specifically include resistance training in the weight room, plyometrics, and various methods or devices for overloading the athlete while running, which can include pushing or dragging sleds, partner-resisted running, or using other resistive elements like a parachute to induce larger force outputs from the athlete.

Speed-Endurance

Speed-endurance refers to the specific metabolic conditioning necessary to sustain running or agility speed over an extended period of time or in order to achieve maximal acceleration or speed during repetitive sprint actions. Developing speed-endurance is specific to the sport the athlete is preparing for: a soccer player will engage in sustained efforts with bursts of sprint speed throughout a match, while a basketball player is generally going to sprint more frequently and at higher speeds more frequently with breaks in play to facilitate recovery. Speed-endurance can be improved upon by performing multiple sprinting bouts for conditioning purposes, and can include running hills, dragging sleds, timed runs over a specific distance, etc. For many athletes, a combination of higher intensity sprint activities and sustained heart rate cardiovascular training will serve to enhance endurance at speed and duration.

Sprinting

Flight Phase and Support Phase

Sprinting is an activity that requires an athlete to repeatedly launch the body forward with maximal velocity and acceleration, and with regards to human movement is unique because of the multiple phases of movement that occur. The flight phase of a sprinting or running action is the phase in which one leg has pushed forcefully from the ground and is in the air, generally with the knee above hip level. The support phase of a sprint or running action is when one leg is acting as the support anchor for the torso and oppositional leg that is engaged in its flight phase. Sprint or running action are considered single leg, or unilateral, actions because of the separate flight and support phases. Waling and other bipedal activities are considered bilateral actions as they alternate between single and double support phases without a flight phase.

There are two primary components that form the support phase. The first component is propulsion, which is the forceful application of the foot to the ground in order to generate maximal force to move the body forward with maximal velocity. The second component to the support phase is braking, which is the application of the foot to the ground, eccentrically loading the leg muscles in order to slow the body's momentum to change direction or in order to completely stop. These two components make up the two most significant elements of sprinting and running action as an athlete moves the body forward rapidly and the other brings the body's momentum to a stop.

Recovery Phase

During the sprinting action, the recovery phase is essential to optimal running mechanics but also in obtaining the highest velocity and lowest times possible. The recovery phase serves as the period

Copyright © Mometrix Media. You have been licensed one copy of this document for personal use only. Any other reproduction or redistribution is strictly prohibited. All rights reserved.
This content is provided for test preparation purposes only and does not imply an endorsement by Mometrix of any particular political, scientific, or religious point of view.

of time in which the hip, knee, and ankle are positioned for ground contact as the leg swings forward. The importance of the recovery phase is essential for maximal force production and highest achievable velocities for an athlete, as this phase is the portion of the sprint action where all of the joints in the lower body need to be aligned properly in order to produce the highest reactive forces to the ground in order to propel the body forward. If an athlete presents with odd joint angles, either high hip position, ankle being plantar flexed instead of dorsiflexed, or knee pointed towards the ground instead of upwards, then an athlete will produce slow times and poor ground contact mechanics.

Stride Frequency and Stride Length

Stride frequency refers to the rate of strides that occur during a sprint or running action over a specific distance. Stride length refers to the distance an athlete is able to cover per completed stride. These two elements are interrelated due to the relationship between distance covered per stride and the number of strides required to complete a specific distance. The greater the stride length, the fewer strides required to complete a distance, which is commonly seen with elite-level athletes. Athletes that try to overstride or struggle with reduced stride length require technical coaching and retraining for sprint-related actions in order to perform optimally during competition.

Overstriding and Understriding

Overstriding occurs when an athlete attempts to outreach their leg length in order to cover more ground during a sprint action. Overstriding causes a significant change in the mechanics of the action that can range from overextension of the hips, poor foot contact position, and a vertical torso. Understriding occurs when an athlete takes smaller strides during a sprint action which can be found in an athlete that may think they are covering more ground by moving their feet more quickly, or by having weaknesses or tight muscles in the kinetic chain that will not allow the athlete to reach for ground efficiently or comfortably. To address both overstriding and understriding, a coach will need to spend one-on-one time with the athlete to make corrections and form a plan to maintain and make the technical changes permanent. With regards to understriding, an athlete may lack strength and flexibility in key muscles involved in sprinting actions, which can be addressed via resistance training, flexibility and mobility activities to improve on this technical error.

Common Technical Errors and Corrections

There are several common errors that can be discussed for technical correction. The most common errors of sprinting include arms crossing over the midline of the torso in a side to side action, premature upright posture, the appearance of "bouncing" during the sprint, and hyperextension or flexion of the neck. To correct improper arm action, practicing proper arm swing during lower-level running activities is necessary. To correct premature upright posture, an athlete needs to improve push-off force, maintain forward trunk, and keep the eyes focused on the ground without raising the head. Correcting "bouncing" vertically during a sprint can be done by lengthening the push-off phase by placing chalk marks along the ground at specific intervals in order to increase the stride rate. To correct hyperextension of flexion of the neck, the athlete should maintain normal head position with eyes focused straight ahead.

Sprint Resistance Techniques

Sprint resistance techniques for sprint training involve increasing the effect of gravity on an athlete's body during sprint action, which can include using harnesses, parachutes, weight vests, sleds, running uphill, or up a staircase. Maintaining proper movement mechanics is important when using resistance methods for sprint training, as loads greater than 10 percent of an athlete's body weight will negatively impact sprint performance as the athlete works to muscle through the resistance via strength instead of an explosive action as intended. Using sprint resistance for speed

Copyright © Mometrix Media. You have been licensed one copy of this document for personal use only. Any other reproduction or redistribution is strictly prohibited. All rights reserved.
This content is provided for test preparation purposes only and does not imply an endorsement by Mometrix of any particular political, scientific, or religious point of view.

development is intended to improve the athlete's explosive strength capacity and increase stride length.

Spring Assistance Techniques

Spring assistance techniques for sprint training involve creating an overspeed effect on the athlete during sprint action without altering normal mechanics. Spring assistance methods for speed development include downhill running on a shallow slope of three to seven degrees, high-speed towing via a harness or stretch cord, or other methods that will generate an overspeed effect. Spring resistance methods are intended to increase stride rate and improve an athlete's ability to accelerate to maximal speed with less effort and energy expended. Similar to sprint resistance, spring assistance methods need not exceed a 10 percent increase in velocity in order to prevent athletes from leaning back or overstriding in an attempt to brake and protect themselves.

Special Endurance

Special endurance refers to the physiological capacity needed to perform maximal or near-maximal efforts in sport-specific exercises or movements. Special endurance is a specialized variation of speed endurance and requires two specific elements: the metabolic power to perform the specific tasks and skills at the desired intensity level, and the metabolic work capacity to repeat efforts at this intensity level. Performing sport-specific movement patterns or exercises at near-maximal or maximal levels will generally require breaking down selected patterns from the sport and implementing the necessary movement skills into a repetitive drill that requires brief periods of rest and multiple bouts of the drill.

Agility

Agility can sometimes be confused with linear speed or other athletic qualities. Agility is specific to an athlete's capacity to explosively change directions, velocities, or modes. In sports, there are transitions of movement types, changes of pace, and changes in body positions that impact the rate of speed an athlete is able to sustain in order to perform such tasks at high rates of speed. Training an athlete to change directions explosively can be achieved with a wide range of skills and directionally-based challenge drills. If an athlete plays a sport where transitions from running to jumping are necessary, this quality can be trained by having an athlete perform drills similar to their sporting activities, such as plyometric drills involving an athlete dropping from a box and sprinting forward, or performing bounding-related activities into a sprint. Agility, like speed development, is an expression of an athlete's ability to generate force. The primary method of addressing deficiencies in this area is with resistance training and making the athlete stronger.

Training for Muscular Hypertrophy

Training for muscular hypertrophy generally requires prescribing a moderate to higher number of repetitions per set to result in higher training volumes. Using a moderate six repetitions per set to higher 12 repetitions per set will require using lower percentages of an athlete's one-repetition maximum, and will reduce the impact the training will have on strength levels other than the trained repetition ranges. If the hypertrophy desired is specific to a particular muscle group, then the use of multiple exercises, usually three per muscle group, can have a substantial impact on muscle growth. Using three different exercises per muscle group can impact the total training volume significantly and would need to be accounted for by the strength and conditioning coach.

Training for Muscular Endurance

Training for muscular endurance requires the athlete to perform numerous repetitions, at least 12 per set, for two to three working sets. Training for muscular endurance, when compared to training for muscular hypertrophy, involves using lighter loads and higher training volumes and will have

Copyright © Mometrix Media. You have been licensed one copy of this document for personal use only. Any other reproduction or redistribution is strictly prohibited. All rights reserved.
This content is provided for test preparation purposes only and does not imply an endorsement by Mometrix of any particular political, scientific, or religious point of view.

very little overall impact on neural fatigue, strength gains, muscular growth, and stress. Another area of differentiation between training for endurance and muscular hypertrophy is the number of exercises used, as muscular endurance usually only uses one exercise per body part.

Muscle Balance

Muscle balance is an essential element to the resistance training program because overemphasizing certain muscle groups over others can alter length-tension relationships along the body's joints and impact the kinetic chain negatively. Without proper programming balance, the body will alter movement patterns in order to produce the necessary force needed to perform the lifts and perform in competition. These alterations, over time, will lead to increased injury rates. In order to prevent this from occurring, the strength and conditioning coach must build balance between the muscle groups at intersecting joints. This does not necessarily mean equalizing strength in antagonist muscles groups, but improving the strength ratios, i.e., hamstring to quadriceps strength at 3:4, will prevent significant injuries and joint breakdown over time.

Multi-Joint Exercises

Multi-joint movements, which include body weight and any externally loaded movement pattern, provide the greatest stimulation of muscle tissue and the highest capacity for loading through increased resistance and training volumes, but also provide significant benefits to the collegiate athlete when working under time constraints that limit the duration of training sessions. When designing training programs for collegiate athletes, designing a program to meet the needs of the sport is essential, but a strength coach must also work under constraints that are beyond their control, and this includes working under NCAA guidelines for practice times, as well as working under the specific guidelines from the coaching staffs of the team they are responsible for preparing.

Assistance Exercises

Assistance exercises are movements that recruit smaller muscle groups, i.e., upper arm, calves, abdominals, or lower back, and involve one primary joint, single-joint movements, while primarily serving to balance out muscular deficiencies or to strengthen an injured area upon return to training. Programming assistance/single-joint movements can vary significantly as they will not be overly draining to the nervous system, nor will they cause significant metabolic fatigue due to the small volume of muscle tissue involved and intensity of loading limitations. A strength coach may choose to program a standing barbell curl to stimulate the biceps brachii for three sets of 12 repetitions for the first and second weeks, and increase the sets to four and reduce the repetitions to eight per set in the third and fourth weeks. This will increase the work capacity and hypertrophy of the biceps in first two weeks, and place an emphasis on strength and hypertrophy in the last two weeks.

Primary Exercise

A primary (or core) exercise is defined as a movement that recruits a single large muscle or multiple muscle groups, requires movement at multiple joints, and are selected as primary movement because of similarities to muscle and joint actions in an athlete's sport. These movements form the basis of an athletic training program because they require significant physical effort and mental focus to properly execute. Core exercises focus on improving performance in these movements in various ways that can be readily altered to fit a wide range of sport-specific athletic needs. Core exercises are superior to single joint movements for enhanced athletic performance because these movements produce greater benefit such as greater lean mass gains, improved coordination, and increased strength in specific muscle groups and the whole body. These movements also lend themselves to tracking progress easily by any selected method a coach

Copyright © Mometrix Media. You have been licensed one copy of this document for personal use only. Any other reproduction or redistribution is strictly prohibited. All rights reserved.
This content is provided for test preparation purposes only and does not imply an endorsement by Mometrix of any particular political, scientific, or religious point of view.

prefers, i.e., increased repetitions at a certain weight, increased repetition maximums, increased one-repetition maximum, etc.

Structural Exercise

Structural movements are core exercises that load the spinal column of an athlete, either directly or indirectly. These exercises include back squats, overhead and horizontal pressing variations, barbell lunges, front squats, and deadlifts. These movements form the foundation of a training program because they load multiple joints, recruit substantial amounts of muscle tissue, allow for variation in loading and volume parameters to elicit a wide array of physiological response, and can be used in nearly every sports training program because these movement patterns are ubiquitous throughout all sports.

Power Exercise

A power exercise is a structural exercise, as the spine is loaded during power movements that requires very quick and explosive muscle actions from start to finish. Power exercises include any Olympic weightlifting movement regardless if the movement is performed with a full catch or without. Other movements that can be considered power movements include traditional barbell (or dumbbell) movements that are loaded in a way that implement speed and total force produced are the emphasis instead of intensity of load which will reduce implement speed. Power movements must be selected based on the sport-specific needs of the athlete.

Open and Closed Skill Classifications

Closed agility skills are programmed and predictable, or stable, environments. Open skills have non-programmed and unpredictable, or unstable, environments. Closed agility skills allow the athlete to determine their movements with the primary objective to solidify and optimize performance, i.e., pro-agility drill. Open agility skills emphasize responding to changes in environment, unanticipated situations, or stimuli quickly and effectively, i.e., open-field dodging in team games. Using a closed skill approach to agility training allows for a coach to assess an athlete and directly address agility-specific weaknesses or technical flaws. An open skill agility training approach will allow a coach to utilize the unpredictable nature of this type of drill to mimic a competitive environment.

Continuous, Discrete, and Serial Skill Classifications

Continuous agility skills are tasks that have no discernible beginning and no specific ending point. Discrete agility skills have a distinct beginning and end point and emphasize a specific task which is generally oriented to improving strength and power. Serial agility skills are drills composed of a combination of discrete and continuous skills performed in a sequence, with successful performance of each subtask determining the overall outcome of the drill. Continuous skills are generally performed in a forward direction and tend to be at submaximal to low speeds due to the cyclical nature of the drills, and can be used to develop proper running technique, jumping, galloping, or backpedaling. Discrete agility drills are used when improving strength and power are desired in a specific skill or movement pattern, i.e., squat patterns used to improve defensive ready stance for a football offensive lineman, or catch and throw a medicine ball. Serial agility skill drills are related specifically to the athlete's sport as these drills will combine elements of continuous and discrete drills by scheduling drills from specialized motor tasks to generalized tasks in order to meet the needs of their sport.

Exercise Order

Exercise order is the sequence that the selected movements will be performed. Structuring the training program in order of most technical and metabolically demanding exercises to those that

Copyright © Mometrix Media. You have been licensed one copy of this document for personal use only. Any other reproduction or redistribution is strictly prohibited. All rights reserved.
This content is provided for test preparation purposes only and does not imply an endorsement by Mometrix of any particular political, scientific, or religious point of view.

are less demanding is key when attempting to improve strength, power, address technical issues an athlete may have, increase muscle mass, or improve muscular endurance. Power movements, specifically the Olympic lifts, are the most technically demanding, require the greatest focus, and place the athlete under substantial metabolic demands which are the primary reasons for placing these movements first in a training session. Core, or structural movements, will generally occur after the power movements, or first if power movements are not included, as these movements require technical mastery, load the spine, place substantial metabolic demands on the athlete and affect multiple joints. Lastly, single-joint or assistance movements are placed at the end of the training session as these movements do not require technical mastery, impact a single joint, a small amount of muscle, and are not neurologically demanding.

Overload

Overload refers to the loading placed on the structures of the body that are active during a specific movement. Overloading, or progressive overload, refers to gradually increasing the amount of external resistance an athlete must work against during training-related activities. The overloading of the body's structures will produce positive changes in bone density, muscular strength, muscle size, and body composition over time. Increasing an athlete's ability to perform work against external resistance is clearly of great benefit to the athlete, but there is a point when an athlete will see diminishing returns when pursuing larger lifts as the body will not simply improve in this area exponentially. With stronger athletes, more specifically power sport athletes, there is a tendency toward pursuing increased training loads at all costs, and this mentality requires a strength coach to monitor progression more closely and to take greater precautions regarding safety and injury risks during training.

Mechanical Work

Mechanical work is defined as the product of force and displacement (W= F[s]). The work an athlete is capable of performing is related to the demands placed on the body via external loading and the body's ability to produce metabolic energy. Being able to accurately determine the amount of mechanical work and metabolic demands placed on an athlete is extremely important, as this will allow the strength and conditioning coach to properly plan and structure the training program and to avoid overreaching and overtraining.

Traditionally, work or (when regarding resistance training) "loading" is determined by multiplying the weight lifted by the number of repetitions and then summing the values for the entire training session to assess the work performed during the session. Load volume and intensity of loading are interrelated, as the amount of weight on an implement will impact the number of times the implement will be lifted. Intensity of loading serves as an indicator of the quality of the work performed, i.e., 80 percent of one-repetition maximums (RM) for five reps is a higher quality of work than 65 percent of one RM for five reps. Being able to assess the quality of work and the total volume of work performed during a training session will provide more in-depth insights into progress of the athlete over time than simply using one RM as the primary indicators of progress.

Primary Resistance Training Goal

The primary resistance goal is set based on the cumulative assessments that are performed prior to initiating a training program. These include the movement and physiological analysis of the sport, the athlete's training background and experiences, as well as injury history and current physical capacities that are assessed through various testing procedures, i.e., one-repetition maximums, vertical jumps, 40-yard dash, etc. The primary resistance training goal must focus on one area to improve during a training segment in order to concentrate on improving this area as much as possible. The primary resistance training goal can change based on the sport season, i.e., offseason,

Copyright © Mometrix Media. You have been licensed one copy of this document for personal use only. Any other reproduction or redistribution is strictly prohibited. All rights reserved.
This content is provided for test preparation purposes only and does not imply an endorsement by Mometrix of any particular political, scientific, or religious point of view.

preseason, in-season, or postseason, in order to ensure various capacities are trained and weaknesses are addressed, with the greatest emphasis on the sport-specific demands being addressed during the preseason and in-season periods.

Split Routine

A split routine is a modification of the training week for intermediate or advanced trainees that involves segmenting the training week by breaking down the training sessions by movements or muscle groups performed. This approach includes separating upper and lower body movements into different training sessions where they will receive the emphasis for that day, which allows for greater training loads and volumes to be used during those sessions. Traditionally, this approach involves altering the training intensities and volumes from day to day, i.e., 80 percent loading on upper body on the first day for the base movement, and the following upper body session may call for 90 percent loading, and is very helpful in allowing an athlete to recover from the training sessions due to the nonconsecutive nature of the upper body days.

Training Frequency

Training frequency is a reference to the number of training sessions that are completed in a specific time period, usually limited to a specific sport season. Training frequency is very important for an athlete because exposure to training stimuli is the means by which physiological changes occur, and training too often or having too many rest days can impact an athlete negatively. Determining an optimum training frequency for an athlete is a key element of the training program and can be properly assessed by evaluating the athlete's training status, projected exercise loading parameters, sport season, exercise selection and type, as well as various other issues such as life stress.

Circuit Training

Circuit training is a method of condensing the amount of work an athlete is going to perform by having them move from movement to movement with minimal rest between sets. This arrangement can consist of power movements, core/structural movements, and assistance movements, tapering from most demanding to least demanding. This approach reduces the total training time for the athlete, produces enhancements in cardiorespiratory function and muscular endurance, and can enhance mental acuity under fatigued conditions. An athlete that needs to reduce their body fat may also utilize this approach as the metabolic cost of circuit training is significantly higher than other resistance training methods.

1-RM

Establishing a one-repetition maximum (1-RM) for an athlete or a group of athletes in power and structural movements is very important when attempting to design a training program, as the 1-RM will serve as the primary guide for determining the load parameters for individual training sessions, load-volumes for training weeks, as well as establishing the overall purpose and goals of the training segment. Once the training segment has been completed, retesting the 1-RM is necessary for determining the progress that has been made over the course of the segment, but also is important for determining the overall purpose and goals for the next training segment.

Repetition Maximum

The repetition maximum is a test of an athlete's ability to lift the most weight for a specific number of repetitions, i.e., a 5 RM. Similar to the 1-RM test, the repetition maximum serves as a guidepost for an athlete's ability to perform work at a certain percentage of their projected or actual maximum. This information is very useful when attempting to assign loading parameters, as it can clarify weaknesses an athlete may have performing repetitions that may not arise during a single-repetition maximum, i.e., a fast twitch athlete performing superiorly in the 1-RM test but struggling

Copyright © Mometrix Media. You have been licensed one copy of this document for personal use only. Any other reproduction or redistribution is strictly prohibited. All rights reserved.
This content is provided for test preparation purposes only and does not imply an endorsement by Mometrix of any particular political, scientific, or religious point of view.

to reach a 5-RM with 70 percent of their 1-RM. The repetition maximum provides clarity when assigning training loads, whereas the 1-RM will require a projection calculation for loads at specific percentages of load.

Primary Resistance Training Goal

The primary resistance training goal is determined from the athlete's testing results, movement and physiological analyses, and the sport season of the athlete. Once the primary resistance goal has been set, the strength and conditioning coach will use the repetition maximum continuum to assign training loads and volumes for the program based on the 1-RM or the repetition maximum performances of the athlete. If the primary goal is strength or power, training loads will need to be heavy with lower training volume. If the goal is hypertrophy, then moderate loading and higher volumes can be used. If muscular endurance is the primary goal, then light loads and higher total training volume can be used.

Percentage-Based System

The force velocity curve plays a significant role when determining if a movement is a power or structural movement. Power movements are most effective when performed using moderate loading parameters, and structural movements can be used effectively in multiple loading segments for different training goals. Using a percentage-based system allows the athlete to follow this guideline more closely and avoid using weights that are too heavy for improving force production, although using the percentage-based system to determine training volume parameters is challenging due to the nature of power movements and the difficulty of performing higher-repetition tests with these movements because of their highly technical nature. Assigning training loads according to the velocity of the movement and using no higher than five repetitions per set are the keys to using power movements successfully.

Two-for-Two Rule

The two-for-two rule is a conservative approach to increasing the training loads an athlete uses during a training segment. This method requires an athlete perform two additional repetitions at a specific training load over the prescribed repetitions in the final set in a given movement, and must be able to achieve this in two consecutive training sessions. At the next training session, the load is increased. The two-for-two rule provides structure to increasing the training load used per session, which allows for an athlete to progress consistently by requiring sustained performance during the training segment in order to increase training load.

Primary Guidelines When Training for Strength and Power

When assigning training loads and training volumes, determining the optimal number of repetitions per set to achieve the desired goal is most important, as this will determine the total volume and the loading used per set. When training for maximal strength gains, an athlete will usually perform no more than six repetitions per set and as few as one repetition per set for two to six total sets, which will yield a low training volume per session. Power training will generally require a lower training volume per session due to the high neurological and metabolic demands, along with fewer goal repetitions per set at lighter training loads because the emphasis is on velocity and controlling for fatigue. The traditional sets and reps recommended for power training are one to five repetitions for three to five sets.

Varying Training Loads and Volumes

The purpose of altering training loads and volumes over the course of a training program is to allow for adequate recovery of the muscles and central nervous system in order to avoid entering into an overtrained state. The strength and conditioning coach can avoid overtraining the athlete or

Copyright © Mometrix Media. You have been licensed one copy of this document for personal use only. Any other reproduction or redistribution is strictly prohibited. All rights reserved.
This content is provided for test preparation purposes only and does not imply an endorsement by Mometrix of any particular political, scientific, or religious point of view.

athletes by reducing and rotating training loads of other training sessions after a "heavy" training session, i.e., "light" and "moderate," in order to facilitate recovery while sustaining training frequency and volumes. Rotating the loading parameters between, light, heavy, and moderate can be used for a variety of training goals and frequencies, while also serving as a method for addressing the physical stress of practice or competition by applying this concept.

Factors Limiting an Athlete's Ability to Increase Training Loads

There are numerous factors that can impact an athlete's ability to add additional weight to their training loads. These factors cover a wide array of possibilities that include training too frequently, emphasizing assistance exercises over core exercises, not following prescribed training load intensities, inappropriate training goals, poor nutrition, poor sleep, etc. The strength and conditioning coach can monitor for these possibilities by tracking the performance of the athlete, locate the trend, and then communicate with the athlete about making changes to their approach to training or addressing the possibility of sleep, nutrition, or other issues.

Functional Capacity

Using the heart rate for prescribing aerobic training intensities is extremely common, and this is due to the relationship between heart rate and maximal oxygen consumption. Functional capacity, or the heart rate reserve (HRR), refers to the difference between an athlete's resting heart rate and maximal heart rate, and this serves as a useful method for prescribing aerobic training intensities. The reason that this method is effective is partly because of the relationship between heart rate and maximal oxygen consumption, but also because, over time, the athlete's resting heart rate will decrease because of training and the heart rate reserve will increase, allowing the athlete to work longer at moderate intensities and accumulating less fatigue.

Training Intensity

Training intensity, when regarding aerobic training, specifically refers to the effort or energy expended during a training session. Training intensity when discussing resistance training refers to the training volume and the intensity of the loading per movement. Aerobic training intensity is intended to provide a guideline for training related to the heart rate, which will significantly impact the volume and rate of oxygen consumption as well as the duration of the training session. An aerobic athlete training at higher intensity levels will improve cardiovascular and pulmonary function in order to improve oxygen uptake in the working muscles.

AMHR, the Karvonen Method, and Percentage of MHR for Assigning Training Intensities

Age-predicted maximal heart rate (AMHR) is a formula that can be used to quickly estimate the maximal heart rate capacity of an athlete based strictly on their chronological age. The Karvonen method uses resting heart rate, AMHR, and desired intensity to calculate the target heart rate for a training session. Percentage of maximal heart rate (MHR) is a calculation of training intensities commonly based on the age-predicted maximal heart rate multiplied by the desired range of intensities, for example, an athlete training between 70-85 percent MHR. Age-predicted maximal heart rate is a generalized estimation and can result in significant differences in heart rate projections when compared to actual heart rate capacity, either high or low. This is one possible limitation to using age-predicted maximal heart rate in an equation, as generally gathering real data, either in a laboratory or via heart rate monitors during training sessions, will generate the most accurate and reliable data upon which to base intensity prescriptions.

Copyright © Mometrix Media. You have been licensed one copy of this document for personal use only. Any other reproduction or redistribution is strictly prohibited. All rights reserved.
This content is provided for test preparation purposes only and does not imply an endorsement by Mometrix of any particular political, scientific, or religious point of view.

Rest Periods

Rest periods are intended to allow an athlete to adequately recover between sets as well as during transitions between movements. The length of time between sets and movements is determined by the resistance training program goal, the intensity of the loading parameters, and the athlete's training status. If a training program is oriented towards maximal strength gains, then the core movements will require longer periods of time between sets in order to facilitate adequate neural and muscular recovery. The determination of rest periods is not solely based on loads lifted or training goal, but can also be established based on the type of movement, muscles used, and repetitions performed. This would mean that an assistance exercise such as lying triceps extension requires less rest between sets than a structural movement such as the power clean or squat, even without consideration of the loads lifted in the core movement.

Exercise Relief Patterns

Rest relief patterns during speed development periods or even in special endurance training periods are used to facilitate physiological recovery, either partial or complete recovery, between bouts of the selected exercise. Depending on the focus of the training period, the strength and conditioning coach can alter work-to-rest ratios to facilitate the desired physiological responses that need to improve. Longer rest periods facilitate complete recovery of the nervous and muscular systems that will allow for maximal performance and speeds to be achieved, which is essential when assessing or retesting an athlete. Briefer rest periods will facilitate partial or incomplete recovery between bouts and can be used to condition an athlete with cardiovascular weaknesses by allowing for more recovery and can also be manipulated to push a well-conditioned athlete to a higher performance level. Generally, brief rest periods will be used for conditioning purposes and can be tapered across a training period as a form of progression.

Neural Potentiation

Potentiation is a neurophysiological response that increases the contractile capacity of muscles via alteration of the force-velocity curve due to stretch, which also increases neural drive to the working muscles. Potentiation functions to increase the muscles' capacity for force production, either utilizing heavy training loads or performing ballistic activities that are similar to the desired movement pattern or sport activity, and is a possible method for improving performance prior to high intensity activities such as maximum barbell lifts, timed sprints, vertical jump tests, etc. A strength and conditioning coach can elicit better performance during testing periods by having an athlete perform body weight jumps, medicine ball throws/tosses, or reactive jumps in order to increase high-threshold motor unit recruitment through excitation of the nervous system and stretch response in the active muscles.

Relationship Between Impulse, Power, and Developing Speed and Agility in Athletes

An impulse is a shift in momentum due to a force, and is measured as the product of force and time. Power is defined as the rate in which work is done, and is represented mathematically as (Force [Velocity]). Speed and agility are dependent on an athlete's impulse and power capacities, as rapid changes in direction are dependent on impulse, and an athlete's ability to perform work is dependent on power. With regards to athlete preparation, power and impulse are interrelated because, in many instances in a game or match, an athlete will require either more power or greater impulse in order to achieve a directive, and as such, sport-specific activities are essential for maximizing these two variables in order to develop the athlete's capacities fully.

Copyright © Mometrix Media. You have been licensed one copy of this document for personal use only. Any other reproduction or redistribution is strictly prohibited. All rights reserved.
This content is provided for test preparation purposes only and does not imply an endorsement by Mometrix of any particular political, scientific, or religious point of view.

Velocity Specificity

Velocity specificity refers to the relationship between a selected mass and the final movement velocity achieved with that mass. Generally, velocity specificity is a selected method for manipulating force using traditional resistance training methods, but it can also be an integral factor when working in speed-specific periods in a training program. To alter the relationship of the athlete's mass to the total force produced, the athlete can work against additional resistance, which will cause the athlete to generate more total force but reduce the movement speed because of the increased loading. Once the athlete is unloaded, as is generally believed but not conclusively proven in research, he or she will achieve higher velocities because the loading has been reduced.

Reactive Ability

Reactive ability specifically relates to an athlete's capacity for reactive force generation via the stretch-shortening cycle. This capacity is specific to an athlete's ability to produce force through the ground in order to propel the body in a specific direction. An athlete can improve reactive ability by using plyometric and explosively-based training methods. Using these methods will require an athlete to produce large forces rapidly while also having the flexibility to include reactive movements that require an athlete to change direction in a variety of planes, including lateral jumping, horizontal to lateral bounding, or box jumps from different heights.

Reaction Time

Reaction time refers to an athlete's ability to respond to a visual or auditory stimulus. Reactive ability refers specifically to the capacity of an athlete's stretch-shortening cycle to react to a rapid stretch or loading of a muscle and redirecting that energy into maximal force generation. Reaction times cannot be altered significantly because an athlete's capacity to process information at a faster rate is not readily trainable, as many of the processes required to process information are determined by the central and peripheral nervous systems. Reaction times do not correlate with performance in explosive activities.

Maximal Aerobic Power

Maximal aerobic power (VO_2 max) is the maximal rate of oxygen that can be consumed during exercise. Maximal aerobic power is an indicator of an athlete's endurance capacities at submaximal exercise intensities. Improving an athlete's VO_2 max will enhance the athlete's ability to not only consume oxygen, but to deliver oxygen to the working tissues via different mechanisms such as increased mitochondrial density at the muscle or enhanced enzyme activity in the Krebs cycle of electron transport chain. VO_2 max is not the only component necessary to excel as an endurance athlete, as lactate threshold, exercise economy, and fat utilization as a primary fuel source are also, if not more, important than VO_2 max.

Lactate Threshold

The lactate threshold is a significant indicator for work capacity and physical endurance, as this is the work rate or percentage of VO_2 max where a specific concentration of blood lactate is observable or is the point at which blood lactate concentration levels begin to accumulate over resting values. The longer an athlete is able to sustain a high rate of work without crossing the lactate threshold—which causes a significant feeling of fatigue and impacts mental acuity—the longer and harder an athlete will be able to work. Significantly enhancing an athlete's ability to perform work will improve their resilience in competition and allow the athlete to sustain higher rates of effort throughout the competition and competitive seasons.

Copyright © Mometrix Media. You have been licensed one copy of this document for personal use only. Any other reproduction or redistribution is strictly prohibited. All rights reserved.
This content is provided for test preparation purposes only and does not imply an endorsement by Mometrix of any particular political, scientific, or religious point of view.

Maximal Lactate Steady State

Similar to lactate threshold, the maximal lactate steady state refers to work capacity. The maximal lactate steady state refers to the exercise intensity at which the maximal rate of lactate generation is equal to the maximal rate of lactate clearance from the blood. The maximal lactate steady state serves to indicate the intensity at which an athlete is able to sustain work without crossing the lactate threshold and accumulating fatigue rapidly. The lactate threshold is simply the point at which the athlete begins to accumulate lactate more quickly than can be effectively cleared from the blood. Lactate threshold will provide information on the intensity level at which the athlete will crossover, while the maximal lactate steady state will provide information on the relative intensity level and the duration for which the athlete can maintain the balance between lactate accumulation and clearance, providing specific information that can be used to modify training intensities and total time needed to improve this capacity over a training cycle.

Exercise Economy

Exercise economy is a measure of the energy needed during exercise, or general activity, at a specific velocity. Exercise economy is a measure that provides insight into the individual athlete's training and movement economy when running, cycling, etc. An athlete with a high training economy will use less energy to reach and sustain a specific velocity than an athlete with a lower training economy. Evaluating an athlete's exercise economy is essential for a strength and conditioning coach working with endurance athletes, as training economy can be impacted through modifications in movement mechanics, i.e., altering stride length in a runner, or stroke mechanics for a swimmer.

Progression

Progression refers to the changes in training program parameters to elicit additional training adaptations in order to continue athletic development. Progression methods can vary significantly depending on the specific athletic qualities of a sport. As a strength and conditioning coach, the training parameters used during a training block will require significant thought and a thorough evaluation of the needs of the athletes, but commonly used approaches to eliciting further adaptations during a training phase include altering rest periods between sets, increasing training density, adding training volume, changing hand or foot position, or reducing training load intensities to emphasize speed of movement.

Training Session Duration and Training Progression

Training session duration is very important for aerobic athletes as the duration of a training session will be predominantly determined by the training intensity prescribed prior to the training session. If an athlete trains at a higher intensity level (85 percent of VO_2 max), the training session will be significantly shorter because of the accumulation of lactate in the working tissues, while lower intensity sessions (70 percent of VO_2 max) could last for several hours. Progression models primarily manipulate the three key elements of aerobic training: frequency, training intensity, and duration. Duration and progression for aerobic athletes do not necessarily differentiate from other athletes, but they have distinct differences as duration of a training session for an aerobic athlete could be measured via total time or in distance covered, and progression for an aerobic athlete is not necessarily tracked via sets and reps but via decreased times across specific distances.

General Adaptation Syndrome

General adaptation syndrome (GAS) describes the human body's response to external loading, i.e., a barbell or dumbbell which represents a greater stress than previously applied. The initial phase of GAS is the alarm phase, which involves soreness, increased stiffness, and decreased performance.

Copyright © Mometrix Media. You have been licensed one copy of this document for personal use only. Any other reproduction or redistribution is strictly prohibited. All rights reserved.
This content is provided for test preparation purposes only and does not imply an endorsement by Mometrix of any particular political, scientific, or religious point of view.

The second phase is the resistance phase, which is the period of time that the body adapts to the stressor and normal function resumes. The third phase of GAS is supercompensation, which sees the body adapt and manifest adaptations in the form if increased performance, greater muscle mass, strength, etc. If training stress persists for too long, then a fourth phase will take place, called the exhaustion phase, and this results in decreased training performance, overtraining, and possible injury.

Supercompensation

Supercompensation is part of the general adaptation syndrome, and is the phase in which an athlete exhibits the positive training adaptations from the training program. These adaptations include increased muscle mass, increased stored muscle glycogen, increased work capacity (i.e., VO_2 increase, muscular endurance), increased neurological adaptations, etc.

Sport Seasons

Endurance athletes require a significant amount of training volume in order to be successful, and they have four periods in the sport season to develop the required capacities: base training period (offseason), preseason, competition (in-season), and active rest (postseason). The base training period requires an athlete to develop the base cardiorespiratory capacities necessary to train more intensely in the preseason and perform during the competition season and is highlighted by lower intensity and longer duration training sessions with increases in intensity only occurring once the athlete has acclimated and is absolutely necessary for progression. The preseason period is highlighted by a focus on increasing training intensity, reducing or stabilizing duration, and including various methods into the training system in order to address weaknesses and prepare for the competition season. The competition season is primarily oriented to athlete readiness for the competitive events, which requires low-intensity and short duration sessions prior to the event with an emphasis on weaknesses and stabilizing strengths in other training sessions. The active rest period is intended to facilitate recovery from the competition season, and should include reduced training volumes and intensities with enough overall exercise to maintain a strong baseline cardiorespiratory fitness level.

Periodization

Periodization is the systematic approach to organizing the strength and conditioning program, and includes all resistance training, flexibility and mobility work, conditioning and sport-related activities. Periodization is the preplanning of training loads, load-volumes, and is structured to produce physiological adaptations over a set period of time by increasing certain variables that will challenge the athlete and cause adaptive response to the training stress. Periodized training segments are specifically organized to fit the sport season and sport-specific activities of the athlete to elicit the desired training adaptations to improve competitive athletic performance.

Training Macrocycle

A training macrocycle is the primary developmental objective for a training program or system that is in place in order for an athlete to achieve peak performance prior to competition. The macrocycle consists of an entire year's training program, or is also representative of a multiple-year developmental plan, and is broken down into smaller periodized units that are intended to develop specific athletic traits throughout the course of the macrocycle. An example of a macrocycle would be segmenting the year into offseason, preseason, in-season, and postseason training periods.

Mesocycle

The purpose of a mesocycle is to segment the overall macrocycle into training periods of two- to six-week blocks that are structured to achieve specific physiological adaptations/training

Copyright © Mometrix Media. You have been licensed one copy of this document for personal use only. Any other reproduction or redistribution is strictly prohibited. All rights reserved.
This content is provided for test preparation purposes only and does not imply an endorsement by Mometrix of any particular political, scientific, or religious point of view.

outcomes. An example mesocycle could resemble (1) preparatory phase- anaerobic work capacity/strength or (2) hypertrophy-endurance-aerobic capacity/ muscular hypertrophy.

Microcycle

The microcycle is the smallest training segment in periodization models. This period is concerned with weekly or daily training variables that allows for consistent monitoring of an athlete's or groups of athletes' training progress. The microcycle allows for minor adjustments intra-training week that can significantly impact athlete progress over a microcycle. The microcycle also plays a significant role in tapering an athlete for competition season or peaking for a single competition.

Preparatory Phase

The preparatory phase is, generally, the longest training segment in the traditional periodization format. This training period usually occurs when there are few (if any) competitions and very few sport-specific skill practices or game preparation sessions. This is generally considered the offseason and preseason preparation period. This phase is highlighted by lower intensity activities that, over time, are transitioned into higher intensity levels and training volume.

Hypertrophy/Endurance Phase

A hypertrophy/endurance phase takes place in the early stages of the preparatory phase, could possibly last up to six weeks, and consists of lower intensity loading with higher training volumes. This portion of the preparatory phase is intended to increase an athlete's lean body mass, increase physical endurance, or both.

Basic Strength Phase

The basic strength phase is intended to increase the strength of the primary muscle groups involved in the sporting events an athlete competes in. This phase emphasizes similar motor patterns to the competitive sport, but also involves the inclusion of higher intensity methodologies (plyometrics, sprints) along with increasing training load and decreasing training volumes to emphasize strength development in the target muscle groups.

Strength/Power Phase

The strength/power phase is the last segment of the preparatory phase, and is highlighted by an increase in training intensity to pre-competition levels. This phase consists of performing explosive/power movements at high training loads and reduced total volumes. The primary differentiation of the basic strength and strength/power phase is that loading strategies for power movements are not governed by the percentage maximum approach of basic strength work, as this training segment relies heavily on implement velocity and speed of movement in comparison to absolute strength.

First Transition Period

The first transition period is the training segment, usually one week of reduced training intensity, immediately prior to the competition period. This transition period between the preparatory period and the competition period allows an athlete a brief period of time to recover mentally and physically in preparation for the competition period.

Competition Period

A competition period is designed to achieve peak strength and power through increased training load and decreased training volumes. This is also a period in which sport skill technique and in-game strategies increase dramatically in preparation for competition.

Copyright © Mometrix Media. You have been licensed one copy of this document for personal use only. Any other reproduction or redistribution is strictly prohibited. All rights reserved.
This content is provided for test preparation purposes only and does not imply an endorsement by Mometrix of any particular political, scientific, or religious point of view.

Second Transition Period

The second transition period, or active rest period, usually consists of a one- to four-week training block that focuses on non-structured, non-event specific recreational activity that is performed at low-level intensity for reduced volumes. The purpose of this training phase is to reduce sport-specific activity following a competitive season or competitive event, as this phase is structured to reduce mental stress from training and preparation, while also preparing the athlete for increased training volume and loading intensity in upcoming training segments.

Unloading/Deloading Week

The unloading/deloading approach is a training week that utilizes reduced training volumes and loading intensity to prime the athlete for an increased workload (volume, intensity, or both) in the next training phase. The unloading/deloading week allows for the athlete to recover from prior training segments, continue to train the necessary neural patterns, and will allow for supercompensation to take place in order to perform at a high level in the next training segment.

Linear Periodization

Linear periodization is an approach to athlete preparation that refers to the increasing training intensity over a mesocycle. This approach is used in sporting events that require an athlete in peak condition for competition, such as track and field or Olympic weightlifting. This approach is very successful with athletes that participate in a sporting event that competes at specific times, usually including periods of time between competitions.

Undulating/Nonlinear Periodization

Undulating/nonlinear periodization is characterized by alterations in training load intensity and training volume for the primary movements in a training session and across a training week. Undulating/nonlinear periodization may lead to greater strength increases in comparison to the linear periodization model, but also may cause less cumulative central nervous system fatigue for an athlete as loads are modified intraweek/training microcycle. Research on the progress of athletes engaging with these two models is mixed.

Injury Analysis

An injury analysis will provide insight into an athlete's health history and possible training limitations. An injury analysis serves as an assessment of common joint injury sites, based on the sport, as well as possible muscle injuries. A portion of the injury analysis involves having the athlete perform specific movements to assess general movement capabilities by grading the quality of performance on a numerical scale, i.e., body weight squat on a scale of 1-5, and totaling the score at the end of the assessment to determine what issues need further attention in a training program or possibly increasing flexibility in mobility to enhance joint and muscular flexibility. Being aware of the specific injury issues or movement limitations an athlete has allows for a specific course of action to be taken by the strength and conditioning coach that will reduce the impact these issues have over the course of the training program, but also, by reducing their impact over time, the athlete will spend less time on the injured list and more time on the field and ultimately have a longer competitive career.

Indication for a Rehabilitating Athlete

Indications are used by strength and conditioning coaches to determine a course of action that is appropriate for an injured athlete, generally regarding overall treatment, conditioning, or strength-related programming of the non-injured areas of an athlete's body. An example of an indication is a

Copyright © Mometrix Media. You have been licensed one copy of this document for personal use only. Any other reproduction or redistribution is strictly prohibited. All rights reserved.
This content is provided for test preparation purposes only and does not imply an endorsement by Mometrix of any particular political, scientific, or religious point of view.

baseball pitcher that has an injured left elbow, and performs lower body strength work to maintain lower body functionality.

Contraindication

A contraindication is a specific movement pattern, sport-related activity, or general activity that is determined to be dangerous to an athlete because of an injury. This is an important issue to be aware of so a strength and conditioning coach can be sure that the training plan for an injured athlete does not perform any dangerous activities.

Macrotrauma

A macrotrauma occurs when a specific tissue of the body suddenly becomes overburdened, causing a significant disturbance in the quality and health of the effected tissue. A macrotrauma can take place at any tissue site and can include broken bones, contusions, or lacerations, to name a few possibilities.

Dislocation and Subluxation

The difference between a dislocation and a subluxation is the severity with which the joint is displaced from the joint articulation surfaces. A subluxation represents a partial displacement from the articulation surfaces, while the dislocation is a complete disruption of the joint from the articulating surfaces.

Contusion

A contusion is a type of macrotrauma that takes place in soft tissues, primarily in muscle tissue. The injury will usually be caused by a direct impact to the muscle tissue resulting in significant accumulation of blood and various fluids into the surrounding tissues. A contusion is a very severe type of bruising which can lead to an athlete missing significant practice or game time, depending on location and severity of the injury.

Sprains and Strains

A sprain is macrotrauma to the ligaments of a joint, and is given a grade according to severity: first-, second-, and third-degree sprain. A strain is macrotrauma to muscle tissues that results in partial or complete tears in the tissue and is determined to be a first-, second-, or third-degree strain.

Microtrauma

A microtrauma is an injury that results from overstressing a tissue either through constant training or not allowing for adequate recovery between training sessions. The primary cause of this type of injury is the accrual of either too much or irregular forces on the tissue.

Tendinitis

Tendinitis is the inflammation of a tendon due to joint-specific overuse, training on abnormal or unforgiving surfaces, or increasing training load or volume too quickly during a training period. Risk for tendinitis can be increased by inadequate stretching and conditioning prior to exercise.

Tissue Healing Phases

Inflammation is the first element in the body's injury response and is characterized by a rapid increase in fluid accumulation to the injured tissues, edema, and is accompanied by external redness to the area directly affected and surrounding tissues. The second component of tissue healing is the repair phase, which is characterized by the elimination of nonfunctioning and heavily damaged tissues, and the regeneration of capillaries and collagen fibers. The third component of

Copyright © Mometrix Media. You have been licensed one copy of this document for personal use only. Any other reproduction or redistribution is strictly prohibited. All rights reserved.
This content is provided for test preparation purposes only and does not imply an endorsement by Mometrix of any particular political, scientific, or religious point of view.

tissue healing is the remodeling phase, which is characterized by the newly formed tissues having a chance to improve structural integrity, strength, and develop greater functional capacity.

Closed Kinetic Chain Movement

A closed kinetic chain movement is a movement that limits the free movement of the hand in upper body movements, or the feet in lower body movements. Examples for the upper body include pull-ups and dips. Examples of closed kinetic chain exercises for the lower body would be power cleans and lunges.

Open Kinetic Chain Movements

An open kinetic chain movement allows for the free movement of the hands or feet while under load. Examples of these types of movements in the upper body would include the bench press and biceps curls. Examples of open kinetic chain exercises for the lower body are hamstring curls and leg extensions.

Neuromuscular Control

Neuromuscular control is the ability of an athlete's body to maintain joint integrity based off of feedback from the external environment to the central nervous system. An injured athlete must rebuild not only strength in the injured areas, but also the neuromuscular associations within the damaged tissues. Restoring neuromuscular control in an athlete can involve performing basic movement patterns such as push-ups or a body weight squat on an uneven/unstable surface, or a wide array of implements can be employed to challenge the nervous system, including stability balls and trampolines.

Fibrosis

Fibrosis is a degenerative process associated with aging. Fibrosis is the formation of scar tissue in muscle tissue that, unless pathological, is caused by the body regenerating various tissues over time. These fibrotic tissue formations are primarily composed of collagen and assorted proteins, and are generally located along muscle tissue or in close proximity to joint capsules. This process can negatively impact the health of muscle tissue or the mobility in a joint by physically restricting the tissues from moving normally, which will result in altering movement patterns and generating odd forces in other joints and muscles, resulting in acute and long-term injuries.

Copyright © Mometrix Media. You have been licensed one copy of this document for personal use only. Any other reproduction or redistribution is strictly prohibited. All rights reserved.
This content is provided for test preparation purposes only and does not imply an endorsement by Mometrix of any particular political, scientific, or religious point of view.

Organization and Administration

Feasibility Study

The feasibility study is intended to assess the costs of building/leasing a facility, as well as determining the costs of purchasing/leasing equipment, assessing possible facility locations based on demographics, and services to be offered within the facility. The feasibility study is also intended to assess the conceptual strengths and weaknesses of a facility in order to determine practical viability and make changes to the initial business plan and concept.

Risk Management

A training facility must have policies and procedures in place that address possible areas of liability. Areas of consideration and concern for the facility are handling injury prevention/risk management strategies in place during training sessions, emergency care planning, record keeping, and having liability insurance for the facility that covers all coaches and support staff.

Liability

Liability refers to the legal responsibility that the trainer, strength coach, and other staff members have with regards to the fitness members and athletes that participate in training programs. The duty of the trainer, coach, and staff member is to respond appropriately in the event of an injury as well as taking the correct and necessary steps to prevent injury from improper or dangerous uses of equipment, along with maintaining standard professional practices. Liability is a significant concern because of the types of activities the individual trainee can engage in that are inherently risky, i.e., maximal lifting or Olympic lifting, which may result in injury. The strength coach and other staff members can protect against possible liability issues by maintaining the training space appropriately, monitoring all training sessions according to professional standards, and making sure the facility has all the requisite first aid supplies, i.e., bandages, splints, and even an automated external defibrillator, in order to respond to an emergency properly should the need arise.

Product Liability

Product liability is an area of law oriented to protecting consumers when purchasing products, services, or other types of personal property from various types of companies that include retail stores, manufacturers, etc. A strength and conditioning coach must be aware of this legal area, as the coach offers a wide array of personal and group services and must ensure proper machine maintenance, clean training areas, and general upkeep of the training facility. This area of liability also extends to nutritional supplements, clothing, or other purchasable items from the training facility.

Standard of Care

Standard of care refers to an acceptable level of response to an adverse situation based on a general comparison of individual behaviors between people with similar competencies. The standard of care is essentially used to determine if a person responded reasonably and appropriately according to their education, training, and certification status.

Scope of Practice

The scope of practice is the defined purpose, duties, and legal responsibility for the strength and conditioning professional. The scope of practice effectively delineates the legal obligations and helps to define the protections for the support and coaching staff of a training facility. This also works in establishing effective hierarchy between medical staff and coaching personnel.

Copyright © Mometrix Media. You have been licensed one copy of this document for personal use only. Any other reproduction or redistribution is strictly prohibited. All rights reserved.
This content is provided for test preparation purposes only and does not imply an endorsement by Mometrix of any particular political, scientific, or religious point of view.

Negligence

Negligence refers to the failure of an individual to respond in a situation in an expectant and logical manner as a person with similar training and background would respond under proximal circumstances. For negligence to occur, there must be a duty for an individual to act, and the failure to act or respond with adequate standard of care represents a breach of that duty. The breach of duty results in some form of damage, i.e., bodily harm or economic harm. The damages occur as a result of proximate cause, which is the predictable and reasonable unfolding of the sequence of events.

Assumption of Risk

Assumption of risk is an acknowledgement of an athlete that the practice of strength and conditioning has inherent risks, and they have understood the inherent risks involved and chosen to participate. The risks associated with strength and conditioning, or other associated sporting activities, must be covered thoroughly with each individual athlete and a signed document should be obtained as acknowledgement of the risks and for records purposes.

Statute of Limitations

The statute of limitations is a clearly defined period of time in which legal action may be taken by an individual in pursuit of restitution of damages. This is a particular area of concern for maintaining accurate records and preserving them over time in order to protect against legal action years after an accident or disputed event.

Eligibility Criteria

Eligibility criteria are a clearly defined facility access criteria that establishes who may or may not access the training facility. The eligibility criteria is generally specific to the type of training facility being operated, i.e., monthly membership, one-on-one training, or group- or class-oriented facilities, but also refers to terms of continued access which should include facility etiquette and policies for removal or membership revocation.

Copyright © Mometrix Media. You have been licensed one copy of this document for personal use only. Any other reproduction or redistribution is strictly prohibited. All rights reserved.
This content is provided for test preparation purposes only and does not imply an endorsement by Mometrix of any particular political, scientific, or religious point of view.

Testing and Evaluation

Establishing an Athletic Profile

Establishing an athletic profile will help the strength and conditioning coach select tests relevant to an athlete's sport. These tests must be reliable and repeatable at various periods in a training program. Having a standard athletic profile for an athlete or specific sport team will help the strength and conditioning coach to develop athletes over time and maintain a consistent approach over many training cycles.

Purpose of Testing in Three Testing Windows

The strength and conditioning coach must perform various types of tests in order to determine athlete competency, strength, flexibility, speed, etc. and plan the training program accordingly. The appropriate testing methodology involve pre-test, which occurs prior to beginning a training program; the mid-test, which occurs during the training program to assess mid-point effectiveness; and lastly the post-test, which can occur prior to or after a competition to determine overall program effectiveness.

Testing Segments

The three significant testing periods for strength and conditioning coaches include the pre-test, mid-test, and post-test. The pre-test is significant as this test is performed prior to beginning a training program and establishes baseline performance indicators for athletic performance. The mid-test can be performed once or as many times as needed, depending on the length of event preparation, and is used to determine progress from pre-test results and is used in evaluating success of the current training program and is essential for determining course of action in the upcoming training periods. The post-test is performed after the completion of the training program in order to determine overall success and athletic progression.

Field Test

A field test is used as a non-laboratory method of testing an athlete's physiological capacities and can include speed testing, field VO_2 testing, anaerobic power, etc. The purpose of the field test is to place the athlete in a proximal competition setting for familiarity purposes to create a more accurate environment for testing procedures. This approach also reduces the dependence on expensive equipment, enhances athlete comfort, and is generally not a time-intensive process.

Measurement

Measurement is essential for the strength and conditioning coach. There are a myriad of measurements that can, and must, be taken often in order to ensure athletic progress and performance improvements are taking place in accordance with the training program. Measurement includes essential elements of training that includes anthropometrics, vertical jump height, body composition, and flexibility, but also includes physiological indicators such as anaerobic power, resting metabolism, blood lactate levels, etc. if equipment is available and proper training has been undertaken for safety and quality assurance purposes.

Low-Speed Muscular Strength

Low-speed muscular strength refers to the maximal force an athlete can produce in a single maximum effort by lifting a weight that requires a one-repetition maximum. This loading intensity does not allow for a barbell to be moved with great speed or velocity. Testing an athlete's one-

Copyright © Mometrix Media. You have been licensed one copy of this document for personal use only. Any other reproduction or redistribution is strictly prohibited. All rights reserved.
This content is provided for test preparation purposes only and does not imply an endorsement by Mometrix of any particular political, scientific, or religious point of view.

repetition maximum to determine absolute strength will provide significant insight into the real strength capacity of the athlete but will also inform proceeding training programs.

High-Speed Muscular Strength/Anaerobic Muscular Power

High-speed muscular strength/anaerobic muscular power refer to an athlete's ability to produce high amounts of force with high rates of speed/velocity to produce contractile force against a resistance. The difference between high-speed muscular strength/anaerobic muscular power and low-speed muscular strength is the rate of speed/velocity that the resistance moves. The movement choices for the two movements are significantly different as well, as the high-speed muscular strength movements consists of the core Olympic lifts or vertical jumping, while the low-speed muscular strength tests usually include testing a squat or bench press maximum.

Local Muscular Endurance

Local muscular endurance refers to the ability of a specific muscle group or groups to perform repetitive submaximal contractions in a continuous fashion for several seconds or minutes. The strength and conditioning coach could choose to perform this test using a body weight movement such as chin-ups, or a fixed load on a barbell performing any barbell-based movement they chose.

Aerobic Capacity/Power

Aerobic capacity is the highest capacity that an athlete can utilize through oxidation of various available energy substrates, i.e., carbohydrates, fats, and proteins. The differences between the aerobic and anaerobic capacities are the systems they are governed by in order to produce energy for muscular contractions. The aerobic system relies on oxygen to break down the needed energy substrate for contraction force, while the anaerobic system relies on the breakdown of glycogen or the phosphagen system to produce contractile forces.

Agility

Agility refers to an athlete's ability to alter their direction through stops, starts, and rapid changes in direction at high rates of speed. Testing this physical trait can involve performing cone drills where various running movements and transitions can be used to determine an athlete's agility against time, or a series of coach-directed changes in direction can be used and compared against a clock or other athlete's performances.

Speed

Speed is the rate an object moves over a specific distance in a measured period of time. Speed is tested in specific distances, generally no greater than 200 meters. Testing an athlete's speed is an evaluation of how quickly they move over a specific distance, and anything greater than 200 meters will rely on physical work capacities that can be confounding for assessing an athlete's speed.

Flexibility

Flexibility is defined by the range of motion that a joint in the body is able to move. A strength and conditioning coach can utilize a variety of tools, goniometers, sit and reach boxes, or simply have an athlete lightly warm-up and perform specific stretches to evaluate the range of motion in specific joints and stretching patterns either dynamically or statically.

Body Composition

Body composition is a test that determines the composition of fat and fat free mass of an athlete. Body composition is a significant measure in determining the overall leanness of an athlete and can be utilized as a gauge of health status as well. Being overly fat can be detrimental to athletic performance, specifically in sports where running, jumping, or changing directions suddenly are a

Copyright © Mometrix Media. You have been licensed one copy of this document for personal use only. Any other reproduction or redistribution is strictly prohibited. All rights reserved.
This content is provided for test preparation purposes only and does not imply an endorsement by Mometrix of any particular political, scientific, or religious point of view.

factor. Being too lean can impact performance as well, which is counterintuitive, but in sports such as distance running, triathlons, or decathlons, having some body fat is helpful for energy production purposes.

ANTHROPOMETRY

Anthropometry is the use of measurement to determine the length of body segments, girth of various muscle groups, total body weight, and height of an athlete. Measurements are an effective tool for assessing physical changes that occur during a training cycle that may be indicative of lean mass gains or fat loss if measurements are significantly different pre-test to post-test.

TYPES OF VALIDITY

Construct validity essentially is the elemental form of validity as a testing procedure must actually measure the phenomena being tested, and if the test does not then it is not a valid method of evaluation. Face validity asserts that a testing procedure appears on a superficial level, or to the casual observer, to measure what is being tested. Content validity refers to the professional observer that a testing procedure evaluates all primary and secondary athletic components relative to a specific sporting event.

RELIABILITY

Reliability refers to a testing procedure's reproducibility and procedural stability. Interrater reliability refers to the test evaluator's ability to accurately and uniformly perform testing procedures in order to gather accurate testing samples across multiple test evaluators. Test-retest reliability refers to variations in multiple test results from a single test observer utilizing the same testing methodology and measurement tools.

INTRASUBJECT VARIABILITY

Intrasubject variability refers to variations in performance by a single test subject during multiple testing bouts of a single test procedure. An example of intrasubject variability is an athlete performing multiple vertical jump tests and experiencing significantly different results across the length of the testing procedure either due to lack of effort, technical flaws, or fatigue.

INTRARATER VARIABILITY

Intrarater variability refers to multiple test observers obtaining similar testing results for a single testing session or across multiple testing procedures. Intrarater variability can be minimized by training the test observers in the testing procedure and testing device calibration.

EVALUATION

A strength and conditioning coach must evaluate the results of testing individual athletes in order to accurately assess development. Evaluation of testing data can involve simply using testing samples for a single athlete, or can include using statistical analysis techniques that involve comparative study of multiple athletes across a single training segment, or multiple years of development, in order to determine individual progress and assessing overall facility and coaching success.

FORMATIVE EVALUATION

The formative evaluation is used to monitor an athlete's progress throughout a training program, but is also used as an evaluation of the methodological approach of the training program and can even be used to determine training program performance norms and outcomes. The formative evaluation can be used to illuminate programming or athlete weaknesses as well as determining overall program success.

Copyright © Mometrix Media. You have been licensed one copy of this document for personal use only. Any other reproduction or redistribution is strictly prohibited. All rights reserved.
This content is provided for test preparation purposes only and does not imply an endorsement by Mometrix of any particular political, scientific, or religious point of view.

Difference Score

A difference score is a comparative analysis between an athlete's initial performance on specific testing/assessment procedures and the post-test performance data in the same tests/assessments. Difference scoring can be informative on changes in athletic performance across a training period, but has limitations in actually assessing the success or failure of a training program. These weaknesses include assessing athletes that begin a training program with a higher training status, as their performance will not change as drastically as a newer trainee. A second limitation can be athletes reserving maximal performance for the post-test window and not test at maximal ability during the pre-test assessment.

Descriptive Statistic

Descriptive statistics are statistics collected from a population in order to quantify the data comparatively using central tendency and standard deviations in order to assess performance across the entire group. This data can be used by a strength and conditioning coach to assess the performance of an entire team, or all athletes in an athletic program.

Central Tendency

Central tendency is a set of descriptive statistics that are clustered around a central data point or points. This data can be assessed as a mean, or average of the scores; a median, which is the middle of the scores assessed in magnitudes; and mode, which refers to the scores that appear most often. Using central tendencies can help a strength and conditioning coach determine who the outlier performers are, either positively or negatively, while also assessing what the needs for the majority of the athletes in the program are at that time. This data can help establish training program changes overall, as well as helping to bring to light possible individual alterations that can be made to help the negative outliers improve and progress more toward the mean.

Standard Deviation

The purpose of the standard deviation is to determine the rate of variation between scores that occur around the mean. Using standard deviation to assess the performance of a group of athletes will differentiate the athletes from one another, but will also determine which athletes are the performance outliers. This type of analysis can assist with program progression.

Review Video: Standard Deviation
Visit mometrix.com/academy and enter code: 419469

Percentile Rank Approach

Using the percentile rank system to determine an athlete's performance can be used as a motivational tool for poor performers to encourage better effort in the training program, or can be used as incentive for the more highly ranked athletes to stay on top of the rankings system by continuing to train hard and preserve their ranking.

Copyright © Mometrix Media. You have been licensed one copy of this document for personal use only. Any other reproduction or redistribution is strictly prohibited. All rights reserved.
This content is provided for test preparation purposes only and does not imply an endorsement by Mometrix of any particular political, scientific, or religious point of view.

CSCS Practice Test #1

Want to take this practice test in an online interactive format?
Check out the bonus page, which includes interactive practice questions and much more: **mometrix.com/bonus948/cscs**

1. An athlete who participates in intense exercise for hours, such as endurance running or cycling events, and consumes primarily only water, is in danger of:

a. Dehydration
b. Iron-deficiency anemia
c. Hyponatremia

2. How can improving flexibility positively impact performance?

a. It speeds up neural transmissions to the brain.
b. It enhances aerobic stamina.
c. It provides the ability to apply force over a greater range of motion.

3. Which statement about reinforcement is TRUE?

a. Only positive reinforcement increases the probability of a given behavior occurring.
b. Use of reinforcement is preferable to punishment.
c. Reinforcement can be used to increase or decrease a given behavior.

4. Which would NOT be part of a list of job objectives for the strength and conditioning professional?

a. Provide targeted rehabilitation for injured athletes.
b. Develop training programs that take athletes' injury status into account.
c. Design strength programs that reduce the likelihood of injuries.

5. What is the correct position for the shoulders in the starting position for the snatch and the clean?

a. Slightly behind the bar
b. Over or slightly in front of the bar
c. Slightly in front of the hips

6. What happens during the drive phase of utilizing a rowing machine?

a. The hips and knees extend.
b. The torso flexes.
c. The elbows extend.

7. What is the difference between the stiff-leg deadlift and the Romanian deadlift (RDL)?

a. Where the movement ends
b. Where the knees flex during the movement
c. Where the movement begins

Copyright © Mometrix Media. You have been licensed one copy of this document for personal use only. Any other reproduction or redistribution is strictly prohibited. All rights reserved.
This content is provided for test preparation purposes only and does not imply an endorsement by Mometrix of any particular political, scientific, or religious point of view.

8. An obstacle course athlete is training to climb ropes more effectively. Which exercise would be the MOST appropriate selection for this goal?

a. Lat pulldown
b. Lateral shoulder raise
c. Flat dumbbell fly

9. The 12-minute run test was used to assess an athlete's strength. This testing situation is best described as:

a. High reliability, high validity
b. High reliability, low validity
c. Low reliability, high validity

10. For which type of athlete would complex training be MOST appropriate?

a. Track & field athlete
b. Swimming athlete
c. Skiing athlete

11. Which option would be LEAST likely to result in overtraining?

a. Reducing the recovery time during high-intensity interval training
b. Doubling the percent of the training volume
c. Changing the exercise modality from weight machines to free weights

12. Which best describes the use of progressive-part training in learning the squat clean?

a. Practice multiple variations on the clean in a randomized order, such as hang power clean and hang squat clean.
b. Practice the squat clean in slow motion with a PVC pipe.
c. Practice power cleans and front squats by themselves, then practice them together as a squat clean.

13. Which of the following is NOT accurately characterized as a test of local muscular endurance?

a. Maximum distance run in 12 minutes
b. Maximum pull-ups in 1 minute
c. Maximum push-ups to failure

14. What would be the MOST reliable condition for obtaining body mass measurements?

a. In the morning, before intake of food or fluids
b. After a workout
c. At the end of the day, with adequate hydration

15. Which of the following is a unilateral movement that would target the rhomboids?

a. One-arm dumbbell bench press
b. Lat pulldown
c. One-arm dumbbell row

Copyright © Mometrix Media. You have been licensed one copy of this document for personal use only. Any other reproduction or redistribution is strictly prohibited. All rights reserved.
This content is provided for test preparation purposes only and does not imply an endorsement by Mometrix of any particular political, scientific, or religious point of view.

16. The average daily nutrient requirement that is adequate for meeting the nutritional needs of most healthy individuals within a given life cycle is termed the:

a. Recommended Daily Allowance (RDA)
b. Dietary Reference Intake (DRI)
c. Estimated Average Requirement (EAR)

17. In what plane of motion should an athlete be viewed for plyometrics to ensure a correct landing position?

a. The frontal plane
b. The sagittal plane
c. The transverse plane

18. What would be an example of negligence for a strength and conditioning professional?

a. The strength and conditioning professional forbids an athlete from entering the weightlifting floor due to wearing improper shoes.
b. The strength and conditioning professional allows athletes to bench press unsupervised, and one athlete gets injured.
c. The strength and conditioning professional finds broken equipment, so athletes have to do a circuit for their workout to take turns on the remaining equipment.

19. Which is an example of an anabolic hormone?

a. Thyroid hormone
b. Insulin-like growth factor (IGF)
c. Cortisol

20. Which statement about creatine is TRUE?

a. Creatine must be obtained through supplemental forms.
b. Creatine is most effective with a loading dose over a period of days.
c. Creatine tends to promote weight loss due to increasing metabolic rate.

21. The first step in the heart's electrical activity, represented by the P-wave on an ECG, is what?

a. Repolarization of the atria
b. Depolarization of the ventricles
c. Depolarization of the atria

22. The aerobic fitness of two athletes is being compared. If we have a measurement for each of them in mL of O_2 per minute, what needs to be done next to provide an accurate comparison and see who is more aerobically fit?

a. Multiply their scores by the rate pressure product.
b. Add their resting heart rate to each of their scores.
c. Divide their scores by each of their weight in kilograms.

23. For which type of athlete would unilateral training be MOST suitable?

a. An athlete seeking to develop strength
b. An athlete recovering from injury
c. An athlete whose sport involves movement into the transverse plane

Copyright © Mometrix Media. You have been licensed one copy of this document for personal use only. Any other reproduction or redistribution is strictly prohibited. All rights reserved.
This content is provided for test preparation purposes only and does not imply an endorsement by Mometrix of any particular political, scientific, or religious point of view.

24. Which of the following would be an example of positive punishment?

a. Having an athlete do five extra minutes of conditioning for being five minutes late to practice
b. Providing a prize for the top-scoring athlete in each season's game
c. Taking away an athlete's team captain status upon observing abusive behavior toward other teammates

25. In testing a group of athletes, the head coach enforces a standardized rest period between 1-RM attempts, while the assistant coach does not enforce a standardized rest, allowing athletes to perform attempts when they feel ready. This difference describes effects on:

a. Intrasubject variability
b. Inter-rater reliability
c. Discriminant validity

26. Where can a muscle generate the most force, and why?

a. At less than its resting length, because this reduces the joint angle
b. At its resting length, because the maximal number of crossbridge sites are available
c. At more than its resting length, because a longer lever arm means more torque

27. Which sport would be most likely to have a relatively HIGH recruitment of type I fibers and a relatively LOW recruitment of type II fibers?

a. Marathon running
b. Olympic weightlifting
c. Hockey

28. An athlete on the track team discloses to the strength and conditioning professional that they have been restricting their food and are fearful of gaining weight. How can the strength and conditioning professional BEST help this athlete?

a. Document the issues and advise the athlete that they may have anorexia.
b. Refer the athlete to a more specifically qualified professional.
c. Provide the athlete with resources on treating and managing disordered eating.

29. What is the functional component of the neuromuscular system?

a. The motor unit
b. The muscle fiber
c. The myofilament

Copyright © Mometrix Media. You have been licensed one copy of this document for personal use only. Any other reproduction or redistribution is strictly prohibited. All rights reserved.
This content is provided for test preparation purposes only and does not imply an endorsement by Mometrix of any particular political, scientific, or religious point of view.

30. An athlete is performing a plyometric push-up and has lowered their chest toward the floor as shown. They are now in the position just before they are about to explosively push off. What would be the name of this phase?

Licensed Under CC BY-SA 3.0 (creativecommons.org/licenses/by-sa/3.0/)
https://commons.wikimedia.org/wiki/File:USMC-120120-M-OB827-142.jpg

a. Eccentric phase
b. Concentric phase
c. Amortization phase

31. For which type of athlete would eccentric loading in resistance training be MOST appropriate as a main focus of the training program?

a. Hockey player
b. Rower
c. Long-distance runner

32. What is the role of a synergist in muscular movement?

a. To indirectly assist in movement
b. To act as the prime mover
c. To decelerate the movement

33. A strength and conditioning professional works at a facility that requires injured athletes to have a medical clearance form before returning to training. Such a requirement is an example of:

a. Procedures
b. Policies
c. Standard of care

34. What is an important consideration in using the 1-RM power clean as a test protocol for athletes?

a. It should not be paired with any other test protocol due to high metabolic demand.
b. It requires a spotter for safety.
c. It is highly technical, so it may not be reliable or valid on an athlete who is inexperienced.

35. Which component is the rate-limiting step in glycolysis?

a. Adenosine monophosphate (AMP)
b. Creatine kinase
c. Phosphofructokinase (PFK)

Copyright © Mometrix Media. You have been licensed one copy of this document for personal use only. Any other reproduction or redistribution is strictly prohibited. All rights reserved.
This content is provided for test preparation purposes only and does not imply an endorsement by Mometrix of any particular political, scientific, or religious point of view.

36. Which two variables receive the most attention across the periods of a periodization training plan?

a. Volume and intensity
b. Intensity and exercise selection
c. Frequency and volume

37. Which is NOT a muscle that is primarily stretched in the spinal twist static stretch?

a. Erector spinae
b. Iliopsoas
c. External oblique

38. A strength and conditioning professional is considering using the pro agility test for assessing a group of hockey athletes. What would be an important consideration of using this test?

a. For the greatest sports-specificity, a test on ice would be preferable.
b. The pro agility test will not measure change of direction, which is critical for hockey players.
c. The test should be paired with an assessment of maximal strength on the same day for the most valid results.

39. In which period of the sport season would it be BEST for a soccer team to develop aerobic endurance?

a. Off-season
b. Preseason
c. In-season

40. Which would be the BEST aspect of technique to emphasize for achieving a rapid stride rate in sprinting?

a. Maintaining upright posture
b. Full-range-of-motion arm swings
c. Brief ground contact times

41. Which of the following is best avoided during stretching?

a. Activation of the muscle spindle
b. Creating autogenic inhibition
c. Stimulating the Golgi tendon organ

42. An athlete wishes to strengthen their technique with the power clean. Which exercise would be the BEST selection to supplement their training?

a. Romanian deadlift (RDL)
b. Barbell bench press
c. Barbell step-up

Copyright © Mometrix Media. You have been licensed one copy of this document for personal use only. Any other reproduction or redistribution is strictly prohibited. All rights reserved.
This content is provided for test preparation purposes only and does not imply an endorsement by Mometrix of any particular political, scientific, or religious point of view.

43. Which is NOT a major muscle involved in this movement?

Licensed Under CC BY-SA 3.0 (creativecommons.org/licenses/by-sa/3.0/)
https://commons.wikimedia.org/wiki/File:DumbbellBentOverRow.JPG

a. Middle trapezius
b. Posterior deltoids
c. Subscapularis

44. What is the basis behind using diaphragmatic breathing as a performance-enhancing technique?

a. It allows mental rehearsal of potentially stressful events.
b. It increases parasympathetic activity.
c. It enhances arousal through release of neurotransmitters.

45. A female volleyball athlete obtains the following scores in testing. What training outcome should be the focus in the athlete's periodized plan going forward?

Pro agility test: 5.2 seconds
1-RM bench press: 108 lbs/49 kg
Vertical jump: 26 inches/66.04 cm

a. Improving power
b. Improving strength
c. Improving agility

46. Which of the following is an example of a biaxial joint?

a. The elbow
b. The ankle
c. The shoulder

47. If an athlete trains aerobically and their body adapts to have a greater stroke volume, what effect will this have on cardiac output?

a. Decreased cardiac output
b. No effect on cardiac output
c. Increased cardiac output

Copyright © Mometrix Media. You have been licensed one copy of this document for personal use only. Any other reproduction or redistribution is strictly prohibited. All rights reserved.
This content is provided for test preparation purposes only and does not imply an endorsement by Mometrix of any particular political, scientific, or religious point of view.

48. Cross-country athletes are going through a circuit. The circuit exercises are arranged in the following order. Which choice would be the BEST fit to go in the blank, based on the existing order?

1. Lunge
2. Vertical chest press
3. Step-up
4. Low-pulley seated row
5. ____________
6. Shoulder press machine

a. Seated leg curl
b. Pec deck
c. Triceps pushdown

49. What would enhance the reliability of a flexibility assessment for an athlete?

a. Performing a standardized warm-up and standardized stretching before the assessment
b. Performing a set amount of ballistic stretching before the assessment
c. Performing the assessment multiple times throughout the season at varied times of day

50. Which substance is released from the sarcoplasmic reticulum to control muscle contraction?

a. Hemoglobin
b. Myosin
c. Calcium

51. For optimal safety and function, what should weightlifting platforms be primarily made of?

a. Turf
b. Wood
c. Tile

52. Which statement about the Valsalva maneuver is FALSE?

a. It can make lifting heavy loads easier.
b. It involves a closed glottis with contracted abdominals and rib cage muscles.
c. It is potentially dangerous due to decreasing blood pressure.

53. Which of the following is a closed kinetic chain exercise?

a. Lateral raise
b. Push-up
c. Dumbbell bench press

54. Which neurotransmitter is responsible for causing excitation of the sarcolemma and therefore muscle contraction?

a. Troponin
b. Action potentials
c. Acetylcholine

Copyright © Mometrix Media. You have been licensed one copy of this document for personal use only. Any other reproduction or redistribution is strictly prohibited. All rights reserved.
This content is provided for test preparation purposes only and does not imply an endorsement by Mometrix of any particular political, scientific, or religious point of view.

55. Anabolic steroids are derived from which hormone found naturally in the body?

a. Human growth hormone
b. Epinephrine
c. Testosterone

56. In the presence of overtraining syndrome (OTS), which of the following would INCREASE?

a. Heart rate
b. Performance
c. Force production

57. A coach provides their athletes with two choices of skills to work on and whether to do them before or after conditioning drills. This is an example of:

a. Negative reinforcement
b. Extrinsic motivation
c. Self-controlled practice

58. A strength and conditioning professional is administering a test battery to a baseball team. What would be the MOST logical sequence?

a. 1-RM bench press, 505 agility test, skinfolds
b. Skinfolds, 505 agility test, 1-RM bench press
c. 505 agility test, skinfolds, 1-RM bench press

59. An athlete sustains a partial tear of their anterior cruciate ligament during a soccer match when colliding with the opposing team's goalie. This type of injury is termed a:

a. Sprain
b. Contusion
c. Strain

60. What type of training program would have the greatest effect on EPOC?

a. High-intensity interval training
b. Aerobic training performed below 50% of VO2 max
c. Sports-specific dynamic stretching

61. Which modality for older adults would be the most useful for muscular strength and postural stability?

a. Machine-based resistance training
b. Treadmill walking
c. Resistance training with free weights

62. Which two minerals warrant particular attention for athletes to ensure they are consuming adequate amounts?

a. Calcium and zinc
b. Magnesium and iron
c. Iron and calcium

63. Which is NOT an effect of resistance training?

a. Increased bone mineral density
b. Increased muscle fiber cross-sectional area
c. Increased blood flow to cartilage

Copyright © Mometrix Media. You have been licensed one copy of this document for personal use only. Any other reproduction or redistribution is strictly prohibited. All rights reserved.
This content is provided for test preparation purposes only and does not imply an endorsement by Mometrix of any particular political, scientific, or religious point of view.

64. What is the primary issue with this spotting technique in the dumbbell bench press?

Licensed Under CC BY-SA 3.0 (creativecommons.org/licenses/by-sa/3.0/) https://commons.wikimedia.org/wiki/File:US_Navy_101122-N-7948R-111_Chief_Warrant_Officer_Jose_Martinez_performs_dumbbell_chest_presses_in_the_gymnasium_aboard_the_amphibious_dock_landing.jpg

a. The spotter should not be touching the athlete.
b. The athlete should not be spotted at all for safety concerns.
c. The spotter should be spotting at the athlete's wrists.

65. Which of the following plyometric exercises has BOTH a horizontal and a vertical component for the direction of the jump?

a. Depth jump
b. Lateral barrier hop
c. Standing long jump

66. For testing athletes on the 1-RM bench pull, which condition would result in an invalid repetition?

a. The athlete utilizes a pronated grip on the barbell.
b. The athlete's feet are off the ground.
c. The athlete raises the bar 2 inches to the underside of the bench.

67. Can muscle fiber types change with specific training?

a. No, muscle fiber types are genetically determined.
b. To an extent, some subtypes can change.
c. Yes, any muscle fiber type can change to another type with the right stimulus.

68. An athlete using a rowing machine first practices the drive of the legs, and then practices the pull of the arms. This best describes:

a. Simplification
b. Repetitive-part training
c. Fractionalization

69. Athlete A gets excited and pumped up by the cheers of the crowd, while the same cheering makes Athlete B nervous and edgy. The difference here best illustrates which theory?

a. Catastrophe theory
b. Inverted-U theory
c. IZOF theory

Copyright © Mometrix Media. You have been licensed one copy of this document for personal use only. Any other reproduction or redistribution is strictly prohibited. All rights reserved.
This content is provided for test preparation purposes only and does not imply an endorsement by Mometrix of any particular political, scientific, or religious point of view.

70. Which is NOT one of the major muscles utilized in this movement?

Licensed Under CC BY-SA 3.0 (creativecommons.org/licenses/by-sa/3.0/)
https://commons.wikimedia.org/wiki/File:Leg_press_(cropped,_flipped).jpg

a. Biceps femoris
b. Vastus lateralis
c. Gastrocnemius

71. A basketball athlete has mastered the stiff-leg deadlift and the deadlift. Which is the BEST choice of exercise to progress them to next, based on these movements and the needs of their sport?

a. Hip sled
b. Bent-over row
c. Power clean

72. What type of carbohydrate molecule is fiber?

a. Monosaccharide
b. Polysaccharide
c. Disaccharide

73. Which of the following is NOT a component of creating a mission statement?

a. The target clientele
b. What makes the service unique
c. The hours and location of the facility

74. Which of the following energy systems is anaerobic?

a. Krebs cycle
b. Glycolysis
c. Electron transport system

75. Which macronutrient would be most important during an activity like sprinting?

a. Carbohydrate
b. Protein
c. Fat

Copyright © Mometrix Media. You have been licensed one copy of this document for personal use only. Any other reproduction or redistribution is strictly prohibited. All rights reserved.
This content is provided for test preparation purposes only and does not imply an endorsement by Mometrix of any particular political, scientific, or religious point of view.

76. An athlete is motivated to spend extra time in the weight room because they enjoy the feeling of getting stronger. This best describes:

a. Drive theory
b. Selective attention
c. Intrinsic motivation

77. What is considered to be one of the reasons behind caffeine's effectiveness as an ergogenic aid?

a. It enhances the formation of ATP, improving muscular power.
b. It stimulates protein synthesis for greater muscular strength.
c. It increases use of fat as a fuel, sparing glycogen.

78. Which of the following is NOT a sign or symptom of ergogenic aid abuse?

a. Increased sarcopenia
b. Increased liver damage risk
c. Increased blood pressure

79. A coach is targeting the behavior of athletes in cleaning up the weight room after their conditioning sessions through providing praise. This target behavior is termed:

a. Positive reinforcement
b. An operant
c. Enhancing self-efficacy

80. An advanced athlete performs a workout with a strength focus on 2 days of the week, a workout with a power focus on 2 days of the week, and a workout with a hypertrophy focus on 1 day of the week. This best describes:

a. Linear periodization
b. Nonlinear periodization
c. Microcycle periodization

81. Which of the following is critical for a strength and conditioning professional in order to be a first responder?

a. Having a certification in first aid, CPR, and AED use
b. Having the ability to activate the emergency medical system
c. Having and storing signed waivers for all individuals using the facility

82. Which of the following is NOT part of the axial skeleton?

a. The scapulae
b. The coccyx
c. The sternum

83. An athlete is performing a training program on the back squat over a period of weeks. If the athlete performs 4 sets of 3 reps, what weight is needed to lift for a volume-load of 2,580 lbs (1,172.7 kg)?

a. 215 lbs/97.73 kg
b. 200 lbs/90.9 kg
c. 195 lbs/88.64 kg

Copyright © Mometrix Media. You have been licensed one copy of this document for personal use only. Any other reproduction or redistribution is strictly prohibited. All rights reserved.
This content is provided for test preparation purposes only and does not imply an endorsement by Mometrix of any particular political, scientific, or religious point of view.

84. In which technique would observation of horizontal displacement be used to ensure the athlete is generating force correctly?

a. Z-Drill
b. Y-Shaped Agility
c. A-Skip

85. Which exercise selection would have the most optimal osteogenic stimuli?

a. Biceps curl, seated chest press
b. Power clean, deadlift
c. Seated calf raise, lying leg curl

86. Which relaxation technique for improved performance is characterized by an attentional state that focuses on body sensations like warmth or heaviness?

a. Autogenic training
b. Systematic desensitization
c. Attentional control

87. Which of the following correctly lists body composition measurement methods from MOST valid and reliable to LEAST?

a. Skinfolds; DEXA scan; Assessing body weight with a scale
b. Underwater weighing; Skinfolds; Circumferences
c. Circumferences; Skinfolds; DEXA scan

88. An athlete is cleared to return to practice after an ankle sprain. Which of the following tests would be the BEST choice to assess the stability of each leg?

a. T-test
b. Star excursion balance test
c. Overhead squat

89. Which of the following is the MOST effective form of PNF (proprioceptive neuromuscular facilitation) stretching?

a. Hold-relax with agonist contraction
b. Hold-relax
c. Contract-relax

90. Which of the following is the best example of a contraindication?

a. Near-maximal loads are avoided in an athlete's program leading up to the day of competition.
b. Open kinetic chain exercises are avoided for an athlete due to a healing ACL injury.
c. Free weights are avoided for newer athletes, who begin with machines instead.

91. A distance running athlete is currently running four times per week at an intensity of 65-75% of their target heart rate for 30 minutes each time. Assuming the intensity is kept the same, which is the BEST choice for the next week's progression?

a. Perform running 3x a week, with each run at 30 minutes.
b. Perform running 5x a week, with each run at 35 minutes.
c. Perform running 4x a week, with 2 runs at 36 minutes and 2 runs at 30 minutes.

Copyright © Mometrix Media. You have been licensed one copy of this document for personal use only. Any other reproduction or redistribution is strictly prohibited. All rights reserved.
This content is provided for test preparation purposes only and does not imply an endorsement by Mometrix of any particular political, scientific, or religious point of view.

92. Which of the following is the largest contributor to an individual's total energy expenditure?

a. Basal metabolic rate (BMR)
b. Physical activity
c. Thermogenesis

93. A strength and conditioning specialist is working with a lacrosse team for the first time. After evaluating the needs of the sport, what action is most appropriate to come next?

a. Evaluate the athletes' body composition and select sports-specific exercises.
b. Evaluate the athletes' training status and perform physical testing.
c. Evaluate the athletes' risk for injury by having them perform power exercises.

94. Which of the following plyometric exercises does NOT require a countermovement?

a. Jump over barrier
b. Lateral push-off
c. Standing long jump

95. A 43-year-old cycling athlete seeks to train at 65-75% of their target heart rate range. The athlete's resting heart rate is 53. Using the Karvonen method, what is the correct training intensity for this athlete?

a. Approximately 143 to 165 beats/min
b. Approximately 134 to 146 beats/min
c. Approximately 115 to 133 beats/min

96. The picture shown is the ending position for which stability ball exercise?

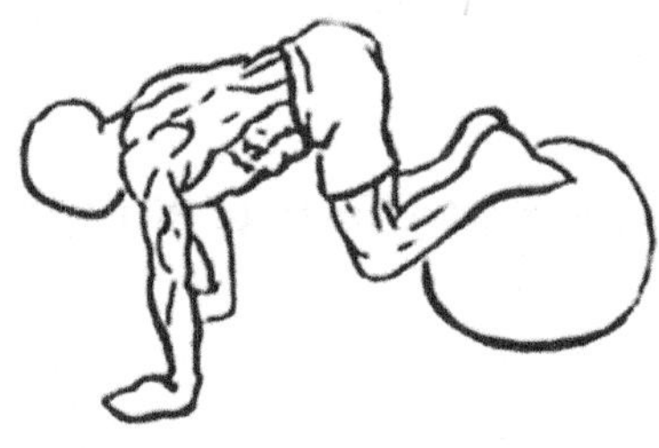

Licensed Under CC BY-SA 3.0 (creativecommons.org/licenses/by-sa/3.0/)
https://commons.wikimedia.org/wiki/File:Exercise-ball-pull-in-2.gif

a. Stability ball rollout
b. Stability ball pike
c. Stability ball jackknife

97. When would the amortization phase occur in a cycled split squat jump?

a. During the landing in the lunge position
b. During the preparatory countermovement
c. During the explosive phase

Copyright © Mometrix Media. You have been licensed one copy of this document for personal use only. Any other reproduction or redistribution is strictly prohibited. All rights reserved.
This content is provided for test preparation purposes only and does not imply an endorsement by Mometrix of any particular political, scientific, or religious point of view.

98. A football team performs the same quick feet lateral agility drill using agility ladders, tires, and then cones. This is an example of:

a. Discovery
b. Segmentation
c. Variable practice

99. Which of the following athletes is likely to have the highest training volume in their program for resistance training?

a. Marathon runner
b. Bodybuilder
c. Football lineman

100. Which of the following orders of exercises would be the BEST selection to maintain good technique and movement quality for an athlete?

a. Bench press, push jerk, lying triceps extension
b. Push jerk, bench press, lying triceps extension
c. Lying triceps extension, bench press, push jerk

101. What information must be known about an athlete in order to assign MET values to prescribe exercise intensity?

a. The athlete's maximal oxygen uptake
b. The athlete's resting heart rate
c. The athlete's height and weight

102. Which of the following BEST describes proper mechanics of the foot strike during running gait?

a. The midfoot strikes the ground first, and weight is transferred laterally.
b. The heel strikes the ground first, and weight is transferred forward.
c. The ball of the foot strikes the ground first, and weight is transferred forward.

103. A test is performed on an athlete three times within a week, resulting in highly variable scores. This test likely has:

a. Low validity
b. Low reliability
c. Low credibility

104. Of the three types of levers in the body's musculoskeletal system, which one typically has the greatest mechanical advantage?

a. First-class lever
b. Second-class lever
c. Third-class lever

105. Which blood pressure response would be most likely during aerobic exercise?

a. Decreased systolic blood pressure, slightly increased diastolic blood pressure
b. Increased systolic blood pressure, slightly decreased or maintained diastolic blood pressure
c. Increased systolic blood pressure, increased diastolic blood pressure

Copyright © Mometrix Media. You have been licensed one copy of this document for personal use only. Any other reproduction or redistribution is strictly prohibited. All rights reserved.
This content is provided for test preparation purposes only and does not imply an endorsement by Mometrix of any particular political, scientific, or religious point of view.

106. A RAMP protocol is being used to create a warm-up for a soccer athlete. The first activities are ones that elevate the heart rate, such as short shuttle runs and side shuffles, and the warm-up continues with lunging and rotating patterns. What type of activity would come next for an effective RAMP warm-up?

a. Sport-specific soccer agility drills
b. Dynamic stretches
c. Longer-distance running

107. A strength and conditioning specialist ensures that the battery of tests for a gymnastics team covers measures of power, strength, and flexibility. This best describes an example of:

a. Test-retest reliability
b. Intra-rater variability
c. Content validity

108. An athlete who is new to the back squat is performing it with just a light barbell under the coach's direction. This is an example of:

a. Segmentation
b. Simplification
c. Repetitive-part training

109. Muscles responsible for maintaining posture would have a high composition of which type of muscle fibers?

a. Type I
b. Type IIa
c. Type IIx

110. An athlete in a state championship soccer match has a game in the morning and another game in the late afternoon. Which is the BEST choice for their optimal performance?

a. Consume food or drink that is high in carbohydrate immediately after the first match and at regular intervals throughout the day.
b. Consume approximately 25-50 extra grams of higher-fat foods to preserve lipid stores in the body.
c. Supplement with 2 grams per kilogram body weight of creatine in the 3 days leading up to the soccer matches.

111. If two athletes have the same skill level and motivation toward a task, which one will typically be the better performer?

a. The one who has set an outcome goal
b. The one with a high motivation to avoid failure
c. The one with higher self-efficacy

112. A workout is designed for an athlete focused on pushing and pulling movements. Which of the following series of exercises would be the best fit?

a. Bench press, deadlift, calf raise
b. Triceps dip, push-up, lunge
c. Bench press, seated row, pec deck

Copyright © Mometrix Media. You have been licensed one copy of this document for personal use only. Any other reproduction or redistribution is strictly prohibited. All rights reserved.
This content is provided for test preparation purposes only and does not imply an endorsement by Mometrix of any particular political, scientific, or religious point of view.

113. Which statement about resistance training programs for youth is TRUE?

a. Youth can expect decreased bone mineral density from training.
b. Youth should not be expected to perform at the same neural skill levels as adults.
c. Youth will improve muscle force production but not muscle mass.

114. Which of the following would NOT be a positive effect on performance from doing a proper warm-up?

a. Increased core temperature
b. Lowered viscous resistance in muscles
c. Decreased metabolic reactions

115. The strength and conditioning specialist for a wrestling team changes up the team's training cycle each month with a new block of exercises. Such a cycle is best described as a:

a. Microcycle
b. Macrocycle
c. Mesocycle

116. For which training goal would it make the MOST sense to progress a resistance training program by decreasing the rest period?

a. Strength
b. Power
c. Endurance

117. Which of the following describes correct posture for the acceleration phase of a sprint?

a. Upright posture with shoulders over hips
b. Slight spinal flexion with neck slightly extended
c. Natural forward trunk lean, head in line with the spine

118. Which type of grip is most effective for Olympic lifting movements such as the snatch or clean?

a. False grip
b. Pronated grip
c. Hook grip

119. An athlete consuming a meal two hours before a competition should consume approximately __ gram/kg body weight of carbohydrate.

a. 0.5
b. 1
c. 2

120. In testing maximum muscular strength with 1-RM, what is the ideal number of attempts after the warm-up?

a. 5-8
b. 1-3
c. 3-5

Copyright © Mometrix Media. You have been licensed one copy of this document for personal use only. Any other reproduction or redistribution is strictly prohibited. All rights reserved.
This content is provided for test preparation purposes only and does not imply an endorsement by Mometrix of any particular political, scientific, or religious point of view.

121. A training program that does not include adequate rest and variance of training protocol would likely have what main effect on the endocrine system?

a. Increased testosterone production
b. Increased growth hormone production
c. Increased cortisol production

122. An athlete is performing a log press. What is the most optimal point in the movement for the athlete to exhale?

a. While pressing the log upward
b. Before pressing the log
c. While lowering the log back down to the shoulders

123. What is torque as it relates to muscle force?

a. The degree to which a force tends to rotate an object around a specific fulcrum
b. The time rate of doing work
c. The product of muscle force and displacement

124. What would be the best example of using knowledge of performance feedback for an athlete running a 100 m dash?

a. Showing the athlete a video of their running form in slow motion
b. Telling the athlete how quickly they ran the 100 m
c. Having the athlete observe other athletes to compare their form

125. An athlete has sustained a second-degree lateral ankle sprain as of five days ago. Which set of movements would be MOST appropriate to include in their training program?

a. Balance training on wobble board, abdominal crunch
b. Stationary bicycle, single leg squat
c. Abdominal crunch, stationary bicycle

126. When considering how to build a new facility, what is the minimum recommended amount of space per athlete?

a. 100 square feet
b. 250 square feet
c. 50 square feet

127. What is the proper height of the box to use when performing a barbell step-up?

a. When the foot is on the box, there should be a 90-degree angle at the knee joint.
b. When standing behind the box, the box should come to the midpoint of the athlete's tibia.
c. When standing to the side of the box, it should be level with the top of the athlete's patella.

128. An athlete sets a goal to perform ten extra minutes of skill work, three days a week for the rest of the preseason. This is an example of a:

a. Process goal
b. Psychological goal
c. Outcome goal

Copyright © Mometrix Media. You have been licensed one copy of this document for personal use only. Any other reproduction or redistribution is strictly prohibited. All rights reserved.
This content is provided for test preparation purposes only and does not imply an endorsement by Mometrix of any particular political, scientific, or religious point of view.

129. A group of male basketball athletes had the following scores for 1-RM testing on the power clean.

Athlete 1: 93 kg/205 lbs
Athlete 2: 98 kg/215 lbs
Athlete 3: 89 kg/195 lbs
Athlete 4: 100 kg/220 lbs

Which statement is INCORRECT?

a. The mean of the scores is 95 kg/208.8 lb.
b. There is no mode for these scores.
c. The median of the scores is lower than the mean.

130. Which of the following is a best practice for safety in administering tests?

a. Supervise a cooldown with active recovery after higher-intensity testing.
b. Avoid any practice attempts to reduce fatigue.
c. Perform non-fatiguing tests like weight or flexibility at the end of the session.

131. A male athlete weighs 63 kilograms and is 1.8 meters tall. In what BMI classification does this athlete fall?

a. Underweight
b. Normal weight
c. Overweight

132. Which would be most likely to increase risk of osteoporosis in a female athlete?

a. Presence of the female athlete triad
b. Using multi-joint resistance training exercises
c. Participating in regular resistance training during childhood

133. A facility supervisor is deciding where to put a tall cable machine in the layout of their facility. The best place for the machine is:

a. Near an entrance
b. In the middle of the room
c. Along a portion of the wall

134. What would be the role of the phosphagen system in a marathon run?

a. Less active at the start of the run, then becomes more active as additional glycogen is needed
b. Not active at all because a distance run is an aerobic activity
c. Active at the start of the run, then becomes less active

135. An Olympic lifting athlete is consuming a reduced calorie diet to make their weight class. Which macronutrient will they likely need more of?

a. Carbohydrate
b. Fat
c. Protein

Copyright © Mometrix Media. You have been licensed one copy of this document for personal use only. Any other reproduction or redistribution is strictly prohibited. All rights reserved.
This content is provided for test preparation purposes only and does not imply an endorsement by Mometrix of any particular political, scientific, or religious point of view.

136. Which of the following is FALSE about fats (lipids)?

a. High levels of high-density lipoproteins (HDL) are associated with increased heart disease risk.
b. The body can store far greater amounts of lipids than carbohydrate.
c. Some amounts of cholesterol are required for bodily functions.

137. Which of the following work:rest ratios would be MOST suitable for a program utilizing interval training?

a. 3:1
b. 1:1
c. 5:1

138. In Olympic lifts like the clean and the snatch, when does extension of the hips, knees, and ankles occur?

a. During the first pull
b. During the second pull
c. During the catch

139. An athlete's program is progressing them to utilizing the two-handed kettlebell swing. Which is the BEST selection of movements that would likely indicate the athlete is ready to progress to the two-handed kettlebell swing if they can perform them correctly?

a. Upright row and push jerk
b. Good morning and bent-over row
c. Hammer curl and abdominal crunch

140. Performing a sit-up requires ____ of the low back in the ___ plane.

a. flexion; transverse
b. extension; sagittal
c. flexion; sagittal

141. At which phase of movement does the push jerk differ from the push press?

a. In the starting position
b. In the dip of the preparation phase
c. In the catch

142. Which of the following would be an example of a superset?

a. Dumbbell bench press and one-arm dumbbell row
b. Deadlift and seated leg curl
c. Back squat and squat box jump

143. A rugby player's 1-RM bench pull from the previous season is 220 lbs/100 kg. In retesting their 1-RM, which weight is most appropriate for their first attempt?

a. 132 lbs/60 kg
b. 121 lbs/55 kg
c. 110 lbs/50 kg

Copyright © Mometrix Media. You have been licensed one copy of this document for personal use only. Any other reproduction or redistribution is strictly prohibited. All rights reserved.
This content is provided for test preparation purposes only and does not imply an endorsement by Mometrix of any particular political, scientific, or religious point of view.

144. Where is the barbell's starting position for a hang power clean?

a. On the floor
b. Resting on the anterior deltoids
c. At midthigh or slightly above/below the knees

145. Which food would be most suitable for an athlete to consume close to competition time?

a. Mini bagel with fruit
b. Meat and cheese burrito
c. Leafy green and bean salad

146. Muscle hypertrophy occurs due to what biological process?

a. Increased number of myofibrils in the muscle
b. Increased collagen synthesis
c. Increased mitochondrial density

147. Which of the following is the correct description of the proper anatomical site to obtain a thigh skinfold?

a. A vertical fold halfway between the hip and knee joints on the anterior portion of the thigh
b. A horizontal fold halfway between the hip and knee joints on the posterior portion of the thigh
c. A diagonal fold halfway between the hip and knee joints on the lateral portion of the thigh

148. Movement of the skeletal system is created by which action?

a. Muscles pulling on tendons
b. Tendons pulling on joints
c. Joints pushing on muscles

149. An athlete who is at beginner-level skill and is asked to perform a complex task will likely have ____ arousal compared to an athlete with higher-level skill performing the same task.

a. lower
b. higher
c. equal amounts of

150. Which type of injury is significantly more common in female athletes than in male athletes?

a. ACL tear
b. Lumbar vertebrae fracture
c. Lateral ankle sprain

151. An athlete performs a set of pull-ups and then performs a set on the lat pulldown machine. This is an example of:

a. A push-pull exercise order
b. A split routine
c. A compound set

Copyright © Mometrix Media. You have been licensed one copy of this document for personal use only. Any other reproduction or redistribution is strictly prohibited. All rights reserved.
This content is provided for test preparation purposes only and does not imply an endorsement by Mometrix of any particular political, scientific, or religious point of view.

152. Creating an interval training program to stress the phosphagen system would involve:

a. Long duration, high intensity, near-complete recovery between sets
b. Short duration, lower intensity, minimal recovery intervals
c. Short duration, high intensity, near-complete recovery between sets

153. Which of the following situations best describes predictive validity?

a. A coach compares the scores of basketball athletes' anaerobic capacity and agility with the athletes' number of steals and assists per game.
b. A coach administers tests during the midpoint of the baseball season to see if performance has improved from the start of the season.
c. A track coach trains their assistant coaches in a standardized training protocol for all speed assessments.

154. An athlete is performing a bench press with resistance bands attached at each end of a barbell. Which point in the movement will have the highest resistance load?

a. At the liftoff of the bench press
b. At the lockout of the bench press
c. In the descent phase of the bench press

155. An athlete desires to start using creatine for enhanced performance. What should be considered FIRST before incorporating use of an ergogenic aid?

a. The athlete's method of strength and conditioning and their nutritional habits
b. The athlete's weight for the appropriate creatine dosage
c. The athlete's competition season schedule to structure an appropriate dose and taper of creatine

156. In performing the snatch, which of the following would be a technique error?

a. The feet leave the ground in the second pull.
b. The athlete performs the catch with flexion at the knees.
c. The hips rise before the shoulders in the first pull.

157. How does tendon insertion affect force production at a given muscle or muscle group?

a. A tendon insertion closer to the joint center means greater potential force production.
b. Tendon insertion does not have an impact on force production.
c. A tendon insertion further from the joint center means greater potential force production.

158. Which BEST describes overreaching or functional overreaching (FOR)?

a. Excessive training that results in long-term decreased performance
b. Excessive training that results in short-term decreased performance
c. Excessive training that results in maintaining performance levels by avoiding high intensities

159. An athlete who consumes a vegan diet asks the strength and conditioning professional about the best way to eat for performance. How can the strength and conditioning professional BEST help this athlete?

a. Direct the athlete to the MyPlate resource for general guidance.
b. Recommend specific amounts of plant-based foods that are good sources of protein.
c. Encourage the athlete to work with a sports dietitian.

Copyright © Mometrix Media. You have been licensed one copy of this document for personal use only. Any other reproduction or redistribution is strictly prohibited. All rights reserved.
This content is provided for test preparation purposes only and does not imply an endorsement by Mometrix of any particular political, scientific, or religious point of view.

160. A needs analysis is being conducted for a basketball athlete. Which type of test and corresponding training movements would be MOST appropriate to the needs of their sport?

a. T-test; hang clean, push press
b. Standing long jump test; stability ball pike, hip sled
c. Star excursion balance test; plyometric chest pass, front & side plank

161. Which test would be the most appropriate choice for basketball players to best simulate the specific needs of the metabolic system?

a. 12-minute run
b. 300-yard shuttle
c. Overhead squat

162. What are the general recommendations for utilizing carbohydrate loading before an aerobic endurance event?

a. Consume 1.0 to 1.6 grams of carbohydrate per kilogram of body weight over a 24-hour period before the event.
b. Consume 16 ounces of carbohydrate-containing sports drink in the 2 hours before the event.
c. Consume 8-10 grams of carbohydrate per kilogram of body weight in the three days before the event.

163. Which of the following is NOT a general goal and approach for the fibroblastic repair phase of injury?

a. Prevent excessive muscle atrophy
b. Provide relative rest
c. Provide submaximal exercise

164. What is responsible for the bone modeling that increases as a response to resistance training?

a. Hyaline cartilage
b. Osteoblasts
c. Fascia

165. Which of the following jumps would have the greatest rate of stretch during the eccentric phase?

a. Countermovement jump
b. Approach jump
c. Static squat jump

166. In a periodization program, which of the following would be the BEST example of supercompensation?

a. An athlete plans to increase their running distance gradually leading up to their next race.
b. An athlete performs successively more difficult plyometric exercises over a period of weeks and improves their sprint speed.
c. An athlete's sleep suffers long-term, and their technique deteriorates as a result.

Copyright © Mometrix Media. You have been licensed one copy of this document for personal use only. Any other reproduction or redistribution is strictly prohibited. All rights reserved.
This content is provided for test preparation purposes only and does not imply an endorsement by Mometrix of any particular political, scientific, or religious point of view.

167. The head basketball coach at a high school has the junior team watch the varsity team's technique in passing the ball. This is an example of:

a. Observational practice
b. Guided discovery
c. Augmented feedback

168. The lactate threshold would be ___ in a trained athlete over an untrained individual.

a. higher
b. lower
c. the same

169. An athlete reads and signs a form that outlines the nature of participating in fitness testing along with the risks and benefits. This BEST describes:

a. Informed consent
b. Risk management
c. Waiving liability

170. Which structure facilitates activation of the muscle when a change in muscle length is sensed?

a. Golgi tendon organ
b. Muscle spindle
c. Motor units

171. The breakdown of carbohydrate (from muscle glycogen or blood glucose) to replenish ATP describes what?

a. Glycolysis
b. Oxidative phosphorylation
c. Gluconeogenesis

172. Which is NOT part of the five-point body contact position for supine exercises on a bench?

a. Both shoulders are firmly on the bench.
b. Both elbows are firmly on the bench.
c. Buttocks are evenly on the bench.

173. Which of the following is NOT a way to impose the overload principle?

a. Increasing rest periods between sets and exercises
b. Utilizing more complex exercises
c. Adding a second session during one of the week's training days

174. Which of the following exercises would benefit MOST from the use of the Valsalva maneuver?

a. Kettlebell swing
b. Back squat
c. Seated leg curl

Copyright © Mometrix Media. You have been licensed one copy of this document for personal use only. Any other reproduction or redistribution is strictly prohibited. All rights reserved.
This content is provided for test preparation purposes only and does not imply an endorsement by Mometrix of any particular political, scientific, or religious point of view.

175. If a training program's goal is to improve force development and force production of the core, which exercise would be the MOST appropriate selection?

a. Power clean
b. Curl-ups on an unstable surface such as a Swiss ball
c. Abdominal crunches using a weight machine

176. Consider the following battery of tests:

Vertical jump
300-yard shuttle
1-RM back squat

Which sport would be the MOST appropriate choice for using these tests?

a. Wrestling
b. Basketball
c. Rowing

177. An athlete begins to run at a moderate intensity. What will be the PRIMARY reason for their increase in ventilation?

a. Increased tidal volume
b. Increased plasma diffusion
c. Increased minute ventilation

178. Which food is a high source of vitamin C?

a. Fish
b. Oranges
c. Fortified milk

179. When considering how to build a new facility, knowing the number of athletes who would use the facility at any given time is critical in order to understand:

a. The scheduling of the staff
b. The choice of equipment selection
c. The traffic flow of the facility

180. An athlete is feeling their heart race and muscles tense in the evening before a championship game. They are likely experiencing:

a. High state anxiety; high arousal
b. Low somatic anxiety; high arousal
c. High trait anxiety; low arousal

181. During a seated leg extension exercise, which muscle is performing a concentric contraction?

a. Semitendinosus
b. Vastus lateralis
c. Biceps femoris

182. What does the Yo-Yo intermittent recovery test assess?

a. Aerobic capacity
b. Maximum muscular power
c. Agility

Copyright © Mometrix Media. You have been licensed one copy of this document for personal use only. Any other reproduction or redistribution is strictly prohibited. All rights reserved.
This content is provided for test preparation purposes only and does not imply an endorsement by Mometrix of any particular political, scientific, or religious point of view.

183. Of the listed choices, which exercise would be MOST effective for a strength and conditioning professional to use in determining whether a volleyball athlete is ready to begin a plyometric program?

a. Any isometric core variation
b. Any pushing variation
c. Any squatting variation

184. The extent of a body's maturation, such as physical growth and development, is called:

a. Chronological age
b. Training age
c. Biological age

185. An athlete is performing a power clean. Where is the best place for the strength and conditioning professional to spot them?

a. Spot at the elbows
b. No spotting is needed
c. Spot at the wrists

186. The speed of an object plus its direction describes:

a. Acceleration
b. Velocity
c. Power

187. Which type of athlete would have the GREATEST need for considerations of nutrition during their event?

a. A powerlifting athlete
b. A wrestling athlete
c. A long-distance triathlete

188. In the sliding filament theory, the power stroke of myosin crossbridges comes from the breakdown of what?

a. Calcium
b. ATP
c. Sodium

189. After air enters the trachea during inspiration, where does it pass to next?

a. The bronchi
b. The alveoli
c. The capillaries

190. Teammates are helping each other perform the PNF hamstring stretch. For most effective stretching, what should occur during a passive stretch of the hamstring?

a. Concentrically contracting the quadriceps
b. Isometrically contracting the hamstrings
c. Eccentrically contracting the gastrocnemius

Copyright © Mometrix Media. You have been licensed one copy of this document for personal use only. Any other reproduction or redistribution is strictly prohibited. All rights reserved.
This content is provided for test preparation purposes only and does not imply an endorsement by Mometrix of any particular political, scientific, or religious point of view.

191. A program is being designed for an athlete with strength goals. Which choice of load, reps, volume, and rest periods is CORRECT?

a. 67-85% of 1-RM, 1-6 reps, 2-6 sets, rest 2-5 minutes
b. 90-100% of 1-RM, 1-6 reps, 2-3 sets, rest 30 seconds or less
c. 85% or more of 1-RM, 1-6 reps, 2-6 sets, rest 2-5 minutes

192. Which of the following exercises would NOT be performed inside a typical power rack?

a. Barbell good morning
b. Forward step lunge with barbell
c. Seated barbell shoulder press

193. A strength and conditioning professional wishes to select a dynamic stretch that includes the latissimus dorsi. Which would be the BEST choice?

a. Lunge with overhead side reach
b. Inchworm
c. Straight-leg march

194. Which of the following is NOT a test that measures maximum muscular power?

a. Margaria-Kalamen test
b. Hexagon test
c. 1-RM push jerk

195. Considering the phases of new facility design, in which phase is a SWOT analysis performed?

a. Design phase
b. Predesign phase
c. Post design phase

196. An athlete performs 3 sets of 5 reps of a weightlifting exercise. Based on this, their training goal is most likely for:

a. Endurance
b. Hypertrophy
c. Power

197. Why should mirrors in a facility be placed 20 inches above the floor?

a. To accommodate access for people with disabilities
b. To prevent weights from colliding with the mirror and causing breakage
c. To allow coaches to best see the form of all athletes

198. Which plyometric drill would be the BEST selection for a volleyball player with a training goal to improve their spiking of the ball?

a. 4-hurdle drill
b. Single leg push-off
c. Backward skip

Copyright © Mometrix Media. You have been licensed one copy of this document for personal use only. Any other reproduction or redistribution is strictly prohibited. All rights reserved.
This content is provided for test preparation purposes only and does not imply an endorsement by Mometrix of any particular political, scientific, or religious point of view.

199. An athlete performs a 1-RM deadlift of 405 lbs (184.09 kg). If this athlete has a strength goal, what is the MOST appropriate load to use for their training program?

a. 315 lbs (143.18 kg)
b. 332 lbs (150.9 kg)
c. 360 lbs (163.6 kg)

200. A group of football athletes has finished a periodization cycle for strength and is now entering a periodization cycle for power. How will the assigned volume for the power cycle be most likely to differ from the previous volume from the strength cycle?

a. The volume will be lower.
b. The volume will now be dependent on a percent of maximal loads lifted.
c. The volume will be slightly higher.

201. This athlete is performing a forward step lunge with dumbbells. What correction should be made to the athlete's technique?

Licensed Under CC BY-SA 4.0 (creativecommons.org/licenses/by-sa/4.0/)
https://commons.wikimedia.org/wiki/File:Jumping_split_squat_with_dumbbells_3.png

a. The lead knee should stay directly over the lead foot.
b. The trailing knee should not be flexed.
c. The torso should be parallel to the floor.

202. Where do most back injuries occur anatomically?

a. Between L4 and L5, or L5 and S1
b. Between T12 and L1, or L1 and L2
c. Between T4 and T5, or C4 and C5

203. For which type of athlete would it be most suitable to determine the training load using goal repetitions?

a. Distance runner
b. Olympic lifter
c. Professional basketball player

204. Which of the following would be the LEAST appropriate training activity for a group of track and field athletes in the preparatory period of periodization?

a. High-repetition resistance training, such as a circuit
b. Sprinting with increased intensity and decreased volume
c. Longer-distance running

Copyright © Mometrix Media. You have been licensed one copy of this document for personal use only. Any other reproduction or redistribution is strictly prohibited. All rights reserved.
This content is provided for test preparation purposes only and does not imply an endorsement by Mometrix of any particular political, scientific, or religious point of view.

205. Which of the following is INCORRECT in properly spotting an athlete who is performing a barbell bench press?

a. Place the hands in a supinated grip outside the athlete's hands.
b. Keep the hands close to the bar without touching it.
c. Adopt a shoulder-width stance with slight flexion in the knees.

206. Assessing the number of foot contacts would be a way to determine the volume of ____ training in order to safely progress over time.

a. agility
b. high-intensity interval (HIIT)
c. plyometric

207. A sprinter's plan includes high-intensity interval training (HIIT). What intensity will elicit the best training stimulus?

a. 80 to 85% of VO2 max
b. 75 to 80% of VO2 max
c. 90% or more of VO2 max

208. What type of exercise would be most likely to result in increased mitochondrial density if repeated with training?

a. Cross-country skiing
b. 50 m swim
c. Olympic lifting

209. A strongman athlete is doing training with tire flips and log clean-and-press. Which of the following is the MOST appropriate rest period?

a. 1-2 minutes
b. 2-5 minutes
c. 30-90 seconds

210. In an area where physical activity is taking place, relative humidity should not exceed:

a. 60%
b. 50%
c. 70%

211. Which of the following is the correct site measurement for obtaining a waist (abdominal) circumference?

a. Three inches below the xiphoid process
b. At the narrowest part of the torso, halfway between the ribcage and the anterior superior iliac crests of the pelvis
c. At the level of the navel

212. An athlete performing a power snatch senses that their second pull is not quick enough to get the bar overhead. This is an example of:

a. Augmented feedback
b. Intrinsic feedback
c. Explicit feedback

Copyright © Mometrix Media. You have been licensed one copy of this document for personal use only. Any other reproduction or redistribution is strictly prohibited. All rights reserved.
This content is provided for test preparation purposes only and does not imply an endorsement by Mometrix of any particular political, scientific, or religious point of view.

213. Three basic techniques are utilized to flip tires. Which one is pictured?

Licensed Under CC BY-SA 3.0 (creativecommons.org/licenses/by-sa/3.0/)
https://commons.wikimedia.org/wiki/File:US_Navy_120206-N-GC412-386_Airman_Mario_Rojas_flips_a_truck_tire_in_the_hangar_bay_while_exercising_aboard_the_Nimitz-class_aircraft_carrier_USS_Jo.jpg

a. Backlift style
b. Sumo
c. Shoulders-against-the-tire

214. Which of the following best characterizes bulimia nervosa?

a. Muscle wasting and severe weight loss
b. Recurrent consumption of foods in much smaller amounts than would be customarily consumed
c. Cycles of binging and purging accompanied by feeling a lack of control

215. Some athletes on the wrestling team have worked to put on sizable muscle mass yet are considering using steroids, as they perceive themselves as looking weak and too small. This situation best describes:

a. Muscle dysmorphia
b. Anorexia nervosa
c. Muscle atrophy

216. What would be an example of a strength and conditioning professional failing to comply with HIPAA guidelines?

a. Providing an athlete with specific supplement recommendations
b. Leaving broken equipment on the fitness floor without an "Out of Order" sign
c. Sharing an athlete's injury report with the rest of the team to provide injury prevention information

217. A distance running athlete wishes to consume a high GI food before going out for a training run. Which food would be the best choice?

a. White bread
b. Brown rice
c. Glass of milk

218. Which is NOT a role of catecholamines?

a. Increase force production
b. Increase vasoconstriction
c. Increase energy availability

Copyright © Mometrix Media. You have been licensed one copy of this document for personal use only. Any other reproduction or redistribution is strictly prohibited. All rights reserved.
This content is provided for test preparation purposes only and does not imply an endorsement by Mometrix of any particular political, scientific, or religious point of view.

219. Which warm-up movements would be MOST appropriate for a plyometric training program?

a. Depth jump and single-leg Romanian deadlift (RDL)
b. A-skip and forward lunges
c. Heel-to-toe walk and static butterfly stretch

220. What are the two arm positions for the front squat?

a. High bar and low bar
b. Parallel-arm and crossed-arm
c. Closed grip and alternate grip

Copyright © Mometrix Media. You have been licensed one copy of this document for personal use only. Any other reproduction or redistribution is strictly prohibited. All rights reserved.
This content is provided for test preparation purposes only and does not imply an endorsement by Mometrix of any particular political, scientific, or religious point of view.

Answer Key and Explanations for Test #1

1. C: Hyponatremia is a dangerous condition resulting from dilution of blood sodium levels. This may occur when an athlete is losing large amounts of sodium in sweat but is not adequately replenishing the sodium. In this situation, drinking only water is likely not enough to replace the sodium lost in sweat, and the athlete should consume sodium-containing foods or beverages, such as a sports drink.

2. C: Applying force over a greater range of motion (ROM) increases impulse, meaning the athlete can apply force for longer. As an example, if an athlete is sprinting with poor flexibility of the hamstrings, the range of motion over which they can apply force will be smaller than that of a more flexible athlete.

3. B: While both reinforcement and punishment can be used by a strength and conditioning professional or coach, reinforcement is preferable because it focuses on what should be done or is being done well. Reinforcement can be positive or negative, and both are used to increase of the frequency of a desired behavior, ruling out option A and option C. Punishment can also be positive or negative, but it is used to decrease the frequency of a desired behavior

4. A: Targeted rehabilitation for an injured athlete would be in the scope of a sports medicine professional. A strength and conditioning professional's scope includes working with athletes who have injuries and working to prevent injuries from happening, but specific rehabilitation post-injury would be beyond the scope of practice for the role.

5. B: A starting position with shoulders over the bar or slightly in front of the bar for the Olympic lifts helps ensure that the first pull will be effective, with adequate power generation for the second pull.

6. A: The drive phase of using a rowing machine is when the athlete begins to pull with the arms, pushing through the legs as the hips and knees extend.

7. A: The stiff-leg deadlift and the RDL have the same starting position and the same amount of knee flexion throughout the movement (that is, a slight to moderate amount of flexion). However, the RDL's end position is when the bar is aligned with the patellar tendon and the torso is parallel to the floor, so the plates do not touch the floor. In the stiff-leg deadlift, the athlete will lower the bar well past the patellar tendon, to the point of the plates even touching the floor.

8. A: In analyzing the needs of the rope climb movement, it is primarily a pulling movement that requires strength from the muscles of the upper and middle back. Therefore, a lat pulldown would be most effective at working those muscles.

9. B: A test can be reliable (having high consistency or repeatability) without being valid (measuring what it is supposed to measure). In this case, a 12-minute run test could be easily done as a repeated measurement and likely get consistent results, meaning high reliability. However, this test selection is not a valid application for measuring strength, as the 12-minute run measures aerobic capacity.

10. A: Complex training alternates movements that use the stretch-shortening cycle (like plyometrics) with heavy resistance exercises. This is intended to improve stretch-shortening cycle

Copyright © Mometrix Media. You have been licensed one copy of this document for personal use only. Any other reproduction or redistribution is strictly prohibited. All rights reserved.
This content is provided for test preparation purposes only and does not imply an endorsement by Mometrix of any particular political, scientific, or religious point of view.

performance, which is most important in activities that involve rapid changes in velocity like running or jumping.

11. C: Overtraining can occur when an athlete's program exceeds their ability to recover and puts their body systems under excess stress. Overtraining can occur when frequency, volume, and/or intensity are excessive, or when rest and recovery are insufficient. Progressing a program through using a different modality is unlikely to cause overtraining on its own.

12. C: Progressive-part training is useful when a skill is complex or has multiple parts. A squat clean involves both a clean and a squat, and these can be separated into two clear parts. Progressive-part training can be used to practice each part in isolation before putting them together.

13. A: Tests of local muscular endurance require certain muscle groups to perform repeated contractions against submaximal resistance. The 12-minute run is more accurately characterized as a test of aerobic capacity as it is full body and includes the cardiovascular system, not just localized to specific muscle groups.

14. A: Performing body mass measurements in the morning without the influence of external factors like food or drink provides a reliable condition because it is the most easily replicated. The two other conditions could have more variable results due to water weight lost in sweat or weight gained from consuming beverages.

15. C: Unilateral movements work only one side of the body at a time, ruling out the lat pulldown. The rhomboids are targeted in rowing or pulling movements. The bench press does not primarily target them as it is a pushing movement, ruling that out as an option.

16. A: To understand why the other two choices are incorrect, DRIs are overarching sets of nutrient intakes, while the RDA is a *type* of DRI. The EAR describes the average daily nutrient intake that is considered sufficient to meet half of a given healthy population's needs.

17. A: Viewing an athlete from the frontal plane will best allow assessment of the knees being positioned over the toes rather than going inward, i.e., valgus knee. Ensuring proper alignment is critical for safe landing in plyometrics and preventing injury.

18. B: Negligence is the failure to act as a reasonable and prudent person would act under similar circumstances. In this case, a strength and conditioning professional's responsibility is to adequately supervise athletes, so failure to uphold this responsibility is acting in a negligent manner.

19. B: The role of anabolic hormones is to promote tissue building, of which IGF is one example, along with others like testosterone. Thyroid hormone is a permissive hormone, letting other hormones' actions happen, and cortisol is a catabolic hormone involved in the breakdown of proteins.

20. B: Because creatine's method of effectiveness as an ergogenic aid relies on energy metabolism and increasing stored creatine in the muscles, it is best taken over a period of days, such as five days of a loading dose. The other choices are false as creatine occurs naturally in meat and fish, and creatine tends to promote weight gain due to increased total body water.

21. C: The P-wave occurs when cardiac muscle cells change electric potential, causing depolarization of the atria, which is the first step in the heart's electrical activity. Depolarization of the ventricles occurs in the second step, represented by the QRS complex on an ECG. Repolarization

Copyright © Mometrix Media. You have been licensed one copy of this document for personal use only. Any other reproduction or redistribution is strictly prohibited. All rights reserved.
This content is provided for test preparation purposes only and does not imply an endorsement by Mometrix of any particular political, scientific, or religious point of view.

of the atria also occurs during this second step, but its waveform is not typically apparent on an ECG due to being hidden by the QRS complex.

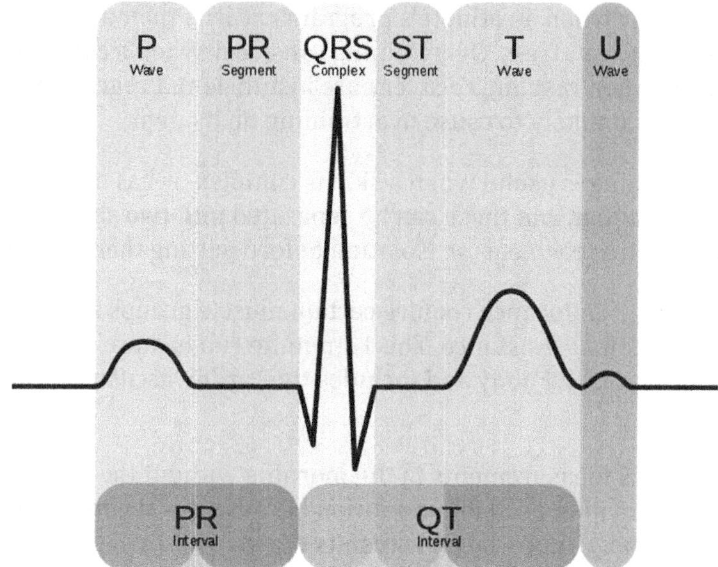

22. C: Measuring aerobic fitness is most accurately done through maximal oxygen uptake, which is measured in mL per kg per minute. Therefore, if our existing measurement is only in mL per minute, the weight of each athlete in kilograms needs to be factored in for a true assessment of each of their aerobic fitness levels.

23. B: Unilateral training works one side of the body at a time. It is best utilized for helping to reduce bilateral asymmetries or rehabilitating an injured athlete to ultimately promote more balanced, bilateral movement.

24. A: In positive punishment, something is presented that is intended to decrease the occurrence of a given behavior, or operant. The coach is presenting the athlete with the penalty of requiring extra conditioning, which is intended to decrease the likelihood that the athlete will be late again in the future.

25. B: Inter-rater reliability refers to the consistency in different raters' agreement on results over time. In this situation, because one coach is not utilizing the same standardized protocol, the results are likely to be more inconsistent.

26. B: A muscle at resting length has the actin and myosin filaments—important components of muscle contraction—next to each other, forming the greatest number of crossbridge sites. A contracted (shortened) muscle or a lengthened (stretched) muscle means there is less overlap between these sites, meaning less potential force production.

27. A: Type I fibers are termed "slow-twitch," as they have a high aerobic capacity and are more resistant to fatigue. High relative involvement of type I fibers is found in longer-duration, lower-intensity activities, like marathon running. Olympic weightlifting and hockey are sports that require rapid force development and high power output, so they would have relatively high involvement of type II fibers instead.

28. B: The role of the strength and conditioning professional is not to diagnose or to treat an eating disorder or a suspected eating disorder, as this is out of the scope of the role, which rules out (A)

Copyright © Mometrix Media. You have been licensed one copy of this document for personal use only. Any other reproduction or redistribution is strictly prohibited. All rights reserved.
This content is provided for test preparation purposes only and does not imply an endorsement by Mometrix of any particular political, scientific, or religious point of view.

and (C). However, it is their responsibility to help the athlete receive proper care and diagnosis through referral to a qualified professional.

29. A: The motor unit activates muscle fibers, using signals from the alpha motor neuron to dictate firing rate or frequency. Myofilaments, like actin and myosin, are components in a muscle fiber that interact for muscle contraction.

30. C: The amortization phase in plyometric movements is the time between the eccentric and concentric phases. Here, the athlete has completed the eccentric lowering and is just about to enact a concentric, explosive action for the plyometric portion of the push-up. The amortization phase must be kept short to best maximize activity of the stretch reflex.

31. A: Eccentric strength is particularly important for activities that require agility—rapid change of direction. Such training allows the neuromuscular system to adapt to decelerating the body appropriately. The other sports listed besides hockey do not involve rapid changes of direction.

32. A: Synergists indirectly assist in movement, such as stabilizing structures so the prime movers, or agonists, can contract, and antagonists can decelerate the movement and provide additional stability.

33. B: Policies refer to a facility's rules and regulations, so any type of requirement that a participant or employee must adhere to would be an example of a policy.

34. C: Athletes who are novice or inexperienced with a given movement or test protocol are not typically good candidates for a valid or reliable assessment. For example, an athlete who does not know how to perform the power clean accurately may obtain a score indicating low strength, when this result is more from their technique versus their raw levels of strength.

35. C: PFK is one of three important glycolytic enzymes that control the process of glycolysis. The reaction that it controls allows cells to metabolize glucose over storing it as glycogen. AMP is a byproduct of ATP hydrolysis, and creatine kinase is a catalyst that synthesizes ATP.

36. A: Volume and intensity will generally receive the most focus across a periodized plan. However, volume and intensity can each be manipulated in various ways, such as the load lifted or the total distance run, for example.

37. B: The spinal twist involves a seated lateral rotation with one leg crossed over the other. As the iliopsoas works primarily to flex the spine and flex the hip, it would be stretched with some type of hip extension or spinal extension movement instead.

38. A: While agility is an important skill for hockey players and the pro agility test does measure change of direction, performing a test that involves sprinting on land will be less sports-specific to emulating the needs of hockey.

39. A: Based on the sport-specific needs of soccer, aerobic endurance is a foundational quality. Such foundational capacities should be built well before the preseason or the in-season, so that the athlete has the proper base for more specialized movements or qualities needed to prepare them for competition.

40. C: Optimal sprinting technique is highly dependent on the correct application of force into the ground. Keeping the ground contact time (the amount of time that the feet are in contact with the

Copyright © Mometrix Media. You have been licensed one copy of this document for personal use only. Any other reproduction or redistribution is strictly prohibited. All rights reserved.
This content is provided for test preparation purposes only and does not imply an endorsement by Mometrix of any particular political, scientific, or religious point of view.

ground) minimal promotes the development of explosive strength, which in turn increases sprint speed.

41. A: The muscle spindle is responsive to rapid changes in muscle length. When activated, the muscle spindle will cause a reflexive muscle action called the stretch reflex in the affected muscle or muscle group. This actually inhibits the muscle from relaxing and lengthening and would be counterproductive for stretching.

42. A: The Romanian deadlift (RDL) closely mimics the transition phase of the power clean as the bar rises just above the knees. Utilizing the RDL would best build strength and proper technique as the athlete goes into the second pull. While the other choices would build strength, they do not have a direct association with similar movements of the power clean.

43. C: The one-arm dumbbell row does not target the subscapularis, which is part of the rotator cuff muscles and is most active during movements that involve some type of rotation (such as internal or external) at the shoulder joint.

44. B: Diaphragmatic breathing is used to promote a relaxation response, where the deep and rhythmic breathing decreases the fight-or-flight response of the sympathetic nervous system, conversely increasing the activity of the parasympathetic system.

45. C: This athlete has obtained scores near the top of the percentiles for the bench press and vertical jump; however, her score for the pro agility test is low (between the 20th and 30th percentile). Therefore, improving her agility would be the priority out of the three options.

46. B: Biaxial means that the joint has movement around two perpendicular axes. This rules out the elbow, as it is a hinge joint with one axis; and rules out the shoulder, which can move freely around multiple axes as it is a ball-and-socket joint. The ankle is the only choice that allows movement around only two axes.

47. C: Cardiac output is the product of stroke volume × heart rate. Thus, if an athlete has a greater stroke volume, this will cause the end product (cardiac output) to increase.

48. A: The existing order of the circuit alternates lower body exercises with upper body exercises. Therefore, the most logical choice for the blank is to select a lower body exercise, since an upper body exercise is before and after it.

49. A: As reliability is the measure of consistency of a test, the more standardized the pre-testing procedure is, the more it will contribute to consistent assessment. Ballistic stretching should not be permitted during flexibility testing as it has a higher risk of injury over benefits.

50. C: Hemoglobin's primary role is to transport oxygen in the blood, not to directly contribute to muscle contraction. Myosin is a type of myofilament that pairs with actin to form crossbridges during muscle contraction, so it plays an important role in muscle contraction but is not a stored substance that gets released. The release of calcium from the sarcoplasmic reticulum is the first step in the sliding filament theory of muscle contraction.

51. B: Wood platforms are the safest choice for weightlifting movements as shoes will not slide on them (like they might on tile), but shoes also should not get caught on them (like they might on turf).

Copyright © Mometrix Media. You have been licensed one copy of this document for personal use only. Any other reproduction or redistribution is strictly prohibited. All rights reserved.
This content is provided for test preparation purposes only and does not imply an endorsement by Mometrix of any particular political, scientific, or religious point of view.

52. C: The Valsalva maneuver does have potential danger associated with blood pressure, such as the risk of blacking out, but this is due to the muscle contraction and closed glottis increasing blood pressure, not decreasing it.

53. B: In a closed kinetic chain exercise, the distal segment(s) are stationary. A push-up is an example of an upper body closed kinetic chain exercise, as the hands are affixed to the floor to perform the exercise.

54. C: While all of these play a role in muscle contraction, acetylcholine is the only listed choice that is a neurotransmitter. Troponin is a protein that binds with calcium in its role in muscle contraction, and action potentials are electrical impulses that release calcium to enable muscle contraction.

55. C: Anabolic steroids are a synthetic version of testosterone. Testosterone by itself is not an effective ergogenic aid due to rapid degradation, so using it as an ergogenic aid requires that it be modified into human-made versions, which provide testosterone in levels exceeding what the body would make naturally.

56. A: OTS is a long-term performance decrease that can result in many body system disturbances, causing undesirable effects like decreased force production. An increased heart rate at rest can indicate that the body is overtraining and not recovering adequately.

57. C: Self-controlled practice is a tactic that can enhance motivation through involving athletes in decision-making (such as providing choices) and promoting their active involvement.

58. B: For the most valid and reliable results out of the three listed tests, non-fatiguing tests should go first, of which skinfolds or other body composition measurements are an example. Agility tests should go next because they are high skill and could be impacted by fatigue from other testing like 1-RM. Out of the choices here, 1-RM would then be the last, as the two tests before are unlikely to significantly affect it.

59. A: The term *sprain* describes trauma to a ligament of the body, and it has three degrees depending on severity. The other terms describe types of trauma to a muscle.

60. A: EPOC, or excess postexercise oxygen consumption, occurs after exercise as the body continues to use oxygen to restore itself back to resting values. Exercise intensity plays the largest role in EPOC, i.e., higher intensities will elicit greater EPOC values. As the other two choices are not high intensity, they are unlikely to elicit a significant amount of EPOC.

61. C: Free weights provide the most direct training stimulus for muscular strength and postural stability. While machines can be used, they will not provide the same level of adaptations. Treadmill walking is a useful form of exercise for the cardiovascular system but would not be the most useful choice for developing strength.

62. C: Failure to consume enough calcium and/or iron can have implications for impaired performance. As iron is needed for oxygen transport, an iron deficiency can lower performance. As calcium is needed for bone density and bone mass, not consuming enough can compromise structural integrity of the bones and increase bone fracture risk.

63. C: Resistance training can boost movement of nutrients to cartilage and prevent it from undergoing atrophy, but as cartilage does not have a blood supply, resistance training would have no effect on blood flow specifically to cartilage.

Copyright © Mometrix Media. You have been licensed one copy of this document for personal use only. Any other reproduction or redistribution is strictly prohibited. All rights reserved.
This content is provided for test preparation purposes only and does not imply an endorsement by Mometrix of any particular political, scientific, or religious point of view.

64. C: Free weight pressing or pushing exercises, such as the dumbbell bench press or dumbbell shoulder press, should be spotted near the wrists. This places the spotter's hands closest to the dumbbells, rather than spotting at the elbow.

65. B: The depth jump has only a vertical component, and the standing long jump has only a horizontal component. However, the lateral barrier jump involves not only jumping high enough to clear the barrier vertically but jumping to the side enough (horizontally) to land on the other side of the barrier.

66. C: For a valid repetition of the 1-RM bench pull, the athlete must lift the bar to touching the underside of the bench. The other two options are proper technique for the athlete's setup in this assessment.

67. B: While the main muscle fiber types, type I and II, are genetically determined, the subtypes can change with training. For example, type IIx can become type IIa. However, the main muscle fiber types are unlikely to significantly change with training—for example, an athlete with mostly type I fibers is unlikely to shift them to type II fibers even with extensive training.

68. C: Fractionalization as a practice technique is characterized by breaking a task into components that normally would occur simultaneously. In this case, a rowing machine uses both the legs and arms at the same time, but this practice technique has the athlete performing each of them independently.

69. C: IZOF, or Individual Zones of Optimal Functioning, notes that individuals have individualized levels of arousal. The same stimulus or emotion can affect two individuals in very different ways.

70. C: The hip sled exercise works the major muscles of the quadriceps group, the hamstring group, and the gluteus maximus. However, it does not primarily work the gastrocnemius, the major calf muscle in the lower leg.

71. C: The power clean would be the most logical continuation in progressing to a more complex movement, as the deadlift closely resembles the transition phase needed in the power clean, and power is a primary need in basketball. While the other two choices could be viable for building strength, they are a less logical progression from the movements the athlete has already mastered.

72. B: Polysaccharides are complex carbohydrates such as fiber, glycogen, and starch built from several molecules of sugar. Monosaccharides are single-sugar molecules like fructose, and disaccharides are two-sugar molecules like sucrose.

73. C: A mission statement should address the target clientele, what service is being provided, and what makes the service unique. While hours and location are important, that information is neither part of conveying why the organization is distinctive nor what it contributes.

74. B: The Krebs cycle and the electron transport system are incorrect choices because they are aerobic, occurring in the mitochondria and requiring oxygen.

75. A: Sprinting would be an anaerobic activity as it requires high power output and rapid muscle contraction speed. Carbohydrate is the only listed choice that can be metabolized without oxygen, making it most critical during an anaerobic activity.

76. C: An individual with high intrinsic motivation for a given activity is motivated from within—that is, they find the activity inherently rewarding and enjoyable.

Copyright © Mometrix Media. You have been licensed one copy of this document for personal use only. Any other reproduction or redistribution is strictly prohibited. All rights reserved.
This content is provided for test preparation purposes only and does not imply an endorsement by Mometrix of any particular political, scientific, or religious point of view.

77. C: Caffeine is thought to improve athletic performance, particularly endurance performance, by increasing fat oxidation through mobilizing free fatty acids. This slows down glycogen depletion, sparing the use of carbohydrates as fuel and thus reducing fatigue.

78. A: Ergogenic aids, such as anabolic steroids, are associated with mood swings and increased aggression and arousal. Sarcopenia is a loss of muscle mass and strength, often associated with the aging process, while ergogenic aids are typically used for effects like *increasing* muscle mass or strength.

79. B: A target behavior, or operant, is one that is manipulated to increase the probability of it happening. In this case, the coach is praising the athletes for cleaning up the weight room, making the cleaning behavior (the operant) more likely to happen in the future.

80. B: Nonlinear periodization, also termed daily undulating periodization, involves large daily variance in the load and volume of exercises performed.

81. A: The principal action in an emergency is to provide immediate care to the affected person. This may require first aid, CPR, or AED, so it is critical that a strength and conditioning professional obtains and maintains a current certification, so they are ready to respond immediately in event of emergency.

82. A: The axial skeleton comprises the skull, all vertebrae from the cervical vertebrae down to the coccyx, the sternum, and the ribs. All other bones, including the scapulae, are part of the appendicular skeleton.

83. A: Volume-load is a way to quantify the work performed in resistance training and involves multiplying the total sets by the reps in each set by the weight lifted per rep. This problem can be solved by working backward—if 2,580 lbs (1,172.7 kg) is the end result, this can be divided by the sets (4), then the reps (3), resulting in the correct weight lifted. This number can be re-checked for accuracy by multiplying 4 sets by 3 reps by the chosen weight.

84. C: In the A-Skip, the objective is to actively drive the swing leg down to the ground while the opposing leg then pops up, and this force generation results in horizontal displacement. The other two techniques involve change of direction and rapid acceleration and deceleration rather than horizontal movement.

85. B: Exercises that promote osteogenic stimuli stimulate formation of new bone by overloading the bone with appropriate stress. The best choices for this training adaptation are movements that are multi-joint and direct forces through the structure of the skeleton. The other two choices are single-joint and/or machine-based and would be less effective at forming new bone growth.

86. A: The relaxation technique of autogenic training has similarities to progressive muscular relaxation, but rather than going through cycles of tensing and relaxing, autogenic training places the attentional focus solely on body sensations, such as sensing heaviness, without using tension.

87. B: Underwater weighing and DEXA are "gold standard" methods that assess amounts of lean mass and fat mass. Skinfolds, when assessed correctly, are more accurate than circumferences as they measure subcutaneous fat and not just girth.

88. B: Because the star excursion balance test assesses one leg at a time for balance and stability, it could assess differences between legs and therefore could gauge an athlete's post-injury performance for this situation.

Copyright © Mometrix Media. You have been licensed one copy of this document for personal use only. Any other reproduction or redistribution is strictly prohibited. All rights reserved.
This content is provided for test preparation purposes only and does not imply an endorsement by Mometrix of any particular political, scientific, or religious point of view.

89. A: The hold-relax with agonist contraction is the most effective form of PNF, as the added concentric contraction of the agonist promotes both reciprocal inhibition and autogenic inhibition.

90. B: A contraindication means that an injury makes a given movement or practice inadvisable, with the assumption that such an action would make the injury worse. Simply avoiding an exercise or movement is not a contraindication as there may be logical reasons for doing so, like in options A and C.

91. C: For safe and effective exercise progression, a general guideline is not to increase the frequency, intensity, or duration by more than 10% each week. Based on the athlete's current amount, they are running 120 minutes per week. Option C adds on 12 total minutes (10% of 120) with the two slightly longer runs. Option A *decreases* the running amount, which does not go toward progression, and option B increases both the days per week and the running amount for a total of 175 minutes, which is far above a 10% increase.

92. A: Basal metabolic rate contributes about 65 to 70% of an individual's total energy expenditure. Out of an individual's total calorie needs per day, the majority of these calories are required by normal body processes like respiration and digestion.

93. B: In the steps of a needs analysis, once the evaluation of the sport's needs has occurred, the strength and conditioning specialist needs to evaluate the athletes on training status and through physical testing and evaluation. This will help determine the program's goal. These lacrosse players may be very untrained athletes in resistance training or may be highly advanced athletes. Performing a step like selecting exercises or using power exercises is jumping ahead before knowledge of the athletes' training status.

94. B: Using a countermovement, such as swinging the arms back for jumping over a barrier or performing a standing long jump, allows the athlete to work at higher velocity and thus to jump higher or farther. Many plyometric drills use a countermovement, but the lateral push-off does not—it simply starts with the athlete standing laterally to a box with the close foot atop the box, then pushing through that foot to jump up.

95. B: The Karvonen method first takes the age-predicted maximum heart rate ($220 - \text{age}$, which in this case is $220 - 43 = 177$). Next, subtract the individual's resting heart rate from the resulting number (which in this case is $177 - 53 = 124$). This number is then multiplied by each end of the range, and the resting heart rate is added back in to each range calculation, where numbers can be rounded to the nearest whole number:

$$(124 \times 0.65) + 53 = 133.6$$

$$(124 \times 0.75) + 53 = 146$$

96. C: The stability ball jackknife begins in a quadruped position with feet on the ball and hands placed on the floor. Unlike the pike, which keeps the legs straight to pull the ball in, the jackknife is performed by flexing the hips and knees to bring the ball closer to the chest, then returning to the start position.

97. A: As the amortization phase occurs between the eccentric and concentric phases, in the cycled split squat jump it would occur as the athlete lands in the lunge position and movement briefly stops. Proper technique to maximize plyometric effects would require that the athlete keep the length of time in this landing position as minimal as possible.

Copyright © Mometrix Media. You have been licensed one copy of this document for personal use only. Any other reproduction or redistribution is strictly prohibited. All rights reserved.
This content is provided for test preparation purposes only and does not imply an endorsement by Mometrix of any particular political, scientific, or religious point of view.

98. C: Variable practice means that variations of the same skill are performed in a single session. Here, the skill is the quick feet lateral agility drill, but the different equipment provides novel variations on the skill.

99. B: Each of the listed athletes has specific needs for their sport or activity that would determine the training goal, whether it is strength, power, hypertrophy, or muscular endurance. An athlete with a hypertrophy goal, such as a bodybuilder, would likely have the highest training volume out of the three due to a moderate to high number of reps per set and doing 3-6 sets per exercise.

100. B: The general principles of exercise order dictate that exercises should be ordered to allow an athlete to exert maximal force and demonstrate proper technique. Power exercises, such as any variation on the Olympic lifts (snatch, clean, press, jerk), are the most taxing as they require the most skill. Working large muscle groups with multi-joint movements should occur next in the order, and then smaller, single-joint movements.

101. A: An MET, or metabolic equivalent, is equal to 3.5 mL per kg of oxygen consumption, the amount of oxygen the body requires at rest. Thus, in order to use METs for intensity, the maximal oxygen uptake must be known so that there is an upper range based on the individual's abilities.

102. B: In proper running gait, the ground force must efficiently dissipate over the foot to carry the body forward. Striking with the heel first allows weight to spread in a gentle rolling manner from the heel all the way through the ball of the foot.

103. B: A test that is reliable has a high degree of consistency or repeatability. Testing an athlete and getting highly variable scores suggests low reliability and could indicate that this test's results are not very meaningful to actually analyze performance improvements.

104. B: A second-class lever typically has the greatest mechanical advantage, because the presence of a long moment arm means that the muscle force can overcome the resistive force. First-class and third-class levers typically have a mechanical disadvantage, because the resistive force is greater than the muscle force.

105. B: Systolic blood pressure increases with exercise as it represents the work of the heart's ventricles to eject blood. Diastolic pressure will slightly decrease (due to vasodilation) or stay the same.

106. B: The RAMP protocol stands for Raise, Activate, Mobilize, Potentiate. The first step is getting the body temperature up via key movements (Raise), and the second step is improving overall movement capacity (Activate). The next step in a RAMP warm-up would be M for Mobilize. The purpose is to bring more mobility into key body segments, such as with dynamic stretches.

107. C: Content validity refers to a test, or battery of tests, covering appropriate component abilities. Since gymnastics requires power, strength, and flexibility, the choice means that the tests should be valid for assessing specific needs of the sport.

108. B: The practice technique of simplification means that the task difficulty is adjusted. Here, a back squat is easier to perform with a light barbell, allowing the athlete to gain practice in proper technique without the task being too difficult.

109. A: Muscles responsible for maintaining posture would be more fatigue-resistant and need to contract at low intensities over long periods of time. This description characterizes type I, "slow-twitch" fibers.

Copyright © Mometrix Media. You have been licensed one copy of this document for personal use only. Any other reproduction or redistribution is strictly prohibited. All rights reserved.
This content is provided for test preparation purposes only and does not imply an endorsement by Mometrix of any particular political, scientific, or religious point of view.

110. A: The primary nutritional goal of this athlete based on their sport and needs is to have adequate recovery between the soccer games. The demands of playing one game and needing to play a second game within the same day are likely to deplete muscle glycogen. Consuming higher-carbohydrate foods or drinks after the first game and at regular intervals will increase muscle glycogen stores and reduce fatigue for the second game.

111. C: High self-efficacy for a given situation means that someone perceives they have the abilities to perform. Self-efficacy can set one athlete above another, as skill and motivation are not enough to promote self-belief.

112. C: The other two choices have at least one movement that is not a push/pull movement, such as lunge or calf raise. Only choice C solely comprises pushing/pulling movements.

113. B: In youth, the nervous system may still be undergoing development, meaning that movements may lack speed or skill. Therefore, youth should not be treated as "small adults" and should have individualized training programs that meet their needs.

114. C: A proper warm-up has many physical effects on the body, and the effect on metabolism is to *increase* metabolic reactions. One way to think of this is that warming up allows us to use energy more efficiently, boosting metabolism.

115. C: A periodization cycle lasting 2-6 weeks is called a mesocycle. A macrocycle is longer, lasting months to a year, and a microcycle is smaller, lasting a few days to two weeks.

116. C: Reducing the rest period for a resistance training program focusing on muscular endurance would be a logical progression in continuing to overload the muscles to work at submaximal levels. However, reducing the rest period for a strength or power goal would likely compromise the success of the movements, since these goals require heavier loads.

117. C: Maintaining a forward trunk lean and keeping the head in line with the spine during the acceleration phase of a sprint helps the athlete to maximize acceleration. Otherwise, bringing the head or torso into a more upright, lifted position can detract from the body's ability to accelerate.

118. C: In the hook grip, the thumb is underneath the index and middle finger, which is the main differentiator from the pronated grip. This hand position allows a strong position for movements requiring high levels of power, like Olympic lifts.

119. B: This amount is likely to provide enough carbohydrate to maximize blood glucose and glycogen while not consuming overly large amounts of food a few hours before competing.

120. C: Performing 3-5 attempts allows an adequate number of trials for an athlete to find their 1-RM while minimizing fatigue that could happen from doing more attempts.

121. C: Failing to vary training and include adequate recovery places more stress on the adrenal system, causing it to release cortisol. Cortisol by itself is not a negative hormone, but having chronic levels in the body in response to excess stress would be undesirable for training adaptations.

122. A: The typical recommendation for resistance training is to exhale during the concentric portion of the exercise, which is where the sticking point occurs. The sticking point at a log press would occur as the athlete presses it upward, so the exhale would reinforce a rigid torso and upright spine for the athlete to ideally pass through the sticking point and successfully press the log.

Copyright © Mometrix Media. You have been licensed one copy of this document for personal use only. Any other reproduction or redistribution is strictly prohibited. All rights reserved.
This content is provided for test preparation purposes only and does not imply an endorsement by Mometrix of any particular political, scientific, or religious point of view.

123. A: Torque can also be conceptualized as a product of force and the length of the moment arm. The other choices describe two other principles involved in movement—power is the time rate of doing work, and work is the product of muscle force and displacement.

124. A: Knowledge of performance feedback allows an athlete to understand their movement patterns, which could be done through videos or other equipment.

125. C: This athlete's injury is relatively recent, so they are in the inflammatory response phase, when resting the affected area is needed to minimize further inflammation. While the athlete is not yet ready to load the healing tissue with a movement like a single leg squat or wobble board balance training, the athlete can maintain their fitness in other ways that utilize other muscle groups or do not directly load the injured area.

126. A: One hundred square feet per athlete is the recommended amount of space for optimal safety and function within the facility.

127. A: Having a 90-degree angle at the knee joint when stepping on the box ensures that it will be high enough to activate the major muscles of the lower body, but not so high that the athlete will have difficulty stepping on it.

128. A: Process goals are focused on action and effort. In this case, the athlete can measure their success by the frequency with which they adhere to this regular behavior.

129. C: The calculated mean is accurate, and each score appears only once, making a mode nonexistent. However, the calculated median of the scores (the average of the two middle-most scores) is 95.5 kg or 210 lbs, which is slightly higher than the mean.

130. A: A cooldown with active recovery like walking and light stretching allows an increased heart rate to gradually return to normal. The other two options are incorrect, as practice attempts are important for familiarity with test procedures, and non-fatiguing tests should be done first in the testing order.

131. B: Body mass index, or BMI, is calculated as weight in kilograms divided by height in meters squared. $\frac{63\text{ kg}}{(1.8\text{ m})^2}$ is equal to 19.4. In BMI classifications, this number falls within the normal weight range, which is 18.5 to 24.9.

132. A: The female athlete triad is characterized by long periods of training where caloric intake is insufficient and menstrual function ceases. Lack of adequate energy intake and hormonal effects can make osteoporosis more likely due to decreased bone mineral density.

133. C: Visibility is an important consideration in the layout of a fitness floor and choosing where to put machines. Tall machines are best placed along the walls, like around the perimeter of the space. This leaves the middle of the room more open for coaches or supervisors to see across the space.

134. C: The phosphagen system's primary role is to fuel high-intensity, short-duration exercise. It derives its fuel from creatine phosphate and ATP hydrolysis, not glycogen breakdown. However, all energy systems are active at any given time, though their involvement depends on the nature of the exercise's intensity and duration. Regardless of the activity, the body's oxygen deficit means that energy is first supplied anaerobically as the aerobic system responds more slowly.

135. C: Consuming higher amounts of protein relative to caloric intake can help to preserve lean muscle if someone is choosing to eat less for a weight loss goal.

Copyright © Mometrix Media. You have been licensed one copy of this document for personal use only. Any other reproduction or redistribution is strictly prohibited. All rights reserved.
This content is provided for test preparation purposes only and does not imply an endorsement by Mometrix of any particular political, scientific, or religious point of view.

136. A: High-density lipoprotein (HDL) is a protective type of cholesterol that lowers heart disease risk. However, other types of cholesterol—such as low-density lipoproteins (LDL) and triglycerides—are associated with increased heart disease risk when found in high amounts in the body.

137. B: Interval training is stressful on the body as it involves training at high intensities close to VO2 max. Thus, keeping the rest equal to the work portion is beneficial. The other two choices have significantly more work than rest in their ratios.

138. B: Extension of the hips, knees, and ankles, otherwise known as triple extension, occurs during the second pull of the Olympic lifts. This is the phase when the most rapid and explosive power is generated.

139. B: Proper form for the two-handed kettlebell swing includes flexing at the hips while keeping the spine in a neutral position. The good morning and the bent-over row would both mimic a portion of the kettlebell swing's movement, so an athlete performing these correctly would be the best choice for indicating they may be ready for such a progression.

140. C: Flexion of the spine is done during movements that involve bending forward, ruling out extension. The transverse plane slices the body into upper and lower sections, where movements occurring in this plane involve rotation. As a sit-up is not a rotational movement, this rules out the transverse plane.

141. C: The push press and push jerk have the same starting position and dip. However, the push press catch position is with the body fully extended, and the push jerk catch position is with the hips and knees in a dipped (slightly flexed) position.

142. A: In a superset, two exercises are performed that target opposing muscle groups or areas. The muscles of the chest and shoulders are an antagonist to the muscles of the back and vice versa. Choices B and C target the same general muscle groups in both exercises.

143. C: The first attempt for a 1-RM should be approximately 50% of the estimated 1-RM weight. In this case, 50% of 220 lbs/100 kg is 110 lbs or 50 kg.

144. C: In the hang power clean, the bar begins at midthigh or slightly above or below the knees. After the bar is initially lifted from the floor for this variation on the power clean, it does not touch the floor again until the repetitions are complete.

145. A: To minimize digestive upset, food consumed close in time to competition should be in small amounts, and high-fat or high-fiber foods (such as choices B and C) are best avoided.

146. A: The cross-sectional area of a muscle fiber enlarges primarily due to increased myofibrils, which then increase the size of the overall muscle. The other choices are possible training adaptations, depending on the stimulus, but are not directly linked with muscle hypertrophy.

147. A: It is important to understand both the anatomical landmarks and the direction for each skinfold, such as the description for the thigh skinfold, as performing a skinfold improperly would compromise the validity of a body composition measurement.

148. A: Muscles function by pulling on bones (never pushing), while tendons are the attachments joining muscles to bones, enabling this movement.

Copyright © Mometrix Media. You have been licensed one copy of this document for personal use only. Any other reproduction or redistribution is strictly prohibited. All rights reserved.
This content is provided for test preparation purposes only and does not imply an endorsement by Mometrix of any particular political, scientific, or religious point of view.

149. B: Arousal is influenced by many factors, but skill level and task complexity are two important ones. A more skilled athlete typically can perform the same task with lower arousal compared to a less skilled athlete.

150. A: Female athletes are approximately six times more likely to have an ACL tear than male athletes. A well-balanced training program that improves knee strength and control is an important preventative measure.

151. C: Both pull-ups and lat pulldowns target the same general muscle group: the latissimus dorsi and the rhomboids. When an individual performs two sequential exercises for the same muscle group, this is called a compound set.

152. C: Stressing the phosphagen system to provoke the most ideal training adaptations would involve near-maximal intensities and adequate recovery to prevent overtraining and foster energy system and muscular adaptations. Regarding the other choices, intensity and duration have an inverse relationship (high intensities cannot be performed for long durations), and lower intensities would not be the most accurate means to stress the phosphagen system.

153. A: Predictive validity describes the extent of a test score aligning with future performance, or in other words, "predicting" it. In the first situation, the coach is assessing if the test scores are transferring into real-life performance in game play.

154. B: Using bands as external resistance to a weighted exercise, such as the bench press, will mean that the maximal amount of resistance is wherever the topmost position of the barbell occurs in the movement, typically the lockout. At the lockout of the bench press, the bands will be stretched to their greatest extent, thus providing the greatest stretch resistance.

155. A: Before utilizing any type of ergogenic aid or sports supplements, an athlete should have an appropriately structured and periodized strength and conditioning program in place and should have sound nutritional practices. These two aspects are foundational to performance. A supplement will not "solve" things like inconsistent training or inadequate nutrient intake.

156. C: For most efficient movement and maximal force generation in the snatch, the hips and shoulders should rise at the same time, keeping the angle of the torso constant relative to the floor.

157. C: When a tendon is inserted further from the joint center, this creates a longer moment arm for muscle force to act. For example, the presence of a patella allows the quadriceps tendon to be further from the knee joint, improving its mechanical advantage.

158. B: Overreaching, or functional overreaching (FOR), is a temporary, short-term response to training overload. While too much overreaching can lead to overtraining, it can be a valid part of training programs to overload the body as long as it is well managed.

159. C: Making specific nutrition recommendations is out of the strength and conditioning professional's scope, unless they also have specific nutrition credentials such as an RD. While MyPlate is a useful general resource overall, athletes who are excluding food groups—such as those eating a vegan diet, which excludes all animal-based products like meat, dairy, and eggs—are highly recommended to work with a sports dietitian so that nutrient requirements for performance can be adequately met.

160. A: Primary needs of basketball include strength, power, and agility. Of the listed choices, the standing long jump and the star excursion balance test are less directly specific to the needs of the

Copyright © Mometrix Media. You have been licensed one copy of this document for personal use only. Any other reproduction or redistribution is strictly prohibited. All rights reserved.
This content is provided for test preparation purposes only and does not imply an endorsement by Mometrix of any particular political, scientific, or religious point of view.

sport than the T-test, as selecting the test is the main key in discerning the right answer. While theoretically any of the resistance training movements could have a case for being used in a basketball player's program, the hang clean and push press go toward maximizing power and jumping needs.

161. B: The 300-yard shuttle test is the most accurate as it measures anaerobic capacity. In basketball, the needs of the metabolic system are primarily for 30-90 second start-and-stop bursts of speed.

162. C: Carbohydrate loading through consuming 8-10 grams of carbohydrate per kilogram of body weight in the three days before an aerobic endurance event can maximize glycogen stores, reducing fatigue from glycogen depletion.

163. B: While the fibroblastic repair phase still warrants careful consideration for the injured area as it is the second phase of three, relative rest is a general goal of the first phase (inflammatory response phase). Once the injured tissue has passed the inflammatory response phase, it can sustain some function and movement and should not need to be isolated with rest.

164. B: Osteoblasts respond to mechanical loading of the bone, such as in resistance training, through laying down collagen which stimulates new bone formation, making the bone stronger.

165. B: The approach jump has the greatest rate of stretch during the eccentric phase and thus results in the highest jump height. This is because this jump, out of the three, uses the quickest and most forceful eccentric phase, meaning the most power can be generated.

166. B: Supercompensation is described as part of the general adaptation syndrome, a model explaining how the body responds to stress. When the body is overloaded with a stressor that is not excessive and is well structured, the body compensates with improved performance.

167. A: Observational practice involves watching the skill or task, whether through other persons, videos, etc. The intent is that watching skills being performed helps improve one's own motor skills.

168. A: The lactate threshold is the exercise intensity where blood lactate begins to abruptly increase and the need for anaerobic energy production also increases. Trained individuals can perform at higher intensities before the lactate threshold occurs.

169. A: When a participant is fully informed (whether verbally or through reading a form) about the risks and benefits of an activity and is permitted to choose whether to participate or not, this describes informed consent.

170. B: Both the muscle spindle and the Golgi tendon organ are types of proprioceptors, which can sense tension in the muscle length. However, only the muscle spindle functions to activate the muscle when a change in length is sensed. The Golgi tendon organ has the opposite function, inhibiting muscle activation when a change in length is sensed.

171. A: Glycolysis allows stored glycogen or glucose to be used as fuel through breaking it down. Oxidative phosphorylation describes resynthesizing ATP as part of the electron transport chain. Gluconeogenesis is when glucose is formed from noncarbohydrate sources.

172. B: The five-point body position allows stability and support for supine exercises like the bench press. However, the elbows do not need to be firmly on the bench, as they should be free to move during such an exercise.

Copyright © Mometrix Media. You have been licensed one copy of this document for personal use only. Any other reproduction or redistribution is strictly prohibited. All rights reserved.
This content is provided for test preparation purposes only and does not imply an endorsement by Mometrix of any particular political, scientific, or religious point of view.

173. A: The overload principle involves imposing a more intense stimulus to stress the body at higher levels than it's used to. Increasing the rest is the only choice that would make a given workout or training program ***less*** intense.

174. B: The Valsalva maneuver is best used for structural exercises that load the spine, such as a back squat, as it can help promote a rigid, neutral spine through alignment and support.

175. A: Using an unstable surface can reduce the rate of force development required during the exercise, so choice B would not be most suitable for this goal. While choice C would isolate the core, there is not evidence that isolating it would improve performance. However, as a power clean is a free weight activity that requires rapid force generation, it would be most effective for the program's goal in activating core musculature in this manner.

176. B: This array of tests will be most sports-specific to basketball, as vertical jumping is required, anaerobic capacity is needed, and muscular strength from the legs is also important. While a case could potentially be made for one or two of these tests being applied to the other choices, neither wrestling nor rowing typically involves jumping, ruling each of them out.

177. A: Tidal volume is the amount of air inhaled and exhaled with each breath and is the primary cause for ventilation increase during low-to-moderate-intensity exercise. Minute ventilation, or the volume of air breathed per minute, does play a role, but it does not start to rapidly increase until higher intensities of exercise.

178. B: Vitamin C is a water-soluble vitamin that also serves as an antioxidant. Colorful fruits and vegetables, including oranges, peppers, tomatoes, and others, are all high in vitamin C.

179. C: Traffic flow is a critical aspect in building and designing a new facility, as understanding the number of athletes who will be using the facility at any given time ensures that everyone can have safe and easy access.

180. A: State anxiety is characterized by an individual's subjective perception of feeling apprehensive or uncertain about a situation, which is typically accompanied by arousal that is not well controlled, leading to symptoms of anxiety like a racing heart.

181. B: A seated leg extension exercise involves a concentric contraction of the quadriceps, since straightening the legs against resistance shortens this muscle group. The vastus lateralis is the only listed choice that is one of the quadriceps muscles. The semitendinosus and biceps femoris are part of the hamstrings.

182. A: The Yo-Yo intermittent recovery test is characterized by short bursts of work in shuttle runs with short recovery periods. This test is preferable to a steady-state aerobic test to mimic the demands of team sports that have frequent starts and stops.

183. C: The demands of volleyball include explosive lower body power like jumping. A plyometric program for volleyball would thus include various types of jumps relevant to the needs of the sport. For safe and effective jumping, proper landing technique is essential, and since most jumps land in a squat variation, using the squat would allow assessment of the athlete's form.

184. C: Of the incorrect choices, chronological age is simply one's numerical age in months or years. Training age is the amount of time that a formal, supervised training program has been followed.

Copyright © Mometrix Media. You have been licensed one copy of this document for personal use only. Any other reproduction or redistribution is strictly prohibited. All rights reserved.
This content is provided for test preparation purposes only and does not imply an endorsement by Mometrix of any particular political, scientific, or religious point of view.

185. B: Power exercises, such as a snatch or clean, should not be spotted. The explosive nature of these movements can result in injury to the spotter and/or the athlete.

186. B: Velocity can be conceptualized as speed with direction. Speed describes only how fast an object is moving, but velocity incorporates the direction. Acceleration would involve changes in an object's velocity, and agility would involve the capacity to change direction while decelerating and re-accelerating.

187. C: Nutrition during an athletic event becomes particularly important when the event is longer than 45 minutes or has multiple events in one day (such as a triathlon). Obtaining adequate nutrients and fluids during the event can ensure the athlete has the best chance of optimal performance. Powerlifting and wrestling are much shorter in duration, so these athletes would not typically need to consume anything during their event.

188. B: ATP's breakdown to ADP and phosphate fuels the pulling action, or power stroke, of the myosin crossbridges as they pull on actin filaments. Calcium is not broken down in this scenario but rather is released from the sarcoplasmic reticulum as an earlier step in the sliding filament theory. Endomysium is the connective tissue surrounding each muscle fiber, so it is not something that gets broken down during muscle contraction.

189. A: The pathway of inspired air in the respiratory system (after air is inhaled through the nose or mouth) is to the trachea, then to the bronchi of each lung, then to the smaller bronchioles, and lastly to the alveoli. The capillaries are a site of exchanging oxygen but are not a direct part of the respiratory system's path during inspiration.

190. A: During a passive stretch in PNF stretching, the agonist (the opposite of the muscle being stretched) should concentrically contract to help relax the antagonist (the muscle being stretched, which in this case is the hamstring).

191. C: The goals of strength, hypertrophy, and endurance are all distinctive. A strength goal has the longest rest but the heaviest load as percent of 1-RM. Choice A has the correct reps, sets, and rest for a strength goal, but the load is incorrect as 67-85% of 1-RM is suited for muscular hypertrophy. Choice B's main issue is the rest period—30 seconds or less would be unrealistic for safely working toward a strength-based goal at high levels of 1-RM.

192. B: The forward step lunge with barbell cannot be performed inside of a typical power rack as the nature of the lunge movement means that the athlete's barbell would collide with the rack structure. However, a rack with supports on the outside could be utilized.

193. A: The lunge with overhead side reach is the only selection that involves overhead reaching with simultaneous lateral bending, which would stretch the latissimus dorsi.

194. B: The hexagon test measures agility, not maximum muscular power. Any 1-RM explosive movement, of which the push jerk is one example, will measure muscular power, and the Margaria-Kalamen test is designed specifically to measure muscular power.

195. B: A SWOT analysis (assessing Strengths, Weaknesses, Opportunities, and Threats) should occur in the second half of the predesign phase. This is an important step before any type of design or construction to ensure the facility will be most successful.

Copyright © Mometrix Media. You have been licensed one copy of this document for personal use only. Any other reproduction or redistribution is strictly prohibited. All rights reserved.
This content is provided for test preparation purposes only and does not imply an endorsement by Mometrix of any particular political, scientific, or religious point of view.

196. C: Out of the listed choices, a power goal would have low repetitions (such as 1-5, depending on type of event) and multiple sets (3-5). While this volume is appropriate for power, the number of reps is too low for a hypertrophy goal or an endurance goal.

197. B: Placing a mirror at least 20 inches above the floor gives a 2-inch buffer to prevent weight plates from damaging or breaking the mirror, since standard weight plates are 18 inches wide.

198. B: The primary jumping needs in volleyball are in a vertical direction. An athlete will have a more powerful and effective volleyball spike if their vertical jump to meet the ball is also effective. The single leg push-off is the only listed choice that involves vertical jumping and thus is most directly applicable to volleyball.

199. C: Load can be expressed as a percent of 1-RM, where the percent range is based on the training goal. For a training goal of strength, a load of 85% or greater of 1-RM is recommended. Multiplying the athlete's 1-RM of 405 by 0.85 yields a number of 344 lbs or 156.36 kg. So, the athlete would need to use a load that is at least this heavy. The other two choices are under the 85%.

200. A: Training for power typically involves complex movements that require technical skills, such as the snatch or the clean and jerk. To emphasize the quality of power movements, the volume is typically lower than the volume in training for strength, due to lighter loads and fewer repetitions.

201. A: In this image, the athlete's lead knee is significantly over the lead foot. This shifts the weight to being too far forward over the knee, rather than evenly balanced between the lead foot and the trailing foot.

202. A: Most back injuries occur between the lowest two lumbar vertebrae (L4 and L5) or between the lowest lumbar vertebra and sacral vertebra (L5 and S1). The discs associated with these vertebrae have very high compressive forces and high levels of torque during loading.

203. A: Using goal repetitions for training load means that the athlete does not need to perform a 1-RM. Maximal strength is not warranted for the needs of a distance runner. Therefore, a method like finding a 12-RM or a 15-RM and having the athlete train to reach that amount of repetitions would be more useful for this athlete.

204. B: The preparatory period of periodization is when athletes should be building a base level of conditioning to prepare for more intense and/or more specialized movements later in the cycle. Once this base is established, the intensity can start to be varied and ramped up. Increasing intensity while decreasing volume is a goal of the competitive period rather than the preparatory period.

205. A: Proper spotting of a movement such as the barbell bench press should have the hand placement in an alternated grip with hands **inside** the athlete's hands.

206. C: Plyometric training's volume is assessed through the number of foot contacts (or catches/throws if upper body movements are performed). Keeping these volumes to the general guidelines for beginner, intermediate, or advanced athletes ensures a proper training load.

207. C: HIIT training requires intensities at 90% or more of VO2 max to properly challenge the anaerobic glycolysis system. HIIT may use durations of 45 seconds up to 4 minutes to elicit such stimuli.

Copyright © Mometrix Media. You have been licensed one copy of this document for personal use only. Any other reproduction or redistribution is strictly prohibited. All rights reserved.
This content is provided for test preparation purposes only and does not imply an endorsement by Mometrix of any particular political, scientific, or religious point of view.

208. A: Mitochondria increase in density as an adaptation to aerobic training, which allows the working muscles to uptake and utilize more oxygen. Cross-country skiing is primarily an aerobic activity with longer duration and lower intensity, where the other two choices are high intensity, short duration, and primarily anaerobic in nature.

209. B: The nature of this athlete's activities means that the training goal is strength/power. This means the athlete is lifting heavy loads and needs more rest for safe and successful completion of the movements. Having rest that is too short may compromise form and technique.

210. A: Relative humidity should not exceed 60%, as anything higher than that can encourage growth of bacteria, leading to potential spread of infections among participants.

211. C: The navel, also known as the umbilicus or belly button, provides an anatomical landmark for an individual's waist circumference. It allows reliable measurements as it is visible and consistent for a given individual.

212. B: Intrinsic feedback comes "from within," generated by an athlete's own senses—as opposed to other types of feedback like augmented feedback that come from an external source, like a coach or a video.

213. B: In the sumo technique, the athlete adopts a wide stance where the feet are significantly wider than hip-width, and the arms are inside of the stance with a narrower grip.

214. C: Bulimia nervosa is characterized by recurrent consumption of foods in significantly ***greater*** amounts than would normally be consumed (the opposite wording choice of option B), also known as binging or binge eating. However, bulimia is distinct from binge eating disorder because individuals then feel compelled to purge food in some way, such as vomiting, where these cycles provoke feelings of being out of control. Choice A describes anorexia instead, as individuals with bulimia are typically normal weight, not underweight.

215. A: Muscle dysmorphia is an altered self-perception where an individual feels the need to increase their body size and muscle mass based on feeling overly small and weak—sometimes resorting to high-risk measures like steroid use.

216. C: HIPAA, or the Health Insurance Portability and Accountability Act, is a federal regulatory law that covers the protection and privacy of individual participants' health care information. The details in an injury report are confidential information that should not be shared without written authorization. The strength and conditioning professional could instead share basic injury prevention guidelines without providing any identifying information that links back to the affected athlete.

217. A: High GI (glycemic index) foods are more quickly digested and absorbed than lower GI foods. White bread is considered a high GI food with a ranking of 70+.

218. B: Catecholamines, like epinephrine, stimulate a fight-or-flight response. Levels of catecholamines increase in the body in response to stress, including the physical stress of exercise. Catecholamines are important for acute strength and power, so increased vasodilation to get more blood flow to the working muscles is one of their roles, not vasoconstriction.

219. B: Warm-up movements should be at a lower intensity that gradually progresses to mimic the demands of the sport or activity. A-Skips and forward lunges fulfill this. The depth jump is itself a

Copyright © Mometrix Media. You have been licensed one copy of this document for personal use only. Any other reproduction or redistribution is strictly prohibited. All rights reserved.
This content is provided for test preparation purposes only and does not imply an endorsement by Mometrix of any particular political, scientific, or religious point of view.

challenging plyometric drill and would not be used as part of the warm-up. In addition, static stretches, like the butterfly stretch, are best avoided before activities requiring strength and power.

220. B: In the front squat, the barbell is held in front of the body, where either the parallel-arm position or the crossed-arm position can be used for placement of the bar on top of the anterior deltoids.

Copyright © Mometrix Media. You have been licensed one copy of this document for personal use only. Any other reproduction or redistribution is strictly prohibited. All rights reserved.
This content is provided for test preparation purposes only and does not imply an endorsement by Mometrix of any particular political, scientific, or religious point of view.

CSCS Practice Test #2

1. When designing a resistance training program for a rugby player, what should NOT be part of a coach's assessment?

a. Training status
b. Health history
c. Movement analysis
d. Comparative strength analysis

2. What substance is involved in muscular contraction at the neuromuscular junction?

a. Serotonin
b. Epinephrine
c. Acetylcholine
d. Creatine phosphate

3. During a pro-agility test, what must occur for the attempt to count?

a. The athlete's hand must touch the cone
b. The athlete's foot must touch each line
c. The athlete must touch the base of each cone
d. The athlete must run past each line

4. A baseball player takes two practice swings before stepping into the batter's box before each at bat during a game. What is this athlete demonstrating?

a. Preparatory routine
b. Procedural routine
c. Performance routine
d. Pattern routine

5. Increasing muscle mass affects the function of which hormone most directly?

a. Cortisol
b. IGF
c. Estrogen
d. Insulin

6. When designing a training program, a strength coach includes a box jump for maximum height in a superset with front squats. The coach is attempting to utilize what neurological phenomenon?

a. Stretch-shortening cycle
b. Myotatic stretch reflex
c. Series elastic component
d. Potentiation

Copyright © Mometrix Media. You have been licensed one copy of this document for personal use only. Any other reproduction or redistribution is strictly prohibited. All rights reserved.
This content is provided for test preparation purposes only and does not imply an endorsement by Mometrix of any particular political, scientific, or religious point of view.

7. When wanting to bring up a lagging body part either to overcome a muscular weakness or increase muscular size, what approach could the strength and conditioning coach insert into the training program for a four- to six-week period?

a. Pre-exhaustion
b. Compound set
c. Circuit training
d. Complex training

8. Where in a muscle are essential elements of muscular contraction (i.e., glycogen, fat, mitochondria) located?

a. Sarcoplasmic reticulum
b. Cytoplasm
c. Sarcolemma
d. Sarcoplasm

9. Under what physiological conditions will gluconeogenesis take place?

a. Periods of starvation
b. Excess carbohydrate consumption
c. Periods of protein deprivation
d. Excess protein consumption

10. What physiological process is responsible for the breakdown of food to release the food's energy resources?

a. Ingestion
b. Excretion
c. Digestion
d. Absorption

11. What percentage of the 1RM would facilitate developing an athlete's ability to accelerate and increase speed?

a. 50-60 percent
b. 40-50 percent
c. 60-70 percent
d. 30-40 percent

12. Which joint is an example of a multiaxial joint?

a. Wrist
b. Vertebrae
c. Knee
d. Shoulder

13. What is the significance of the atrioventricular bundle?

a. The atrioventricular bundle is responsible for monitoring the cardiac rhythm of the heart.
b. The atrioventricular bundle is a key determinant of cardiac rhythm, as it causes the ventricles and atria to relax during diastole.
c. The atrioventricular bundle is crucial for maintaining cardiac rhythm and communicates the signal from the AV node to the left and right bundle branches.
d. The atrioventricular bundle is responsible for regulating the cardiac rhythm during high-intensity exercise.

Copyright © Mometrix Media. You have been licensed one copy of this document for personal use only. Any other reproduction or redistribution is strictly prohibited. All rights reserved.
This content is provided for test preparation purposes only and does not imply an endorsement by Mometrix of any particular political, scientific, or religious point of view.

14. What is the bilateral deficit?

a. Bilateral deficit refers to a neural deficiency when performing bilateral upper-body movements.
b. Bilateral deficit refers to a neural deficiency between the dominant and non-dominant limbs.
c. Bilateral deficit refers to a neural deficiency when performing bilateral lower-body movements.
d. Bilateral deficit refers to a neural deficiency when performing bilateral movements.

15. How is the movement of CO_2 and O_2 controlled during respiratory gas exchange?

a. Movement of CO_2 and O_2 is controlled via a concentration gradient so that the molecule will move from an area of higher concentration to an area of lower concentration.
b. Movement of CO_2 and O_2 is controlled via active diffusion, which requires the activation of specific enzymes to allow CO_2 and O_2 to move into or out of the cell for transport.
c. Movement of CO_2 and O_2 is controlled via an active diffusion process that requires the accumulation of CO_2 and O_2 in the blood to trigger transport processes.
d. Movement of CO_2 and O_2 is controlled via a concentration gradient so that the molecule will move from an area of lower concentration to an area of higher concentration.

16. What does the sarcoplasmic reticulum store that is significant for muscular contraction?

a. ATP
b. Glycogen
c. Sodium/potassium
d. Calcium ions

17. The protein hormone erythropoietin can be used to enhance aerobic endurance. Via what mechanism does EPO improve aerobic function?

a. Increased plasma volume
b. Decreased capacity to carry iron
c. Increased hematocrit
d. Increased renin-angiotensin-aldosterone activity

18. When opening a new strength and conditioning facility, the hiring phase for qualified staff begins during which phase?

a. Pre-operation phase
b. Design phase
c. Construction phase
d. Predesign phase

19. When working with an athlete with limited training experience, what is the most appropriate way to assess strength levels?

a. 15-20 repetition maximum
b. 1-3 repetition maximum
c. 10-12 repetition maximum
d. 6-8 repetition maximum

Copyright © Mometrix Media. You have been licensed one copy of this document for personal use only. Any other reproduction or redistribution is strictly prohibited. All rights reserved.
This content is provided for test preparation purposes only and does not imply an endorsement by Mometrix of any particular political, scientific, or religious point of view.

20. In what tissues can lactate be used as an energy source?

I. Muscle
II. Cardiac muscle
III. Lungs
IV. Brain

a. I and II
b. II and III
c. I and IV
d. II and IV

21. What is the proper orientation for blood pressure notation, and what is considered normal blood pressure?

a. Systole/Diastole; 80/120
b. Diastole/Systole; 120/80
c. Systolic/Diastolic; 120/80
d. Diastole/Systole; 80/120

22. For an athlete who has been in a training program for two years and needed to gain significant muscle mass in the upper torso, quadriceps, and hamstrings, what type of training split would the strength and conditioning coach use?

a. Upper/lower training split
b. Body part split
c. Total body training
d. Leg power/upper hypertrophy

23. During altitude training, there are several acute training adaptations. What are they?

I. Greater availability of bicarbonate
II. Increased pulmonary ventilation
III. Increased myoglobin concentrations
IV. Increased capillary density

a. I and IV
b. II and III
c. IV
d. II

24. When planning training programs for two distinct types of athlete (e.g., a marathon runner and a football player), how should a strength and conditioning coach track training volumes?

a. Duration and load-volume
b. Time and training intensity
c. Total distance and load-volume
d. Duration and work

25. Which selection below represents a first-class lever?

a. Biceps curl
b. DB lateral raise
c. Knee extension
d. Triceps extension

Copyright © Mometrix Media. You have been licensed one copy of this document for personal use only. Any other reproduction or redistribution is strictly prohibited. All rights reserved.
This content is provided for test preparation purposes only and does not imply an endorsement by Mometrix of any particular political, scientific, or religious point of view.

26. During phosphorylation of ATP, what must be added to the adenine, phosphate, and ribose to complete the ATP molecule?

a. Glycogen
b. Inorganic phosphate
c. Glucose
d. Amino acid

27. Which food listed below is primarily composed of dietary fats?

a. Lean ground beef
b. Peanut butter
c. Sweet potato
d. Boneless/skinless chicken breast

28. What is the primary role of the athletic trainer?

a. Assigning training protocols to injured athletes
b. Management and rehabilitation of injury
c. Performing anthropometric measurements
d. Discussing injuries with strength and conditioning coach

29. Why are capillaries significant for optimal function in the vascular system?

a. Transport large volumes of oxygenated blood to working tissues.
b. Transport hormones, exchange fluids, gases, and electrolytes with interstitial fluids throughout the body.
c. Exchange large volumes of CO_2 and O_2 with the lungs.
d. Exchange large volumes of fluids, gases, electrolytes, and various nutrients with the lymphatic system.

30. When performing power cleans, the bar is caught in what position?

a. Full squat
b. Legs straight
c. ¼ squat
d. ½ squat

31. A 200-meter hurdler is about to begin his competitive training season. What training approach would the strength and conditioning coach use to maintain the athlete's explosive and work capacities?

a. Complex training
b. Push/pull split
c. Circuit training
d. Compound sets

Copyright © Mometrix Media. You have been licensed one copy of this document for personal use only. Any other reproduction or redistribution is strictly prohibited. All rights reserved.
This content is provided for test preparation purposes only and does not imply an endorsement by Mometrix of any particular political, scientific, or religious point of view.

32. What is the onset of blood lactate accumulation?

a. Exercise-intensity-induced accumulation of lactate in the blood due to increased buffering capacity and drop in blood pH.
b. Exercise-intensity-induced accumulation of lactate in the blood due to decreased buffering capacity caused by decreased H+ ion activity.
c. Exercise-intensity-induced accumulation of lactate in the blood due to increased H+ ions in the blood and increased buffering capacity eliminating lactate at an insufficient rate.
d. Exercise-intensity-induced lactate accumulation in the blood due to inability to buffer at a sufficient rate.

33. What is the correct staff-to-athlete ratio for a secondary school?

a. 1:15
b. 1:20
c. 1:10
d. 1:30

34. During oxidative phosphorylation, what is the net ATP production, assuming two ATP molecules are consumed during the process?

a. 24
b. 42
c. 38
d. 18

35. If training an athlete to improve work capacity, or a specific characteristic such as speed-endurance, what type of resistance training split and method could be used to enhance the anaerobic conditioning activities the athlete would necessarily undertake?

a. Total body training
b. Circuit training
c. Upper/lower split
d. Body part split

36. Which substance is responsible for supplying the energy for human movement?

a. Glycogen
b. Acetylcholine
c. Adenosine triphosphate
d. Potassium

37. What are the time considerations for assessing local muscular endurance?

a. 10 seconds to 120 seconds
b. 60 seconds to 80 seconds
c. 30 seconds to 40 seconds
d. 180 seconds to 300 seconds

38. What comprises long thin chains of proteins that are arranged into sarcomeres and responsible for muscular contraction?

a. Myocytes
b. Actin
c. Myofibrils
d. Myofilaments

Copyright © Mometrix Media. You have been licensed one copy of this document for personal use only. Any other reproduction or redistribution is strictly prohibited. All rights reserved.
This content is provided for test preparation purposes only and does not imply an endorsement by Mometrix of any particular political, scientific, or religious point of view.

39. When assessing a basketball player's one-legged jumping ability, the strength and conditioning coach notices the athlete does not jump very well off his left leg. What movement pattern and training strategy would the coach select to begin the process of correcting this issue?

a. Include instability training using unstable surfaces
b. Include unilateral lower-body movements
c. Include partner stretching in the warm-up
d. Include additional bilateral lower-body movements

40. What is the all-or-nothing principle of muscular contraction?

a. This principle states that for muscular contraction to occur a variation in signal strength will generate a muscle contraction and the number of motor units activated is determined by the signal strength.
b. This principle refers to the complete muscular contraction that takes place after an action potential has been released onto the sarcolemma of the muscle. If no action potential is present, then there is no contraction.
c. This principle refers to the confounding elements of the nervous system and how variations of neural signaling alter the rate and type of muscular contractions.
d. This principle states that for muscular contraction to occur, an action potential must be present, but the intensity of contraction varies based on the rate of transduction of the signal along the sarcolemma of the muscle.

41. From the prescribed repetition schemes listed below, which will cause the greatest metabolic stress?

a. 3x8 at 70 percent
b. 6x6 at 85 percent
c. 4x4 at 90 percent
d. 4x8 at 70 percent

42. What training adaptation to aerobic exercise increases the end-diastolic volume?

a. Right-ventricle hypertrophy
b. Left-ventricle hypertrophy
c. Right-atrium hypertrophy
d. Left-atrium hypertrophy

43. What phase of an EKG represents ventricular depolarization?

a. P-wave
b. QRS complex
c. Q-wave
d. T-wave

44. What is the most important element to consider when determining the training frequency for an athlete?

a. Sport season
b. Training status
c. Training split
d. Exercise selection

Copyright © Mometrix Media. You have been licensed one copy of this document for personal use only. Any other reproduction or redistribution is strictly prohibited. All rights reserved.
This content is provided for test preparation purposes only and does not imply an endorsement by Mometrix of any particular political, scientific, or religious point of view.

45. When does a muscle act as a synergist?

a. A muscle will act as a synergist when it is necessary to complete a maximal effort lift.
b. A muscle will act as a synergist to absorb force during an eccentric movement pattern.
c. A muscle will act as a synergist when it assists indirectly with a movement pattern.
d. A muscle will act as a synergist when it opposes a specific movement

46. Which substance is heavily involved in muscle anabolism and neurological adaptations?

a. IGF
b. Cortisol
c. Estrogen
d. Testosterone

47. What factor should most heavily influence the type of progression method a strength and conditioning coach uses across the different sport seasons throughout the training program?

a. Increasing training loads quickly
b. Gradual training load increases
c. Reducing injury
d. Controlling training stress

48. During a combine event, there are 12 separate timers during the 40-yard dash event. What is the best approach for accurately collecting and reporting the data?

a. Remove the highest and lowest times and then assess the average
b. Calculate the average of all 12 timers
c. Determine the standard deviation among the times
d. Determine and report the median

49. What connective tissue attaches a muscle to a bone?

a. Ligament
b. Cartilage
c. Tendon
d. Myocyte

50. What percentage of the one-repetition maximum will generally allow an athlete to complete eight repetitions per work set?

a. 86 percent
b. 78 percent
c. 82 percent
d. 90 percent

51. What is the basic function of allosteric binding sites?

a. Allosteric binding sites allow for multiple hormones to bind to a receptor to increase or decrease activity of a primary hormone.
b. Allosteric binding sites allow for substances other than hormones to bind to a receptor to increase or decrease responses to the primary hormone.
c. Allosteric binding sites generate a baseline chemical response triggering increased activity in the primary hormone.
d. Allosteric binding provides a binding site where proteins and other substances inhibit the function of a primary hormone.

Copyright © Mometrix Media. You have been licensed one copy of this document for personal use only. Any other reproduction or redistribution is strictly prohibited. All rights reserved.
This content is provided for test preparation purposes only and does not imply an endorsement by Mometrix of any particular political, scientific, or religious point of view.

52. In the off-season training program, how often should the athlete resistance train?

a. 2-3 training sessions per week
b. 5-7 training sessions per week
c. 3-4 training sessions per week
d. 4-6 training session per week

53. What is the prescribed push-up testing standard from the American College of Sports Medicine?

a. As many repetitions as possible in a two-minute period
b. As many repetitions as possible in a 60-second period
c. As many repetitions as possible, performed continuously, until failure
d. As many repetitions as possible, resting at peak when necessary, for two minutes

54. What is the muscle structure responsible for controlling muscular responses to rapid changes in muscle tension to prevent injury?

a. Golgi tendon organ
b. Proprioceptor
c. Lamellar corpuscle
d. Muscle spindle

55. Which of the terms listed is NOT considered a part of the general adaptation syndrome?

a. Reaction
b. Super-compensation
c. Alarm
d. Overtraining

56. When an athlete is described as being in the "zone" during competition, what is this state identified and how is this characterized?

a. Optimal performance state; athlete is relaxed, focused, and confident.
b. Ideal performance state; athlete is relaxed, focused, and confident.
c. Optimal performance state; athlete is relaxed, fast, energetic, and engaging with teammates.
d. Ideal performance state; athlete is relaxed, fast, energetic, and engaging with teammates.

57. What cardiovascular rhythm is indicated by a resting heart rate of less than 60 beats per minute?

a. Tachycardia
b. Brachycardia
c. Bradycardia
d. Arrhythmia

58. What protein is responsible for initiating muscular contraction?

a. Actin
b. Tropomyosin
c. Troponin
d. Myosin

Copyright © Mometrix Media. You have been licensed one copy of this document for personal use only. Any other reproduction or redistribution is strictly prohibited. All rights reserved.
This content is provided for test preparation purposes only and does not imply an endorsement by Mometrix of any particular political, scientific, or religious point of view.

59. During the starting position of the snatch exercise, what coaching cue should be given to an athlete who starts with his chest over the barbell and hips higher than the shoulders?

I. Squat down with the hips lower than the shoulders
II. Eyes focused straight ahead or slightly downward
III. Shoulders over or slightly in front of the bar
IV. Chest held up and out

a. I and III
b. I and IV
c. II and III
d. I, III, and IV

60. What is the primary goal for the competition period?

a. Increase strength and power gradually
b. Maintain conditioning levels for competition
c. Increase training intensity in preparation for competition
d. Preserve strength and performance levels

61. Which exercises would be selected to generate the highest release of human growth hormone?

I. Compound movements affecting large muscle groups
II. Isolation movements affecting individual muscle groups
III. Loading intensity > 80 percent and higher training volume
IV. Loading Intensity < 70percent and lower training volume

a. I and IV
b. II and III
c. II and IV
d. I and III

62. When establishing baseline testing values, what is the key element for accurately tracking changes over time?

a. Testing frequency
b. Regimented time periods between testing procedures
c. Testing in similar conditions
d. Duration of the testing process

63. What muscle fiber type has the greatest capacity for force production and hypertrophy?

a. Type IIa
b. Type I
c. Type IIb
d. Type IIf

Copyright © Mometrix Media. You have been licensed one copy of this document for personal use only. Any other reproduction or redistribution is strictly prohibited. All rights reserved.
This content is provided for test preparation purposes only and does not imply an endorsement by Mometrix of any particular political, scientific, or religious point of view.

64. When determining the methods to include in a sprint training program, where do sprinting, sprint assistance, mobility, and endurance training fall in order of importance?

I. Sprinting
II. Endurance training
III. Sprint assistance
IV. Mobility

a. I, III, II, IV
b. I, IV, III, II
c. I, III, IV, II
d. I, II, III, IV

65. Which muscle structure is responsible for providing reflex responses to sudden changes in a muscle's length?

a. Extrafusal muscle fiber
b. Golgi tendon organ
c. Muscle spindle
d. Pacinian corpuscle

66. When an athlete is lifting maximal or near-maximal loads throughout a training cycle, what is the most effective method for maintaining progress and balancing training stress?

a. Alternating training loads
b. Varied training load intensity
c. Block training
d. Varied training volume

67. Which of the listed options below is representative of steps an athlete should take to return to normal training processes during the remodeling phase after an injury?

a. Isotonic strengthening to dynamic stretching
b. Concentric strength to eccentric strength
c. Flexibility to eccentric strength
d. Rapid isotonic strengthening to dynamic stretching

68. During muscular contraction, two specific proteins form a cross bridge that generates movement. What are these two proteins called, and for what action during the cross-bridge formation are they individually responsible?

a. Actin is the thin filament and serves as the binding site. Myosin is the thicker filament and forms the crosslink to the actin filament.
b. Troponin is the thin filament and serves as the binding site. Tropomyosin is the thicker filament and forms the crosslink to the actin filament.
c. Myosin is the thick filament that serves as the binding site during muscular contraction. Actin is the thin filament that serves as the crosslink during muscular contraction.
d. Tropomyosin is a long-chain filament that is responsible for cross bridging. Troponin is a long, thick filament that serves as the binding site for myosin.

Copyright © Mometrix Media. You have been licensed one copy of this document for personal use only. Any other reproduction or redistribution is strictly prohibited. All rights reserved.
This content is provided for test preparation purposes only and does not imply an endorsement by Mometrix of any particular political, scientific, or religious point of view.

69. What would be an appropriate primary resistance goal for a lacrosse player in the off-season, which is eight weeks in length?

a. Adding 30 lbs. to overhead press
b. Increasing bench press from 315 lbs. to 385 lbs.
c. Increasing deadlift from 405 lbs. to 415 lbs.
d. Increasing power clean from 265 lbs. to 300 lbs.

70. What occurs after the transduction of an electrical signal at the sarcolemma?

a. Accumulation of an action potential
b. Muscular contraction
c. ATP hydrolyzes, releasing energy for muscular contraction
d. Release of Ca2+ ions into the sarcoplasm

71. When determining the effectiveness of a training program, when should the strength and conditioning coach perform a final review?

a. End of each sport
b. End of the competition year
c. End of the off-season program
d. End of the in-season program

72. An athlete struggling with physical manifestations that affect athletic performance positively or negatively is an example of what type of anxiety?

a. Somatic anxiety
b. Cognitive anxiety
c. Perception anxiety
d. Physical anxiety

73. Which testing procedure represents the BEST layout for a test battery?

I. 1-RM squat
II. Pro-agility
III. Pull-up test
IV. 110-meter sprint test

a. I, II, III, IV
b. II, I, IV, III
c. II, III, I, IV
d. III, I, IV, II

74. During muscular contraction, which section of the sarcomere does not move?

a. H-zone
b. A-band
c. M-line
d. I-band

75. When evaluating the work performed by an athlete during a training session, what essential factor must be most accurately assessed?

a. Mechanical loading
b. External loading
c. Metabolic energy
d. Time

Copyright © Mometrix Media. You have been licensed one copy of this document for personal use only. Any other reproduction or redistribution is strictly prohibited. All rights reserved.
This content is provided for test preparation purposes only and does not imply an endorsement by Mometrix of any particular political, scientific, or religious point of view.

76. Which of the terms listed below represent an area of legal concern that can be mitigated by a clearly defined emergency care plan for a new strength and conditioning facility?

a. Tort
b. Negligence
c. Statute of limitations
d. Eligibility criteria

77. Which neuromuscular structure is responsible for initiating the stretch reflex?

a. Muscle spindle
b. Golgi tendon organ
c. Pacinian corpuscle
d. Extrafusal muscle fiber

78. What structure is found in both the conduction and respiratory zones of respiration?

a. Primary bronchi
b. Alveoli
c. Pleura
d. Bronchioles

79. If sufficient oxygen is not available during glycolysis, what is pyruvate's function?

a. Pyruvate is converted to acetyl coenzyme A to enter the Krebs cycle.
b. Pyruvate is converted to acetaldehyde to produce sufficient ATP.
c. Pyruvate is converted to acetyl coenzyme A, then to alanine, and then to ATP.
d. Pyruvate is converted via fermentation to lactate to produce sufficient ATP.

80. When training an athlete who needs to perform multiple explosive events in brief periods of time, what intensity and repetition range should a strength coach prescribe?

a. ≤ 85 percent, ≤6 repetitions
b. 75-85 percent, 3-5 repetitions
c. 67-85 percent, 3-5 repetitions
d. 80-90 percent, 1-2 repetitions

81. The sarcolemma in striated muscle tissue plays a significant role in muscular contraction. What is the primary function of the sarcolemma?

a. The primary function of the sarcolemma is to conduct electrical signals via the neuromuscular junction.
b. The primary function of the sarcolemma is to conduct electrical signals, via transduction, signaling the release of Ca2+ ions.
c. The sarcolemma is responsible for communication from the central nervous system and the individual muscle cell.
d. The primary function of the sarcolemma is to pump Ca2+ ions into and out of a muscle cell.

82. What is the name of the outermost layer of muscle fiber?

a. Epimysium
b. Endomysium
c. Perimysium
d. Ectomysium

Copyright © Mometrix Media. You have been licensed one copy of this document for personal use only. Any other reproduction or redistribution is strictly prohibited. All rights reserved.
This content is provided for test preparation purposes only and does not imply an endorsement by Mometrix of any particular political, scientific, or religious point of view.

83. When transitioning to a pre-season training period, what modifications will the strength and conditioning coach make to the training parameters for the athletes?

a. Decrease training load intensity
b. Increase training load Intensity
c. Decrease training volume
d. Increase training volume

84. If a marathon runner uses a four- to six-week training block to swim and cycle, this is considered to be what kind of training?

a. Alternative training
b. Neural reprogramming
c. Cross-training
d. General endurance training

85. When evaluating high-school-aged female athletes' body composition using a skin-fold measurement procedure, what sites are tested?

a. Thigh, subscapular
b. Suprailiac, biceps
c. Thigh, abdomen
d. Suprailiac, triceps

86. Under what conditions is using the Valsalva maneuver appropriate and inappropriate?

I. Experienced and properly resistance-trained athletes
II. Under maximal loading during structural exercise
III. Under heavy loading during assistance exercises
IV. When performing heavy-resistance abdominal exercises

a. I and IV
b. II and III
c. I and II
d. II and IV

87. Which enzyme is used as a means of determining a heart attack, kidney failure, or rhabdomyolysis?

a. Creatine kinase
b. Adenylate kinase
c. Riboflavin kinase
d. Myokinase

88. What energy system is supplying the majority of ATP when the body is at rest?

a. Aerobic glycolysis
b. Phosphagen system
c. Anaerobic glycolysis
d. Oxidative system

Copyright © Mometrix Media. You have been licensed one copy of this document for personal use only. Any other reproduction or redistribution is strictly prohibited. All rights reserved.
This content is provided for test preparation purposes only and does not imply an endorsement by Mometrix of any particular political, scientific, or religious point of view.

89. The preparatory phase is the longest training phase in a yearly macro-cycle. What is the primary emphasis for this training phase?

a. Develop basic strength levels
b. Establishing a baseline of conditioning
c. Preparation for higher-intensity loading
d. Initiation of higher training volumes

90. When designing a plyometric training program for younger athletes, what should the focus of the program be?

a. Increased power
b. Increased horizontal jumping distance
c. Skill acquisition and neuromuscular control
d. Skill acquisition and movement-specific strength

91. What is the difference between oxygen debt and oxygen deficit?

a. Oxygen deficit refers to the initial anaerobic energy system contributions, and oxygen debt is the volume of oxygen consumed above resting values.
b. Oxygen deficit is the volume of oxygen consumed above resting values, and oxygen debt refers to the initial anaerobic energy system contributions.
c. Oxygen deficit is the volume of oxygen consumed during rest before exercise, and oxygen debt refers to the difference between the volumes of oxygen consumed between resting and exercise values.
d. Oxygen deficit is the initial aerobic energy system contributions, and oxygen debt is the volume of oxygen consumed during exercise.

92. What periodization model would be most effective for an athlete who has multiple events during a competitive season?

a. Linear periodization
b. Non-linear periodization
c. Matveyev periodization
d. Strategic periodization

93. If a woman over the age of 40 is concerned about the possibility of her bone density decreasing as she ages, which exercises would serve to increase bone density even as she ages?

a. Aerobic exercise
b. Externally loaded resistance exercises
c. Bodyweight exercises
d. Pilates/yoga

Copyright © Mometrix Media. You have been licensed one copy of this document for personal use only. Any other reproduction or redistribution is strictly prohibited. All rights reserved.
This content is provided for test preparation purposes only and does not imply an endorsement by Mometrix of any particular political, scientific, or religious point of view.

94. A track and field coach is designing a training program for a broad jumper. In what order should the selected exercises be performed in this program?

I. Power clean
II. Hamstring curl
III. Reverse hyperextension
IV. Deadlift

a. IV, I, III, II
b. I, IV, III, II
c. IV, III, I, II
d. I, III, IV, II

95. Which situation requires multiple spotters to assist an athlete should they miss a lift?

a. An athlete performing 225 lbs. maximum repetitions test
b. An athlete performing barbell step-ups
c. An athlete overhead pressing 185 lbs.
d. An athlete squatting 450 lbs. in a work-set

96. Who will the strength and conditioning coach have direct and most frequent contact with on the sports medicine team?

a. Team physician
b. Nutritionist
c. Exercise physiologist
d. Sports physical therapist

97. What is the translation point for the muscular and nervous systems?

a. Neuromuscular junction
b. Peduncle
c. Motor neuron
d. Action potential

98. Tapering is an important component of competition preparation. What is NOT a primary benefit to a tapering strategy before competition?

a. Neurological recovery
b. Rehydration
c. Increased glycogen stores
d. Joint/muscle recovery

99. Steroid hormones differ from polypeptide hormones in what way?

a. Steroid hormones are fat-soluble and originate from the gonads and adrenal cortex.
b. Steroid hormones are amino acid based and have multiple binding sites throughout the body.
c. Steroid hormones do not rely on allosteric binding sites the way polypeptide hormones do.
d. Steroid hormones are fat-insoluble, originate from the gonads and adrenal cortex, and rely on allosteric binding sites to affect target tissues.

Copyright © Mometrix Media. You have been licensed one copy of this document for personal use only. Any other reproduction or redistribution is strictly prohibited. All rights reserved.
This content is provided for test preparation purposes only and does not imply an endorsement by Mometrix of any particular political, scientific, or religious point of view.

100. When performing a data analysis on the effectiveness of the strength and conditioning program for three similar female sports - volleyball, basketball, and sprinters and jumpers - the strength and conditioning director should use what statistical approach to the data?

a. Central tendency
b. Difference score
c. Variability
d. Descriptive statistics

101. When evaluating athlete readiness for engaging in a plyometric program, what are the primary considerations?

a. Balance, strength, flexibility, speed
b. Balance, technique, flexibility, strength
c. Strength, technique, balance, speed
d. Flexibility, technique, strength, speed

102. When training an athlete with a weakness in a small muscle group, what type of movement will the strength coach prescribe?

a. Auxiliary movement
b. Assistance movement
c. Core movement
d. Isolation movement

103. What is the primary limitation of trunk plyometrics?

a. Limited stretch-reflex response
b. Too many muscles groups involved
c. Hip flexors overtaking the abdominals
d. Overactive stretch-reflex response

104. When training female athletes or fitness clients, which joint is most at risk for injury because of the anatomical structure of the female body?

a. Shoulder
b. Hip
c. Knee
d. Ankle

105. What determines the energy systems used during a training session?

a. Loading intensity
b. Injury history
c. Session duration
d. Athlete's training capacity

106. The series elastic component of the stretch-shortening cycle is primarily concerned with what structures?

a. Muscle spindle
b. Golgi tendon organ
c. Ligament
d. Tendon

Copyright © Mometrix Media. You have been licensed one copy of this document for personal use only. Any other reproduction or redistribution is strictly prohibited. All rights reserved.
This content is provided for test preparation purposes only and does not imply an endorsement by Mometrix of any particular political, scientific, or religious point of view.

107. Which of the responsibilities below is NOT within the purview of the strength and conditioning coach?

a. Coach team warm-up activities
b. Assess injuries
c. Provide skill and movement corrections during training
d. Develop and implement training programs

108. What causes metabolic acidosis?

a. Rapid decrease in enzyme activity, resulting in increased lactate accumulation.
b. Rapid increase of hydrogen ion concentration in the blood that causes a decrease in blood pH.
c. Rapid increase in hydrogen ion concentration in the blood that causes an increase in blood pH.
d. Rapid increase in enzyme activity, resulting in decreased lactate accumulation.

109. If an aerobic athlete wanted to improve his anaerobic metabolism while enhancing his finishing strength at the end of a race, which of the selected methods below would provide this most effectively?

a. Pace/tempo training
b. Interval training
c. Fartlek training
d. Repetition training

110. What anatomical structure is considered to be the "pacemaker" of the heart?

a. Sinoatrial node
b. Bundle of His
c. Atrioventricular node
d. Purkinje fibers

111. If a training program called for three upper-body training sessions that emphasized upper-body pressing exercises, how would the strength and conditioning coach best create muscle balance in these training sessions?

a. Include horizontal and vertical pulling exercises in all three training sessions
b. Include three lower-body training sessions
c. Perform rotator cuff assistance exercises at the end of each session
d. Include overhead pressing and vertical pulling in one of the training sessions

112. What role does the sympathetic nervous system (SNS) have regarding athletic performance and exercise?

a. The SNS is responsible for the relaxation of the body and is primarily active during periods of digestion and sleep, and plays no role in athletic performance.
b. The SNS is responsible for maintaining the body's homeostatic responses during athletic activity.
c. The SNS is responsible for the direct feedback loops from the periphery to the central nervous system during activity.
d. The SNS is responsible for the potentiation of the body's physiological systems in preparation for physical activity.

Copyright © Mometrix Media. You have been licensed one copy of this document for personal use only. Any other reproduction or redistribution is strictly prohibited. All rights reserved.
This content is provided for test preparation purposes only and does not imply an endorsement by Mometrix of any particular political, scientific, or religious point of view.

113. Utilizing heavy resistance exercises and movements that utilize the stretch-shortening cycle is considered what type of training?

a. Neural manipulation training
b. Combination training
c. Contrast training
d. Complex training

114. Which testing procedure would be the BEST option for assessing an athlete's speed?

a. 400-meter sprint
b. T-test
c. Pro-agility test
d. 150-meter sprint

115. Which fiber type is most important to the endurance athlete?

a. Type-IIa
b. Type-I
c. Type-IIx
d. Type-IIb

116. Morphology of the neuromuscular junction is affected by anaerobic training in what way?

a. Length of nerve terminal branching is increased, and acetylcholine circulation increases
b. Surface area and length of nerve terminal branching is increased, and synapse locations are increased and dispersed more widely
c. Surface area and synapse location are increased and dispersed more widely
d. Surface area is increased, synapse locations are increased and dispersed more widely, and acetylcholine circulation increases

117. Where are the contractile proteins in striated muscle located?

a. Myofilament
b. Myofibril
c. Myocyte
d. Sarcomere

118. What cardiac phase is represented by diastole?

a. Diastole is the phase of the cardiac cycle where contraction of the left ventricle occurs, ejecting oxygen-rich blood toward the working tissues of the body.
b. Diastole is the phase of the cardiac cycle where relaxation of the ventricles and atria allows for the heart to fill with blood.
c. Diastole is the phase of the cardiac cycle where the ventricles relax and the atria contract to move blood into the ventricles in preparation for systole.
d. Diastole is the phase of the cardiac cycle where ventricular contraction occurs, moving blood from the atria to the working tissues of the body.

Copyright © Mometrix Media. You have been licensed one copy of this document for personal use only. Any other reproduction or redistribution is strictly prohibited. All rights reserved.
This content is provided for test preparation purposes only and does not imply an endorsement by Mometrix of any particular political, scientific, or religious point of view.

119. Will increased activity in the parasympathetic nervous system (PNS) affect athletic performance positively or negatively?

a. Increased activity in the PNS will affect athletic performance positively via increased focus and mental acuity, while also enhancing neural signaling for muscular contraction.
b. Increased activity in the PNS will affect athletic performance negatively, as this system is responsible for a reduction in mental focus and body temperature, and is most active during leisure activities.
c. Increased activity in the PNS will affect athletic performance positively via increased activity of the cardiorespiratory and endocrine systems.
d. Increased activity in the PNS will affect athletic performance negatively via decreased neuromuscular activity, increased body temperature, and reduced heart rate.

120. Which enzyme is responsible for catalyzing the cross bridging action in muscular contraction?

a. ATPase
b. Calcium ATPase
c. Amylase
d. Myosin ATPase

121. A high school football coach decides to bench the starting running back after a fumble early in the first half. The coach's decision is an example of what type of reinforcement?

a. Positive punishment
b. Negative reinforcement
c. Negative punishment
d. Positive reinforcement

122. Which of the following movements are open-chain movements?

I. Bench press
II. Lunge
III. Leg curl
IV. Lying triceps exercise

a. I and II only
b. I and III only
c. I, II, and IV only
d. I, III, and IV only

123. What role, if any, does strength play in determining an athlete's maximal sprint velocity?

a. Strength allows an athlete to overcome increased resistance generated on the body as acceleration occurs.
b. Strength is what propels an athlete forward when attempting to accelerate the body.
c. Strength is essential for the initial takeoff to propel the body forward and sustain the sprint effort.
d. No role

Copyright © Mometrix Media. You have been licensed one copy of this document for personal use only. Any other reproduction or redistribution is strictly prohibited. All rights reserved.
This content is provided for test preparation purposes only and does not imply an endorsement by Mometrix of any particular political, scientific, or religious point of view.

124. During the inflammatory phase, what kind of training can be undertaken by the athlete?

a. Maintain strength and endurance in adjacent muscles
b. Isometric contraction of injured area
c. Lightly stretch the injured area
d. Train non-affected muscle using normal processes

125. What is the purpose of an EKG testing procedure?

a. An EKG is a used for determining the blood pressure of an athlete post-training.
b. An EKG is used to measure the brain activity of an athlete during recovery periods post-training.
c. An EKG is used to assess the electrical signals generated during polarization and depolarization of cardiac tissue, which provides insight into the overall function and health of an athlete's heart.
d. An EKG is used to record the rhythm of the heart, assess blood pressure, and generate information regarding the position and size of the patient's heart.

126. Resistance training with a higher volume and brief rest periods will most heavily affect which hormone?

a. Cortisol
b. Testosterone
c. Human growth hormone
d. Insulin

127. When determining the grip width for the snatch, which approach listed below is recommended?

a. ¼ inch outside of snatch rings on barbell
b. Elbow to elbow
c. Wrist to elbow
d. Total wingspan

128. During warm-ups, a lacrosse player notices that his right hamstring is a bit tighter than normal, so he spends an extra five minutes of the warm-up period performing light static and dynamic stretching. He plays and presents with little to no evidence of having any remaining hamstring stiffness. The athlete has taken advantage of what muscle quality?

a. Tension
b. Autogenic inhibition
c. Plasticity
d. Elasticity

129. What is the difference between muscle and resistive forces?

a. Muscular force is generated force, and resistive force is internal force acting on the muscle.
b. Resistive force is force acting on the body, and muscular force is a reflexive responding to the resistive force.
c. Muscular force is generated mechanical force from biochemical reactions, and resistive force is external force acting on the body.
d. Muscular force is generated muscular force, and resistive force is structural resistance in the force-generating muscles.

Copyright © Mometrix Media. You have been licensed one copy of this document for personal use only. Any other reproduction or redistribution is strictly prohibited. All rights reserved.
This content is provided for test preparation purposes only and does not imply an endorsement by Mometrix of any particular political, scientific, or religious point of view.

130. What areas of the body does sarcopenia affect most significantly?

I. Lower limb extensors
II. Lower limb flexors
III. Upper limb extensors
IV. Trunk extensors

a. II and III
b. I and III
c. III and IV
d. I and IV

131. When an athlete drops from the top of a box and first contacts the ground, what are the phases of the stretch-shortening cycle after ground contact has occurred?

a. Reactive, transition, and concentric
b. Eccentric, transition, rebound
c. Eccentric, amortization, concentric
d. Reactive, amortization, rebound

132. What relationships, according to the size principle, affect the recruitment patterns of the central nervous system?

a. Twitch force, nerve signal strength, and rate of force production
b. Size of the motor unit, acetylcholine saturation, and recruitment threshold for each motor unit
c. Twitch force, size of the motor unit, and recruitment threshold for each motor unit
d. Recruitment threshold for each motor unit, Ca+ ion activity, and acetylcholine saturation

133. What energy system is most active during brief, intense muscular contractions?

a. Anaerobic glycolysis
b. Phosphagen system
c. Aerobic glycolysis
d. Gluconeogenesis

134. Which of the bone injuries listed below occurs most frequently?

a. Stress fracture
b. Displaced fracture
c. Comminuted fracture
d. Compound fracture

135. When evaluating areas that an athlete can improve significantly over time, which of the areas listed below is most unlikely to be impacted?

a. Reaction time
b. Stretch-shortening cycle
c. Reactive time
d. Speed-endurance

Copyright © Mometrix Media. You have been licensed one copy of this document for personal use only. Any other reproduction or redistribution is strictly prohibited. All rights reserved.
This content is provided for test preparation purposes only and does not imply an endorsement by Mometrix of any particular political, scientific, or religious point of view.

136. A member of the strength and conditioning facility is wearing blue jeans to train in the facility. What are the proper action/s for a strength and conditioning coach or associate staff member to take for this first-time rule violation?

I. Verbal warning by staff member
II. Dismissal from facility for the day
III. Make member aware of violated rule
IV. Document the offense

a. I and II
b. I and III
c. I, III, and IV only
d. I, II, and III only

137. When preparing for a training session or athletic event, what type of stretching should be avoided?

a. Dynamic stretch
b. Ballistic stretch
c. Static stretch
d. Active stretch

138. Insulin is considered what type of hormone?

a. Catabolic
b. Peptide
c. Steroid
d. Amine

139. Name the phenomenon that causes increased oxygen usage after an intense bout of exercise.

a. Post-exercise oxygen consumption
b. Excess post-exercise consumption
c. Excess post-intense-exercise consumption
d. Excess oxygen consumption

140. Using a superset approach to a training program can be most beneficial during what part of the sport season?

a. Off-season
b. Pre-season
c. In-season
d. Post-season

141. When designing training programs for children, what area of adaptation to resistance training is a concern?

a. Skeletal adaptations
b. Muscular adaptations
c. Cardiovascular adaptations
d. Neuromuscular adaptations

Copyright © Mometrix Media. You have been licensed one copy of this document for personal use only. Any other reproduction or redistribution is strictly prohibited. All rights reserved.
This content is provided for test preparation purposes only and does not imply an endorsement by Mometrix of any particular political, scientific, or religious point of view.

142. What is the primary reason for including an unloading week in a training program?

a. Acclimate to higher training loads during the current training phase
b. Allow the body to recuperate during a week off
c. Prepare the athlete for demands of next training phase
d. Provide a break from training during a competitive season

143. How many pyruvate molecules result from anaerobic glycolysis?

a. 1
b. 3
c. 4
d. 2

144. When training for strength and power, which adaptations will occur most quickly?

a. Neural
b. Muscular
c. Body composition
d. Cardiovascular

145. Why is backpedal running considered to be a specific and independent movement pattern and not simply the reverse of forward sprinting?

a. Mechanical resistance to backpedal running
b. Anatomical and functional symmetry of the leg
c. Alternate muscle firing patterns
d. Different force couplings at the hip and thigh

146. Other than adding additional training load to an athlete, what other mechanisms that utilize the progressive overload principle are acceptable for athlete progression?

I. Increasing repetitions performed at specific loading parameters
II. Increasing work density
III. Increasing number of sets performed at specific loading parameters
IV. Reducing rest periods

a. I, II, III, IV
b. I and III
c. II and IV
d. I, II, and III

147. What is the correct distance for placement of weight trees from lifting equipment?

a. 42 inches
b. 36 inches
c. 54 inches
d. 28 inches

148. According to the law of mass action, what drives the direction of a chemical reaction?

a. The concentration of products and reactants in solution
b. The concentration of products in a solution
c. The concentration of reactants in a solution
d. The concentration of products and reactants along a pressure gradient in solution

Copyright © Mometrix Media. You have been licensed one copy of this document for personal use only. Any other reproduction or redistribution is strictly prohibited. All rights reserved.
This content is provided for test preparation purposes only and does not imply an endorsement by Mometrix of any particular political, scientific, or religious point of view.

149. When adjusting a cam-, pulley-, or lever-based exercise machine, what is the most important consideration for the athlete's body position?

a. Making sure the athlete is aligned with the angle of push or pull
b. Ensuring the primary joint involved in an exercise is aligned with the axis of resistance
c. Being sure to reduce injury possibilities by aligning the body correctly and reducing the weights lifted
d. Discussing optimal body position and demonstrating proper movement execution

150. When considering the needs of an athlete, the sport needs of the athlete are most important. Which athlete listed below would benefit most from a moderate-volume, moderate-intensity training program in the off-season?

a. Swimmer
b. Discus thrower
c. Golfer
d. Football player

151. Which anatomical plane splits the body into left and right segments?

a. Frontal plane
b. Transverse plane
c. Sagittal plane
d. Horizontal plane

152. Rest periods are extremely important for allowing muscular and neural recovery between sets. What is the suggested rest period for an athlete performing four sets of 12 repetitions in the squat?

a. 2-5 minutes
b. 1-2 minutes
c. 45 seconds
d. 20 seconds

153. Under what conditions would using high-GI foods prove most beneficial to an anaerobic power athlete?

a. Post-aerobic training session
b. Post-high-intensity and low-volume resistance training session
c. Post-high-intensity and high-volume Resistance Training Session
d. Post-restorative flexibility training session

154. What is the suggested square-footage recommendation for the stretching area, per athlete?

a. 36-square-foot area
b. 58-square-foot area
c. 40-square-foot area
d. 49-square-foot area

Copyright © Mometrix Media. You have been licensed one copy of this document for personal use only. Any other reproduction or redistribution is strictly prohibited. All rights reserved.
This content is provided for test preparation purposes only and does not imply an endorsement by Mometrix of any particular political, scientific, or religious point of view.

155. A basketball player stands at the free throw line, focused on the rim, and is preparing to shoot the first of two free throw attempts. He effectively ignores the raucous noise of the home crowd and makes both attempts. What ability is this athlete using?

a. Selective focus
b. Limited attention
c. Discriminating focus
d. Selective attention

156. Which of the listed training volumes will affect muscular hypertrophy the most?

a. Five sets of 10 repetitions
b. Five sets of 5 repetitions
c. Three sets of 8 repetitions
d. One set of 15 repetitions

157. When determining what equipment to purchase for a new strength and conditioning facility, this decision should be most heavily influenced by which person?

a. Athletic director
b. Director of business operations
c. Facility manager
d. Strength and conditioning director

158. If a strength and conditioning coach wants to improve sprint speed, what type of plyometric drills would be most effective over a six-week plyometric program?

a. Lower-body plyometrics; jumps in place; box jumps for height
b. Lower-body plyometrics; jumps over an object; standing jumps
c. Lower-body plyometrics; horizontal bounding; single-leg jumps
d. Lower-body plyometrics; single-leg jumps in place; single-leg jumps for height

159. In the modified Matveyev model, in which phase do sport-specific activities begin?

a. Hypertrophy/endurance phase
b. Strength/power phase
c. Peaking phase
d. Basic strength phase

160. Of the following substances, which is NOT considered an ergogenic aid?

a. Protein powder
b. BCAAs
c. Acetaminophen
d. Creatine

161. Which of the training phases below is an alteration to the Matveyev model of periodization?

a. Preparatory phase
b. Strength/power phase
c. Transition phase
d. Competition phase

Copyright © Mometrix Media. You have been licensed one copy of this document for personal use only. Any other reproduction or redistribution is strictly prohibited. All rights reserved.
This content is provided for test preparation purposes only and does not imply an endorsement by Mometrix of any particular political, scientific, or religious point of view.

162. What are the two primary functions of hemoglobin?

I. O_2 transport
II. CO_2 transport
III. Acid base buffer
IV. Deliver nutrients to muscles

a. II and IV
b. I and II
c. I and III
d. All of the above

163. A volleyball player, the team's setter, needs to improve her upper-body strength in the off-season training program. What training load and repetition range would a strength and conditioning coach use to bring about the needed improvement in upper-body strength?

a. 60-70 percent, 4-8 repetitions
b. 70-85 percent, 6-10 repetitions
c. 80-90 percent, 8-10 repetitions
d. 85-100 percent, 4-6 repetitions

164. What is a uniaxial joint?

a. A joint that rotates about a single axis.
b. A joint that is uniplanar in action.
c. A joint that functions in multiple planes of movement.
d. A joint that rotates about a single axis and operates in multiplanar fashion.

165. Using the Valsalva maneuver is helpful when transitioning from eccentric to concentric lifting phases. What is the name for this in-between transition?

a. Sticking point
b. Turnaround point
c. Transition point
d. Isokinetic point

166. When preparing an athlete for competition, what is considered to be the best-practice procedure for stretching, listed in the order in which the exercises should be performed?

I. Sport skill
II. Dynamic stretching
III. Jogging
IV. Bounding

a. III, I, II, IV
b. IV, II, I, III
c. III, II, I, IV
d. I, III, II, IV

167. Inactivity and poor nutritional habits lead to the downregulation of this hormone resulting in significant disease complications over time. What is the hormone?

a. Testosterone
b. Estrogen
c. Growth hormone
d. Insulin

Copyright © Mometrix Media. You have been licensed one copy of this document for personal use only. Any other reproduction or redistribution is strictly prohibited. All rights reserved.
This content is provided for test preparation purposes only and does not imply an endorsement by Mometrix of any particular political, scientific, or religious point of view.

168. Which action is the pulmonary division of the arterial system responsible for carrying out?

a. Carrying oxygenated blood to working tissues.
b. Carrying deoxygenated blood back to the heart.
c. Carrying oxygenated blood back to the heart.
d. Carrying oxygenated blood to the lungs.

169. Cartilaginous and synovial joints differentiate in what specific aspect?

a. Cartilaginous joints do not allow significant movement, and synovial joints allow significant movement.
b. Cartilaginous joints comprise ligaments and tendons but lack the synovial fluid compartments that are found in synovial joints.
c. Cartilaginous joints are tough, fibrous joints and synovial joints are capsulated joints.
d. Cartilaginous joints allow for multiplanar movements, and synovial joints allow movement in two planes.

170. There are several changes in cardiovascular function due to chronic aerobic training; which of the responses below is NOT one of these adaptations?

a. Increased resting heart rate
b. Increased cardiac output
c. Increased stroke volume
d. Decreased heart rate during submaximal exercise

171. If a 100-meter sprinter has a problem with pulling her hamstring frequently, what would be a prescription for her in an off-season program to help eliminate this issue?

a. Increase conditioning work
b. Increase training frequency
c. Focus on developing weaknesses
d. Improve strength ratios at the affected joints

172. When programming power and structural movements in the same session, what repetition ranges and training intensities will the strength and conditioning coach most likely assign?

a. Power, 1-5 repetitions at 80-90 percent intensity; structural, 3-5 repetitions at 70-80 percent
b. Power, 3-5 repetitions at 75-85 percent; structural, 4-6 repetitions at 80-90 percent
c. Power, 3-8 repetitions at 85-90 percent; structural, 10-12 repetitions at 75-85 percent
d. Power, 1-5 repetitions at 70-80 percent; structural, 8-10 repetitions at 80-90 percent

173. Counterconditioning is a combination of two techniques that are utilized to overcome performance anxiety. What are these two techniques?

I. Hypnosis techniques
II. Reciprocal inhibition
III. Cognitive techniques
IV. Somatic techniques

a. I and IV
b. I and II
c. II and III
d. III and IV

Copyright © Mometrix Media. You have been licensed one copy of this document for personal use only. Any other reproduction or redistribution is strictly prohibited. All rights reserved.
This content is provided for test preparation purposes only and does not imply an endorsement by Mometrix of any particular political, scientific, or religious point of view.

174. Caffeine is a heavily studied ergogenic aid and has a myriad of positive effects on performance. Which of the effects listed below is not one of them?

a. Increased fat oxidation
b. Enhanced power production
c. Increased neuromuscular feedback
d. Enhanced memory

175. If equipment limitations are an issue at a training facility, what test could be used most effectively for determining maximum muscular power?

a. Deadlift
b. Vertical jump
c. Pro-agility test
d. Margaria-Kalamen test

176. When a client is performing a bench press, where should the trainer's hands be placed to spot the client effectively?

a. Outside the athlete's hands in an overhand grip
b. Center of the barbell using a pronated grip
c. Outside the athlete's hands in a pronated grip
d. Center of the barbell using an alternated grip

177. When designing a training program, a strength and conditioning coach uses both structural movements and core movements. How are these movements similar and different?

a. Both affect multiple joints and large muscle groups, with core movements requiring higher force outputs as these are speed and power movements.
b. Both affect large muscle groups, but core movements are primarily considered assistance exercises.
c. Both affect large muscle groups, but structural movements are always high-force movements and should be placed first in a training program.
d. Both affect multiple joints and muscle groups, but structural movements load the spine either directly or indirectly.

178. In what energy system is the electron transport system most heavily involved?

a. Anaerobic glycolysis
b. Creatine phosphate system
c. Oxidative system
d. Aerobic glycolysis

179. What are the primary goals for the strength and conditioning program, either as a private company or a university athletic department?

a. Improve speed and agility
b. Decrease potential injury risks and improve performance
c. Develop athletes mentally and physically
d. Individual development through a team setting

Copyright © Mometrix Media. You have been licensed one copy of this document for personal use only. Any other reproduction or redistribution is strictly prohibited. All rights reserved.
This content is provided for test preparation purposes only and does not imply an endorsement by Mometrix of any particular political, scientific, or religious point of view.

180. For many years, daily protein intake for athletes has been recommended at levels similar to the recommendations for non-athlete populations. What is the current recommendation?

a. 0.8 g/Kg of body weight
b. 1.7 g/Kg of body weight
c. 0.8 to 1.4 g/Kg of body weight
d. 1.5 to 2.0 g/Kg of body weight

181. What specialized sensory receptor provides feedback to the central nervous system to alert the body to changes in the external and internal environments?

a. Optical Nerve
b. Olfactory Nerve
c. Motor neuron
d. Proprioceptors

182. An athlete needs to develop specific movement patterns to gain mastery in his sport. What is the guiding principle for this type of training and what skill type needs to be trained?

a. Skill specificity; closed movement skill
b. Practice specificity; open movement skill
c. Skill specificity; open movement skill
d. Practice specificity; closed movement skill

183. Testosterone is the primary sex hormone for males. Where is testosterone produced?

a. Leydig cells
b. Interstitial cells
c. Epididymis
d. Adrenal glands

184. During the repair phase, what is the primary objective of treatment?

a. Optimizing joint function
b. Maintain joint mobility and increase muscular elasticity
c. Prevent disruption of tissue healing
d. Prevent muscle atrophy and joint deterioration

185. What is combination training?

a. A form of interval training
b. A form of cross-training
c. A form of endurance training
d. A form of strength-endurance training

186. When outlining professional responsibilities in the strength and conditioning facility, what position is responsible for supervising the training sessions for the athletes?

a. Athletic trainer
b. Graduate assistant strength and conditioning coach
c. Assistant strength and conditioning coach
d. Head coach of athlete's sport

Copyright © Mometrix Media. You have been licensed one copy of this document for personal use only. Any other reproduction or redistribution is strictly prohibited. All rights reserved.
This content is provided for test preparation purposes only and does not imply an endorsement by Mometrix of any particular political, scientific, or religious point of view.

187. When considering pre-competition food meals, what are the key elements in preparation for the meal that ensure maximum benefit to the athlete?

a. Meal timing, well-tolerated food choices, meal macronutrient content, enjoyable food selection
b. Well-tolerated food choices, high carbohydrate, including lots of water
c. Meal timing, proper hydration procedures, high protein content
d. Meal macronutrient content, low salt, proper carb and protein balance, enjoyable food selection

188. What sport skill and movement pairing below best exemplify the specific adaptations to imposed demands (SAID) principle?

a. Free throw shooting; overhead press
b. Throwing a baseball; squat
c. 100-meter sprinting; barbell row
d. Freestyle swimming; power clean

189. Which pair of muscles have an antagonistic relationship?

a. Biceps and latissimus dorsi
b. Rectus abdominis and erector spinae
c. Quadriceps and sartorius
d. Gastrocnemius and soleus

190. Which of the following injuries is NOT an overuse injury?

a. Stress fracture
b. Contusion
c. Microtrauma
d. Tendinitis

191. Which physiological adaptation is most significant in older males when engaging in high-intensity resistance training programs?

a. Increased bone mineral density
b. Increased muscular strength
c. Decreased muscle mass
d. Increased anabolic hormone activity

192. An athlete has been tested in a laboratory to assess her specific heart rate and training intensities. What approach would be best for determining the athlete's training intensities?

a. Fick equation
b. Heart-rate reserve
c. Karvonen method
d. Age-predicted maximal heart rate

193. When would using a body-part training split be appropriate for an athlete in an off-season training program?

a. Correcting muscular imbalance
b. Increasing muscle size
c. Reducing body fat
d. Recovering from an injury

Copyright © Mometrix Media. You have been licensed one copy of this document for personal use only. Any other reproduction or redistribution is strictly prohibited. All rights reserved.
This content is provided for test preparation purposes only and does not imply an endorsement by Mometrix of any particular political, scientific, or religious point of view.

194. After performing the essential assessments of an athlete's strength, balance, and speed, what is the next step in the process?

a. Perform a vertical jump test to establish a vertical jump baseline
b. Assess movement and flexibility of the athlete
c. Evaluate the athlete's jumping technique
d. Perform multiple jumps in place to assess athlete's elasticity

195. Which valves of the heart are responsible for preventing backflow into the ventricles during diastole?

a. Semilunar valves
b. Aortic valve
c. Atrioventricular valves
d. Tricuspid valve

196. What is the definition of power?

a. Power= work x time
b. Power= work x time/velocity
c. Power= work/time
d. Power= time/work

197. When designing a training program, the first step in this process is to undertake what two-step task?

a. Injury analysis
b. Needs analysis
c. Movement analysis
d. Physiological analysis

198. When working with an older adult who has been diagnosed with osteopenia, what is the key aspect of the evaluation process that ensures the implementation of a developmentally appropriate training program?

a. Strength testing
b. Complete health and movement screenings
c. Aerobic training capacity assessment
d. Anaerobic power testing

199. In the off-season program for a Premier League soccer player, training volume and intensity are characterized by what during the strength/power phase?

a. High intensity; low Volume
b. Low intensity; high Volume
c. Low intensity; low Volume
d. High intensity; high Volume

200. Which of the following exercises does not require a spotter?

a. Barbell row
b. Step-up
c. DB incline press
d. Barbell triceps extension

Copyright © Mometrix Media. You have been licensed one copy of this document for personal use only. Any other reproduction or redistribution is strictly prohibited. All rights reserved.
This content is provided for test preparation purposes only and does not imply an endorsement by Mometrix of any particular political, scientific, or religious point of view.

201. When considering muscular adaptations to long-term aerobic training, which muscle fiber type has the greatest capacity for morphological and physiological adaptations?

a. Type II-b
b. Type II-x
c. Type I
d. Type I-x

202. When performing a PNF hamstring stretching exercise, an athlete contracts the hamstring and then relaxes the muscle to facilitate the passive stretch. How long should the stretch be applied for by the partner?

a. 5 seconds
b. 60 seconds
c. 20 seconds
d. 30 seconds

203. How does ketosis adversely affect an aerobic endurance athlete?

a. Increased substrate circulating in the blood
b. Decreased physical endurance
c. Decreased somatic stress
d. Decreased body fat

204. Which of the movements listed below is an example of neuromuscular control?

a. Jumping in a basketball game
b. Swimming in the ocean
c. Running on a soccer field
d. Changing directions on a tennis court

205. When assigning training volumes during periods of maximal or near-maximal lifting intensities, a coach must consider what specific element when completing a program outline?

a. Increasing total training volumes for the week
b. Current strength levels of the athletes
c. Need for increased recovery time
d. Decreasing rest periods

206. How many vertebrae are there in the human spine?

a. 32-34
b. 29-31
c. 28-31
d. 26-30

207. When setting up for the bench press, which of the body positions below is NOT one of the five points of body contact?

a. Right foot is flat on the floor
b. Shoulders and upper back are on bench
c. Lower back is highly arched to increase spinal stability
d. Buttocks are firmly and evenly placed on bench

Copyright © Mometrix Media. You have been licensed one copy of this document for personal use only. Any other reproduction or redistribution is strictly prohibited. All rights reserved.
This content is provided for test preparation purposes only and does not imply an endorsement by Mometrix of any particular political, scientific, or religious point of view.

208. Addressing a muscular weakness, primarily as a contributor to a compound movement, would require the inclusion of what kind of movements?

a. Power
b. Isolation
c. Structural
d. Assistance

209. What is the primary factor for achieving maximal sprint velocities?

a. Stride length
b. Arm swing
c. Stride frequency
d. Length of recovery phase

210. During the second transition phase, a collegiate baseball player should engage in which of the following activities?

a. Motocross
b. High-intensity interval training
c. Lounging on the beach
d. Free swimming

211. What is an impulse with regard to speed and agility training, and how is this measured?

a. A shift in momentum as a result of force, (Impulse = Force x Time)
b. A shift in momentum as a result of force, (Impulse = Force/Time)
c. The rate of directional change as a result of force, (Impulse = Force x Time)
d. The rate of directional change as a result of force, (Impulse = Force/Time)

212. The feasibility study establishes what essential element for the strength and conditioning facility?

a. Determines facility demographics
b. Outlines services to be provided
c. Establishes total cost
d. Assesses existing locations for facility

213. When attempting to develop speed-endurance, what component of the training program must be considered to improve this specifically?

a. Total training time
b. Exercise relief patterns
c. Training volume
d. Training frequency

214. How can the strength and conditioning coach structure a training session to account for when the athlete is not performing at or near his normal capacities?

a. Use goal repetitions
b. Increase rest periods
c. Reduce training loads
d. Reduce number of exercises

Copyright © Mometrix Media. You have been licensed one copy of this document for personal use only. Any other reproduction or redistribution is strictly prohibited. All rights reserved.
This content is provided for test preparation purposes only and does not imply an endorsement by Mometrix of any particular political, scientific, or religious point of view.

215. From the list of plyometric drills listed below, determine the correct order they should be in from least demanding to most demanding.

I. Jumps over an object
II. Depth jump
III. Box jumps
IV. Vertical jump

a. I, II, III, IV
b. IV, I, III, II
c. IV, III, I, II
d. I, Iii, IV, II

216. A strength and conditioning coach is using a sequenced training model. What should the next training block emphasize if an athlete has just completed a block that emphasizes agility?

a. Strength
b. Stretch-shortening cycle
c. Power
d. Speed

217. Which of the athletes listed below would benefit MOST from a circuit training approach?

a. In-season basketball player
b. Marathon runner
c. Deconditioned football player
d. Off-season golfer

218. A triple jumper is completing training preparations for the World Championships in four weeks. What phase of preparation is the triple jumper in at this point in the training program?

a. Competition; maintenance
b. Competition; end preparation
c. Competition; peaking
d. Competition; transition preparation

219. What is one of the primary adaptations to energy production due to chronic aerobic exercise?

a. Increased mitochondria density in muscle tissue
b. Increased oxygen-carrying capacity of hemoglobin
c. Increased phosphate availability for ATP replenishment
d. Increased glycogen storage capacity

220. Balance between muscle groups is important when designing a training program. What possible negative outcomes are associated with poor muscle balance over the long term for an athlete?

a. Reduction in total body power
b. Increased injury rate
c. Poor work capacity
d. Decrease in athletic performance

Copyright © Mometrix Media. You have been licensed one copy of this document for personal use only. Any other reproduction or redistribution is strictly prohibited. All rights reserved.
This content is provided for test preparation purposes only and does not imply an endorsement by Mometrix of any particular political, scientific, or religious point of view.

Answer Key and Explanations for Test #2

1. D: Comparative strength analysis. A comparative strength analysis is not necessary or essential when initiating a training program, as a comparison of strength levels between two athletes does not provide important information when attempting to establish the core needs of an athlete before developing a training program. When performing an assessment on an individual athlete, the key elements to include are the needs analysis, movement and injury analysis, and evaluating training status and background, along with physiological assessments (strength, endurance, etc.).

2. C: Acetylcholine is the neurotransmitter responsible for inducing the release of sodium ions into the muscle cell that results in muscular contraction. Acetylcholine must accumulate in sufficient amounts at the neuromuscular junction for an action potential to be released onto the sarcolemma, resulting in a muscular contraction.

3. B: The athlete's foot must touch each line. During the pro-agility test, the athlete's foot must touch each line for the testing procedure to count. During this test, the athlete makes three separate changes in direction after a brief sprint. When attempting to run quickly, the athlete may stop short of the line, which means the strength and conditioning coach must be very attentive to the athlete's feet touching each line to qualify the time.

4. A: Preparatory routine. A preparatory routine is a process routine whereby an athlete undertakes specific steps to focus on a specific task. This routine allows an athlete to focus on an immediate task that effectively limits his exposure to negative elements that can negatively affect performance. This routine establishes a consistent approach to stressful situations and allows the athlete to perform consistently.

5. D: Increasing muscle mass will most heavily affect the body's response to insulin. The increase in muscle mass will increase the number of available receptors for the insulin to bind and will decrease blood glucose level at rest.

6. D: Potentiation. Potentiation is a neurophysiological response that increases the contractile capacity of muscles via alteration of the force-velocity curve due to stretch, which also increases neural drive to the working muscles. Potentiation functions to increase the muscles' capacity for force production by generating a reflexive response from the nervous system that can be used to decrease recruitment thresholds for fast-twitch muscle fibers that are necessary to perform strength exercises at or above maximal intensity levels. Using this combined training approach can result in immediate strength increases for a training session and significantly affect strength progression over the course of several weeks.

7. B: Compound set. An athlete needing to improve a muscular weakness or increase the size of a muscle group would benefit significantly in a brief period from using a compound set approach for the affected muscle. Performing multiple movements in sequence to target the muscle group will not require the body to respond to significantly greater stresses to the body, as this method is primarily oriented to forcing the muscle to work for longer periods of time, under limited recovery conditions between movements, to increase nutrient delivery to the training muscle. This increase in blood flow to the muscle will promote growth via increased local protein synthesis, and when coupled with heavier training methods in the early part of the training session will allow the athlete to meet the training goal within the four- to six-week training block.

Copyright © Mometrix Media. You have been licensed one copy of this document for personal use only. Any other reproduction or redistribution is strictly prohibited. All rights reserved.
This content is provided for test preparation purposes only and does not imply an endorsement by Mometrix of any particular political, scientific, or religious point of view.

8. D: The sarcoplasm functions similarly to the cytoplasm in other organisms, and serves as the primary storage site for glycogen, fats, mitochondria, etc. The sarcoplasm of a muscle fiber is analogous to the cytoplasm of other organisms, as it houses essential elements of muscular contraction, such as glycogen, fat, various enzymes, mitochondria, and the sarcoplasmic reticulum.

9. A: Gluconeogenesis is the process of proteins being broken down and converted into glucose for energy production. This is not a common occurrence and generally will only be seen in periods of starvation, extended periods of time with low to no carbohydrate consumption, and exercise bouts greater than 90 minutes.

10. C: Digestion is responsible for the breakdown of food to release the food's energy resources. Ingestion is the intake of food to begin the digestive process, whereas absorption is how the body makes use of the energy resources produced by digestion. Excretion is the elimination of waste that could not be utilized by absorption.

11. A: 50-60 percent. An athlete using 50-60 percent of his 1RM will be able to accelerate the barbell at the desired speeds of approximately 0.08 m/s to facilitate an increase in speed. This percentage of the 1RM is sufficiently heavy enough to require a high force output from the athlete without risking muscular failure, and allows for sufficient training volumes to develop the neurological consistency needed to increase the rate of signaling to the muscles to facilitate the increase in bar speed and over time speed in competition.

12. D: The shoulder joint is an example of a multiaxial joint. A multiaxial joint is a joint that can move in all three perpendicular axes. The other possible joints are uniaxial joints, which allow movement about one axis, and biaxial, which allows movement about two axes of motion.

13. C: The atrioventricular bundle is significant for maintaining the cardiac rhythm. Once the atrioventricular bundle has received the signal from the AV node, the signal is then transmitted to the left and right bundle branches. This signal is significant, as this is a point in conduction that occurs between the atria and ventricles, and is a key element in maintaining constant cardiac rhythm.

14. D: The bilateral deficit refers to a neural deficiency when performing bilateral movements that cause a reduction in total force produced bilaterally when compared to the total of force from a comparable unilateral movement.

15. A: The diffusion of CO_2 and O_2 through the alveoli in the lungs occurs according to a concentration gradient. The concentration gradient is formed by molecules from a higher-concentration region into a region with a lower concentration of molecules, which is dictated by the partial pressure of the gases as well as the concentrations in the capillaries and alveoli. Diffusion is a passive process driven by the motion of the molecules as they transition from regions of higher and lower concentration.

16. D: The sarcoplasmic reticulum is a system of tubules surrounding each myofibril and is responsible for pumping Ca+ ions into the muscle when an action potential releases onto the sarcomere. The sarcoplasmic reticulum is responsible for pumping calcium ions into the muscle to generate a contraction, but is also the site of calcium ion storage; without these essential functions, muscular contraction would not occur.

17. C: Increased hematocrit. Erythropoietin is a protein hormone that stimulates the production of red blood cells. The suggested mechanism for enhancing aerobic endurance performance is increasing hemoglobin levels, the result of increased hematocrit and decreased plasma volume. The

Copyright © Mometrix Media. You have been licensed one copy of this document for personal use only. Any other reproduction or redistribution is strictly prohibited. All rights reserved.
This content is provided for test preparation purposes only and does not imply an endorsement by Mometrix of any particular political, scientific, or religious point of view.

decrease in plasma volume is thought to be caused by downregulation of the rennin-angiotensin-aldosterone axis.

18. A: Pre-operation phase. The pre-operation phase, also known as the start-up phase, of facility planning is the three to four months before opening the facility when the selection and hiring for qualified staff members begins. This is also the period when staff development, in-service, and advanced credentialing standards should be put in place. This is the final stage in the facility planning process.

19. D: 6-8 repetition maximum. When training individuals with limited training experience, the most important component for testing is to ensure maximal safety and to perform the test in a way such that the result is useful for multiple loading intensities. This would require the strength and conditioning coach to use a repetition maximum that would be useful for moderate loading intensities while also being light enough to ensure technique and joint health are not compromised. In the provided example, using a 6-8 repetition maximum is the most effective and safest option for an athlete with limited training experience.

20. D: Lactate is a byproduct of anaerobic glycolysis. Lactate is considered to be a "waste" product and responsible for the "burning" sensation in muscle tissue during intense bouts of exercise. This may not be the case, as recent findings suggest the increased H^+ concentration in the blood is not caused by increased circulation of lactate in the blood, but instead by other mechanisms. Lactate is also used as a fuel source in specific tissues that include the heart and the brain.

21. C: The proper notation for blood pressure places the systolic phase (contraction) of the cardiac cycle over the diastolic (relaxation) phase, and normal blood pressure is considered to be 120 systolic pressure/80 diastolic pressure.

22. A: Upper/lower training split. An upper/lower split training approach will allow the athlete to gain the necessary lean mass in the upper torso, hamstring, and quadriceps because each session will have significantly higher volumes than if the athlete were to train using a total body approach. This body part split will also allow the athlete to use big compound movements, both structural and power movements, without interfering with the recovery of other muscle groups that may be involved in these exercises, as would be the case with a whole-body approach.

23. D: Increased pulmonary ventilation. The acute adaptations are an increase in pulmonary ventilation and cardiac output in both resting and exercising states. Acute adaptations are necessary to stabilize respiration and heart rate due to the decreased partial pressure of oxygen at altitude. Chronic adaptations to altitude training primarily affect cellular function, take place over four to six weeks, and stabilize after this period.

24. A: Duration and load-volume. The method for assessing training volume for an aerobic athlete is to track the duration of his training sessions as a measure of time. To correctly track training volume for a football player, a strength and conditioning coach must keep track of load-volume, which is the quantification of the amount of mechanical work performed by the athlete combined with the metabolic demands associated with that work.

25. D: A triceps extension is a movement pattern that is an example of a first-class lever.

26. B: Adenosine diphosphate is composed of adenine, ribose, and two molecules of inorganic phosphate. From this energy state, ADP can be converted into ATP with the addition of an inorganic phosphate group, which can be achieved through the creatine phosphate energy system.

Copyright © Mometrix Media. You have been licensed one copy of this document for personal use only. Any other reproduction or redistribution is strictly prohibited. All rights reserved.
This content is provided for test preparation purposes only and does not imply an endorsement by Mometrix of any particular political, scientific, or religious point of view.

27. B: Peanut butter. Peanut butter has a caloric density that is primarily derived from fats and fatty acids. The macronutrient composition of an item will determine whether the item is considered a protein, carbohydrate, or fat. This allows for foods that have a composite macronutrient makeup to be delineated based on the predominant macronutrient, for easy and proper categorical assignment.

28. B: Management and rehabilitation of injuries. The primary role of the athletic trainer is to manage and rehabilitate injuries resulting from training, competition, or other physical activity. The athletic trainer can also assign sport-specific exercises intended to prevent injuries, as well as apply prophylactic equipment for practice and competition to prevent injury or provide stability to an injured muscle or joint via bracing or taping.

29. B: Capillaries are the smallest division of the blood vessel and serve as part of the microvasculature. The role of the capillary is to exchange fluids, gases, nutrients, hormones, electrolytes, and other substances with the interstitial fluids from various tissues throughout the body.

30. C: ¼ squat. After reaching triple extension and completing the second pull, the athlete pulls the body under the bar and rotates the arms under and around the bar. At this point, the hips and knees are flexed to a quarter squat position. Once the bar reaches the clavicle and is stopped, the athlete stands from the quarter squat position, thus completing the lift. The quarter squat is preferred over the full catch position because of the inherent injury risks of performing a highly skilled movement pattern with inexperienced athletes. The ¼ squat offers significant benefits over the quarter squat catch position.

31. A: Complex training. An athlete who requires a high work capacity coupled with the ability to be explosive for brief periods of time will benefit most from using a complex training approach, as this will allow the athlete to use low-moderate plyometric activity during the in-season program to maintain explosive capacities and resistance train at sufficient levels to maintain strength. This type of training does not need to be high intensity to be effective, and can allow an athlete to sustain a high level of performance throughout a training season as long as the strength and conditioning coach closely monitors training volume and intensity.

32. D: The onset of blood lactate accumulation is the point at which exercise intensity causes lactate to accumulate in the blood of the participant or athlete at a rate faster than can be buffered. Two separate activities cause this, with the first being the release of H^+ ions into the blood because of the hydrolysis of ATP, and the second being a reduction of available bicarbonate in the blood due to increased physical activity.

33. A: 1:15. The correct ratio of strength and conditioning staff members (e.g., strength and conditioning director, assistant strength and conditioning coaches, and graduate assistants), in a secondary education setting is 1:15. This is established primarily due to the age of the participants, as they will be between 14 and 19 years of age, and the type of training in which the athletes will engage. The ratio for younger athletes to strength staff members at the middle school level is 1:10, while the ratio for university-aged athletes is 1:20, as the trend is for older athletes to require less supervision, as they will be of a higher training age and better suited to training independently due to familiarity with facility rules and avoiding possibly dangerous behaviors.

34. C: Oxidative phosphorylation will generate 40 molecules of ATP after two rotations through the Krebs cycle utilizing one molecule of glucose. This number is then reduced by the two molecules that are consumed during the process to give us 38 net ATP molecules.

Copyright © Mometrix Media. You have been licensed one copy of this document for personal use only. Any other reproduction or redistribution is strictly prohibited. All rights reserved.
This content is provided for test preparation purposes only and does not imply an endorsement by Mometrix of any particular political, scientific, or religious point of view.

35. A: Total body training. An athlete who is trying to improve her speed endurance or anaerobic training capacity would benefit most from engaging in a total body training routine that requires the athlete to train using big compound movements at every training session, most effectively using a superset model, and training frequently throughout the week. This approach would develop the resiliency needed for competition, and with proper movement and training load selection explosive power and strength will also increase significantly.

36. C: Adenosine triphosphate is the energy source that the human body requires to carry out endergonic reactions, i.e., muscular contraction. ATP is composed of an adenine group, a ribose group, and three molecules of inorganic phosphates.

37. A: 10 seconds to 120 seconds. Tests of local muscular endurance can persist for a few seconds to several minutes at a time depending on the amount of resistance that is being used for the testing procedure. Movement selection will affect the time this test will require from an athlete, as a pull-up will require less time than a barbell lunge at 50 percent loading intensity because the amount of work that is possible with each movement is significantly different.

38. C: Myofibrils are the internal structure of the muscle fiber (myocyte) and contain the long, thin chains of protein responsible for contraction of the muscle fiber. Myofibrils comprise long strands of the proteins actin, myosin, and titin. These proteins are arranged along the myofibril into thick and thin filaments, which are arranged into compartments known as sarcomeres. Muscle contraction takes place all along the myofibril as the actin filaments, also referred to as thin filaments, slide along the length of the myosin, also referred to as thick filaments, generating muscular contractions.

39. B: Include unilateral lower-body movements. Addressing a weakness that occurs on one side of the body is most effectively done by training that side of the body. In this example, adding in additional unilateral training volume will be sufficient to help improve the athlete's one-leg jumping ability. This will not create a deficiency in the right side, as both sides will be trained using this approach. Using a unilateral approach does not mean the elimination of bilateral training, as the athlete can continue to train these movement patterns. The strength and conditioning coach may simply add the unilateral training to the program or reduce the bilateral training volume to compensate for the added training volume from the unilateral movements.

40. B: The all-or-nothing principle specifically outlines that if an action potential is released onto the sarcolemma of a muscle, then a contraction will take place, and if there is no action potential present, then the muscle will not contract and remain relaxed. If there is enough action potential, the stimulus is strong enough to contract the muscle fiber. If there is insufficient stimulus, the muscle will not contract.

41. B: 6x6 at 85 percent. In the examples provided, the greatest metabolic stress would occur when the athlete performs 6x6 at 85 percent training load intensity. The total training volume is higher than the other possible selections, but is also trained with a higher training load intensity than the other options, which will require significantly more recovery time before training again. Understanding the relationship between physiological responses and the impact of training load intensity and volume is the key to resistance training programs.

42. B: The muscle fibers of the heart become stretched over time. The left-ventricle experiences the largest change, which allows for a greater end-diastolic volume. This morphological change over time increases the volume of blood ejected during exercise when increased oxygen uptake is essential for the working muscle tissues and athletic performance.

Copyright © Mometrix Media. You have been licensed one copy of this document for personal use only. Any other reproduction or redistribution is strictly prohibited. All rights reserved.
This content is provided for test preparation purposes only and does not imply an endorsement by Mometrix of any particular political, scientific, or religious point of view.

43. B: The QRS complex represents ventricular depolarization of the left and right ventricles. This complex is characterized by three separate components and may not be represented on all EKG tests, considering the brief duration of this segment in normal cardiac rhythm. This signal segment is much larger in amplitude than the P-wave because of the larger mass of the ventricles of the heart in comparison to the atria.

44. B: Training status. Determining an athlete's training status is the key element for determining training frequency. An athlete who does not have a significant training background will require fewer training sessions per week to facilitate improvements, while a more experienced and conditioned athlete will require greater frequency to stimulate progress.

45. C: A muscle will act as a synergist when it is involved indirectly in a movement pattern. A muscle that is acting as a synergist during a movement is acting to stabilize the agonists as force is produced or indirectly assisting in force production. A commonly cited example is any arm curling movement that requires multiple synergists to engage in the movement; assisting in the muscular contraction are the brachialis and brachioradialis muscles, but there are stabilizing muscles along the scapula that work to maintain structural integrity and generate force at the humerus and the scapula.

46. D: Testosterone affects muscular physiology via increased protein synthesis and increased growth hormone production in the pituitary glands. Testosterone can also affect central nervous system adaptations to resistance training by increasing neuronal receptor activity, increasing neurotransmitter activity and availability, and altering structural proteins that facilitate muscular contraction.

47. B: Gradual training load increases. Having a gradual and highly structured approach to training load increases throughout a training program will ensure consistent results and allow athletes to achieve their primary resistance training goals in each sport season. Using an approach such as the two-for-two rule provides structure for gradual training load increases by requiring the athlete to perform two additional repetitions at an assigned training load above the prescribed repetitions during the final set and being able to achieve this result in two consecutive training sessions. Once this has been achieved, the training load will increase.

48. B: Calculate the average of all 12 timers. The most effective approach for reporting the times to the athletes is to take the average of the 12 timers, because the sample size is small and removing any score will affect the accuracy of the reporting, as the differences between the lowest and highest score should be minimal at best. Scores should not be removed unless they are off by more than a second when compared to the other scores, which could indicate user error during measurement.

49. C: A tendon is a fibrous connective tissue made primarily of collagen that connects muscle to bone via the bone periosteum. The tendon bridges the muscle and bone together facilitating movement throughout the body. Ligaments are also dense fibrous connective tissue that connects bone to bone to hold a joint together. Myocyte is another term used for a muscle cell or muscle fiber. Cartilage is a flexible connective tissue found in numerous joints, including the knee, elbow, and rib cage. Cartlidge is more rigid than muscle tissue and absorbs force well, but is less rigid than bone.

50. C: 82 percent. An athlete training in the 80 percent loading intensity range should generally be able to perform eight repetitions. Using a percentage of the 1-repetition maximum chart will provide significant guidance for assigning training load intensities when working in specific

Copyright © Mometrix Media. You have been licensed one copy of this document for personal use only. Any other reproduction or redistribution is strictly prohibited. All rights reserved.
This content is provided for test preparation purposes only and does not imply an endorsement by Mometrix of any particular political, scientific, or religious point of view.

repetition ranges. For example, an athlete can be assigned to use a training load intensity prescription of 75-83 percent when assigned 7-10 repetitions per set, according to the 1-repetition maximum chart.

51. B: Allosteric binding sites allow for substances other than hormones to bind to a receptor to increase or decrease responses to the primary hormone. This allows for feedback loops to maintain tight control over the endocrine system, which is essential for maintaining homeostasis over time and adjusting to changes when necessary.

52. D: 4-6 training sessions per week. During the off-season training program, an athlete should be training as frequently as possible, with four sessions per week being the bare minimum. More experienced athletes should train more frequently to stimulate progress, as training frequency is one of the key elements for athlete development in a resistance training program as the athlete matures in training age and experience. The other aspect in consideration is the lack of other activities to distract from the training program, as there are no sport-specific activities the athlete is engaging in and recovery from session to session can be maximized because energy is solely directed to the training program.

53. C: As many repetitions as possible, performed continuously, until failure. The American College of Sports Medicine standard for the push-up assessment is for the participant to perform as many repetitions as possible in a continuous fashion until failure. There is no time consideration for the testing procedure, and it is simply a test of local muscle endurance in the chest, shoulders, and triceps.

54. A: Golgi tendon organs are responsible for inhibiting tension overload in muscle and tendons when placed under stretch. The GTO achieves this by emitting electrical signals from its sensory neuron to an inhibitory neuron in the spinal cord, which inhibits the motor neuron in the same muscle. This signaling process is very rapid and leads to an immediate reduction in tension within the muscle, preventing excessive loading injuries and even reactive stress injuries.

55. D: Overtraining. Overtraining is not considered part of the general adaptation syndrome. The general adaptation syndrome consists of three-stages: alarm, resistance, and exhaustion. A fourth component can be identified as supercompensation, which can be included after the resistance phase. Overtraining can be considered a symptom of the exhaustion phase of the general adaptation syndrome.

56. B: Ideal performance state; the athlete is relaxed, focused, and confident. The ideal performance state, or "zone," occurs when an athlete can relax, focus, and engage in the competitive activity with joy and confidence, as this allows for the body to respond rapidly and without hesitation.

57. C: Bradycardia is an arrhythmia that is indicated by a resting heart rate below 60 beats per minute. A normal heart rate falls between 60 and 100 beats per minute. Another type of arrhythmia is indicated when resting heart rate is over 100 beats per minute and is known as tachycardia.

58. C: Troponin is the protein responsible for initiating muscular contraction, as this is the location where actin and myosin sites bind forming the cross bridges necessary for contraction to occur. Calcium ions are responsible for initiating the movement of troponin from the myosin binding site, initiating a conformational change. Once this takes place, the myosin cross bridge can be carried out, and muscular contraction can occur.

59. D: I, III, and IV. The proper starting position for the snatch exercise requires the athlete to have feet either hip or shoulder width apart, the hips down below the shoulders, a grip that is wider than

Copyright © Mometrix Media. You have been licensed one copy of this document for personal use only. Any other reproduction or redistribution is strictly prohibited. All rights reserved.
This content is provided for test preparation purposes only and does not imply an endorsement by Mometrix of any particular political, scientific, or religious point of view.

the snatch rings, elbows fully extended, and feet flat on the floor. The body is positioned with the back flat or slightly arched, chest held up and out, head in line with the vertebral column, heels on the floor, shoulders over or slightly in front of the bar, and eyes focused straight ahead or slightly upward.

60. D: Preserve strength and performance levels. The primary focus of the competition period is to maintain the strength and performance levels attained throughout the training program and carry them through the competitive season. Performing a maintenance schedule, as opposed to a peaking schedule, requires the athlete to train using structural and power exercises with moderate training loads and training volumes to sustain performance.

61. D: Compound movements affecting large muscle groups, coupled with higher loading intensities, will result in the highest growth hormone release.

62. C: Testing in similar conditions. To accurately collect testing data over a period, testing conditions must be similar to the original testing period. Adverse testing conditions will affect the athlete being tested, e.g., extreme hot/cold or rainy weather, as will testing on different ground surfaces. Another element for testing is to make sure that the athlete is properly hydrated and properly fed, i.e., not fasted or recently fed. Testing conditions should closely resemble each other as much as possible.

63. C: Type IIb fibers are considered "fast" glycolytic, produce large amounts of force, and possess the greatest capacity for hypertrophy. Type IIb fibers primarily function in high-force, explosive-type movements because of the force generation capacities they possess. This fiber has minimal involvement in moderate duration movements past the initial effort, usually 5-8 seconds, and virtually no impact on sustained muscular contractions and endurance-related efforts.

64. C: I, III, IV, II. The correct hierarchy for developing speed and agility is making sure to properly orient the methodology, which means establishing the primary, secondary, and tertiary methods for inclusion in the program. This would place primary methods first, which consist of sprint and agility training to acquire the correct technical skill and develop the basic patterns first in the training program. Secondary methods would include using specialized techniques to develop acceleration, maximal velocity, or other special skills, and utilizing sprint assistance or sprint resistance techniques to achieve this end. The tertiary methods for developing an athlete's sprint and agility capacities would include mobility, strength, and endurance training.

65. C: Muscle spindle. A muscle spindle is responsible for providing feedback to motor neurons of the spine when a sudden stretching action occurs. After the signal is sent from the muscle spindle to the motor neuron of the spine, the motor neuron then generates a muscular action of the stretched muscle. This is a response arch that occurs as part of the stretch reflex.

66. B: Varied training load intensity. The purpose of altering training loads and volumes over the course of a training program is to allow for adequate recovery of the muscles and central nervous system to avoid entering an over trained state. The strength and conditioning coach can avoid overtraining the athlete or athletes by reducing and rotating training loads of other training sessions after a "heavy" training session, i.e., "light" and "moderate," to facilitate recovery while sustaining training frequency and volumes. Rotating the loading parameters between light, heavy, and moderate can be used for a variety of training goals and frequencies, while also serving as a method for addressing the physical stress of practice or competition by applying this concept.

67. C: Flexibility to eccentric strength. Correctly developing the necessary flexibility and strength capacities to return to training and competition is essential during the remodeling phase of injury

Copyright © Mometrix Media. You have been licensed one copy of this document for personal use only. Any other reproduction or redistribution is strictly prohibited. All rights reserved.
This content is provided for test preparation purposes only and does not imply an endorsement by Mometrix of any particular political, scientific, or religious point of view.

recovery. The proper procedure for returning an athlete to normal training includes transitioning from an emphasis on flexibility to developing eccentric strength in the affected muscle to ensure the injured muscle's ability to load without creating too much stress in the injured tissues.

68. A: Actin is the thin filament, is arranged in a double helix shape, and serves as the binding site for myosin that, with the hydrolysis of ATP, generates a power stroke where the actin will slide past the myosin filament. The movement of actin and myosin is the basis of the sliding filament theory of muscular contraction.

69. C: Increasing deadlift from 405 lbs. to 415 lbs. When setting resistance training goals, the most important factor is ensuring that the final resistance training goal is attainable in the current sport season. In the example provided, the desire to add 15 lbs. to the deadlift is a reasonable goal in the allotted period for the off-season training period. This goal, unlike the others provided, will not require the athlete to engage in any special behaviors or to access substances or specialized training methods to obtain it.

70. D: The sarcolemma is essential in conducting and receiving stimuli from the connecting nerve fibers. The ability of the sarcolemma to transduce electrical signal allows the t-tubules that run from side to side throughout the sarcolemma to release Ca^{2+} ions into the sarcoplasm. The sarcolemma is the cell membrane of striated muscle tissue and is responsible for the separation of each muscle fiber.

71. B: End of the competition year. A full review of the strength and conditioning program should take place at the end of the competitive year, as the post-season period will consist of little training for the athletes, other than general sport activity, and the next competitive season will not begin until the off-season training program begins again. The strength and conditioning coach should evaluate athlete progress over the course of each sport season. A full qualitative review is not required until the end of the competitive season.

72. A: Somatic anxiety. Somatic anxiety is a form of anxiety that causes physical manifestations the person cannot determine the cause of, e.g., butterflies in the stomach before a soccer match. Somatic anxiety can have either positive or a negative impact on performance, as this is dependent on the mental capacity of the person experiencing this type of anxiety. Some athletes can perform under high levels of somatic stress, and others are unable to overcome the stress response and will perform poorly.

73. B: II, I, IV, III. The proper order in the example provided is to do the pro-agility test first, as this test relies on coordinated movement and therefore should occur first before the accumulation of excessive fatigue due to the other testing procedures such as the 110-meter sprint. The 1-RM squat test would occur next, as this is a maximum strength and power test, and likewise, must not occur after a test that accumulates excessive fatigue like the 110-meter sprint test. The 110-meter sprint test would occur next in the battery because this test requires the athlete to achieve maximal velocity; this test should not be placed after a test of local endurance, as fatigue accumulation would affect the testing procedure. The final test in the battery would be the local endurance test, as this test will accrue the highest localized muscular fatigue and would affect the other testing procedures if conducted before the alternatives. Proper testing order in a battery of tests is important, as activities that utilize differing energy systems or require significant levels of movement coordination create different types of fatigue that will limit performance on other tests when not sequenced correctly.

Copyright © Mometrix Media. You have been licensed one copy of this document for personal use only. Any other reproduction or redistribution is strictly prohibited. All rights reserved.
This content is provided for test preparation purposes only and does not imply an endorsement by Mometrix of any particular political, scientific, or religious point of view.

74. B: The A-band contains actin and myosin filaments. The A-band does not move during muscular contraction, while the I-bands and H-zones shorten. The H-zone is a part of the A-band located in the center of the sarcomere where only myosin filaments occur. The I-band is an area that only consists of thin filaments, and is made up of two adjacent sarcomeres. The Z-line occurs in the middle of the I-band and appears as a line running lengthwise throughout.

75. C: Metabolic energy. Physical work is simply the force needed to move an object one meter (work = force x displacement). When assessing the work performed by an athlete, the amount of metabolic energy required to perform the work prescribed must be considered because the metabolic stress placed on the athlete will require sufficient time for recovery and regeneration across multiple physiological systems.

76. B: Negligence. Negligence refers to the failure of an individual to respond in a situation in an expected, logical manner as a person with similar training and background would respond under proximal circumstances. The importance of clearly outlining the emergency care plan is to establish the responsibilities and expectations of the staff members in the training facility. This can significantly mitigate problems that could arise regarding negligence or violation of the standard-of-care expectations for people who should have the essential knowledge and understanding of how to handle challenging emergency situations.

77. A: Muscle spindle. The muscle spindle is the primary proprioceptive feedback structure in the muscle and the most important component in the stretch reflex response. The muscle spindle senses when a rapid stretch is applied to a muscle and reflexively contracts, which serves to potentiate the force-generating capacity of the muscle as well.

78. D: Bronchioles are found in both the conduction and respiration zones. The respiratory bronchioles are responsible for approximately 10 percent of gas exchange during respiration. The division of the terminal bronchioles represents the end of the conduction zone in human respiration and can be identified with the occurrence of alveoli, which represents the beginning of the respiration zone.

79. D: During anaerobic glycolysis, the energy system that is active when oxygen is not readily available, the pyruvate molecule will undergo fermentation, via lactate dehydrogenase and coenzyme NADH, to lactate to produce sufficient ATP. If oxygen is present, then aerobic glycolysis will take place through oxidative phosphorylation, which requires pyruvate to enter the mitochondrion of a cell and then, when oxygen is present, is oxidized and enters the Krebs cycle.

80. B: 75-85 percent, 3-5 repetitions. An athlete who is training for repetitive explosive bouts in competition will need to train at a sufficient threshold to develop the power capacity required, but will also need to do so in a moderate fashion to be able to perform the activity at a high level over time. Training in the 75-85 percent loading intensity range meets the first requirement of using a training load that will require the athlete to move with great force and velocity, and the 3-5 repetitions per set is a sufficient amount of work per set to develop the capacity to produce large force and velocity consistently over a period.

81. B: The sarcolemma is essential in conducting and receiving stimuli from the connecting nerve fibers. The ability of the sarcolemma to transduce electrical signal allows the t-tubules that run from side to side throughout the sarcolemma to release $Ca2+$ ions into the sarcoplasm.

82. B: The endomysium encapsulates each muscle fiber. The perimysium is a layer of connective tissue that groups individual muscle fibers into fascicles. The epimysium is a sheath of dense

Copyright © Mometrix Media. You have been licensed one copy of this document for personal use only. Any other reproduction or redistribution is strictly prohibited. All rights reserved.
This content is provided for test preparation purposes only and does not imply an endorsement by Mometrix of any particular political, scientific, or religious point of view.

connective tissue that covers the entire muscle, including the perimysium and endomysium, and is continuous with the fascia.

83. A: Decrease training load intensity. When preparing to start the pre-season training phase, the strength and conditioning coach does not need to alter his training program significantly from the off-season program. The primary consideration for transitioning into the pre-season phase of the training program is to decrease the training load intensity, as this will allow the athlete to begin to put more energy into sport- and practice-related activities and not negatively affect recovery rates. This change will also reduce the risk of injury heading into the period when the athlete is preparing most heavily for the competitive season, which is about six to eight weeks away when the pre-season is initiated.

84. C: Cross-training. An endurance athlete engaging in alternate methods from event-specific training is considered cross-training. Cross-training for brief training segments in a competition year can assist with the recovery from injury or with general recovery during intense periods of competition preparation. Breaking up training segments allows the muscles to be trained in various ways and provides relief to joints that may be overexposed to stress from preparation for competition.

85. D: Suprailiac, triceps. When testing body composition in high-school-aged female athletes, the test requires that the measurement be taken at the suprailiac and triceps sites. For high-school-aged male athletes, the testing procedure calls for the measurement to be taken at the thigh and subscapular sites. These sites allow for consistent measurement and fall in line with where young men and women from an athletic population will typically store fat.

86. C: I and II. The Valsalva maneuver is appropriate to use with athletes who have been properly trained on movement skill and execution, and those who have substantial training experience. Secondarily, structural exercises that load the spine will require the use of the Valsalva maneuver in some cases to stabilize the spine properly when under heavy training loads. It is important to note that the Valsalva maneuver can lead to a loss of consciousness and requires extreme caution.

87. A: Creatine kinase is an enzyme that potentiates the activity of the replenishment of ATP molecules for energy utilization in the phosphagen system. Creatine kinase elevation in serum blood tests is indicative of muscle damage, whether from a heart attack, kidney failure, or rhabdomyolysis.

88. D: The oxidative system is the primary energy production system at rest and during low-intensity exercise. This system can utilize all three macronutrients as substrate but is predominantly oriented to using fats while at rest (~70 percent) and carbohydrates during low to moderate exercise intensities. Proteins can be broken down into amino acids and then converted to glucose via gluconeogenesis, but this is not a common occurrence and generally will only be seen in periods of starvation and exercise bouts greater than 90 minutes.

89. B: Establishing a baseline of conditioning. The primary focus of the preparation phase is to establish an initial level of conditioning for the athlete, as this will prepare the athlete for upcoming training phases that require higher intensity loading and higher training volumes. The preparatory phase is highlighted by lower training load intensities and higher training volumes, and no sport-specific or skill training. This phase is strictly intended as a developmental stage for future training phases.

90. C: Skill acquisition and neuromuscular control. Considerations for younger athletes include emphasizing fun, the development of proper technical movement patterns, neuromuscular control,

Copyright © Mometrix Media. You have been licensed one copy of this document for personal use only. Any other reproduction or redistribution is strictly prohibited. All rights reserved.
This content is provided for test preparation purposes only and does not imply an endorsement by Mometrix of any particular political, scientific, or religious point of view.

and anaerobic skills necessary to participate in athletic endeavors. Younger athletes will require progression from simple movement skills to more complex skills over time, and consideration for development in the areas of power, strength, and other measurable elements will benefit from the time spent developing proper movement skill and technique execution.

91. A: The oxygen deficit refers to the early initial contributions of the anaerobic energy systems during a bout of exercise until a steady state of oxygen consumption is achieved. Oxygen debt refers to the increased rate of oxygen above resting rates after an intense bout of exercise.

92. B: Non-linear periodization. Using a non-linear periodization model allows the strength and conditioning coach to vary training load intensities and training volumes according to the competition schedule, as there may be significant gaps between events that allow an athlete to increase intensity and training volume for a two- to three-week period in a peaking strategy of sorts to perform above previous competitions. This could also be used in a sport with weekly competitions, e.g., a collegiate football or gymnastics program, as this would allow the strength and conditioning coach to evaluate the needs of the athlete based on the difficulty of the upcoming meet or game and prescribe training volumes and training load intensities accordingly. This approach also allows for significant variation during each training week, as training loads intensity and training volume can be altered day to day if desired.

93. B: Performing resistance exercises, such as barbell movements. Mechanical loading causes osteoblasts to move toward the surface of a bone to begin modeling new bone matrix along the spaces between bone cells, which occurs primarily on the surface of the bone to increase bone density and overall strength.

94. B: I, IV, III, II. The strength and conditioning coach must first consider the needs of the athlete, and in this case, the athlete is a broad jumper and will rely most heavily on the posterior chain to propel the body forward and to spring into action out and across the ground. The selected movements will develop the posterior chain sufficiently and will facilitate improvements in jumping distance. The proper training order must be from most demanding and complex to the least demanding and complex. The correct order for the selection given is power clean, deadlift, reverse hyperextension, and hamstring curl.

95. D: An athlete squatting 450 lbs. in a work set. An athlete performing a squat with 450 lbs. should utilize multiple spotters to protect against injury if the lift is missed. While a 225-lbs. maximum repetition test could require multiple spotters, the loading is not sufficient to command multiple spotters.

96. D: Sports physical therapist. The strength and conditioning coach will have most frequent contact with the sports physical therapist or the athletic trainer. Communication between members of the medical team is essential, and the strength and conditioning coach must stay in frequent contact with the sports physical therapist or athletic trainer. Players of any sport will have injuries, and communicating the athlete's needs is of greatest importance, not just to be able to play in the next game, but also for the athlete to effectively heal and strengthen the affected joint or muscle.

97. A: The neuromuscular junction is the central communication point for the nervous and musculoskeletal systems that lead to muscular contraction. This is the translation point for the nervous system signal (electrical) that is converted into a biochemical reaction and then into movement (mechanical).

98. A: Neurological recovery. Neurological recovery is not a primary emphasis in tapering methods, as tapering involves planned technique work and gradually reducing the training duration and

Copyright © Mometrix Media. You have been licensed one copy of this document for personal use only. Any other reproduction or redistribution is strictly prohibited. All rights reserved.
This content is provided for test preparation purposes only and does not imply an endorsement by Mometrix of any particular political, scientific, or religious point of view.

intensities. The nervous system, due to the repetitive nature of aerobic endurance training, is not taxed as heavily as it is for anaerobic power athletes, and neurological fatigue will not play a significant role in the success or failure of an aerobic athlete's competitive season. Allowing for joint/muscle recovery, rehydrating, and increasing glycogen stores are of greater importance to the aerobic endurance athlete.

99. A: Steroid hormones are fat-soluble and secreted from the gonads and adrenal cortex. Steroid hormones are generally derived from cholesterol and can actively bind to specific receptor sites in specific body tissues, in line with the traditional lock-in-key theory modeling of hormonal interactions.

100. C: Variability. Using variability to assess a large statistical sample is the best approach to evaluating the effectiveness of the program for the total group sample. Standard deviation will separate the data, if the data is normal, which is most probable, according to the best and least responsive to the training program. This will clearly provide insight into the global effectiveness of the program, but not on an individual basis. A program may have some very poor performers, e.g., college freshman with little training experience, who make substantial progress but are still considered below average according to a variability analysis.

101. C: Strength, speed, balance, technique. Before initiating a plyometric training program, an athlete must be assessed for sufficient balance, strength, and speed while also possessing an understanding of proper plyometric technique. These are mandatory elements that must be present before initiating a plyometric training program to reduce the risk of injury, as plyometric movements are high-force, high-velocity movements that carry significant risk if performed incorrectly or with athletes who are not adequately prepared to perform these exercises.

102. D: Isolation movement. When addressing structural weaknesses or a size deficiency in smaller muscle groups, using isolation movements will address the weakness directly. A smaller muscle group will need direct training stimulus to improve neural integration and recruitment patterns, and isolation work will allow the athlete to focus on contracting the weak muscle group and developing the ability to contract the muscle group maximally when using compound movements.

103. A: Limited stretch-reflex response. Trunk plyometrics do not necessarily function the exact same way as upper- and lower-body plyometrics, and this is due to limited stretch-reflex response. The muscles of the trunk do not effectively store elastic energy, which limits the capacity of the trunk musculature to generate reactive force. Research findings suggest that slow response times and lower movement velocities result from the distance between the trunk musculature and the spinal cord.

104. C: Knee. A female athlete is at higher risk for knee injuries, most likely due to the angle of the hip to the knee that is caused due to a widening of the hips at adolescence. Other factors that may be involved in the increased occurrence of knee injuries in women could be the overall increased participation of women in sports, the use of ankle braces, joint laxity, neuromuscular deficiencies, lack of coordination and movement skill, or hormonal changes.

105. C: The duration, or total training time, will determine the energy systems utilized during a training session. The body's ability to use multiple energy systems to meet the specific needs of an individual fall within a finite period for each system, e.g., the phosphagen system persists for approximately six to eight seconds, while aerobic glycolysis can produce energy for several hours.

106. D: Tendon. The series elastic component (SEC) of the stretch-shortening cycle is the most important component of the mechanical model of muscle function. The SEC is predominantly

Copyright © Mometrix Media. You have been licensed one copy of this document for personal use only. Any other reproduction or redistribution is strictly prohibited. All rights reserved.
This content is provided for test preparation purposes only and does not imply an endorsement by Mometrix of any particular political, scientific, or religious point of view.

focused on the role of the tendons and the capacity of the tendon to store and release elastic energy in response to a rapid stretching action.

107. B: Assessing injuries. The strength and conditioning coach is not involved in the assessment of injuries during either a competition or a training session. The strength and conditioning coach should never provide medical advice, as this is not within his scope of responsibilities or the scope of his training and education. In case of an emergency, the strength and conditioning coach can provide CPR/AED or first-aid support until medical personnel arrives. This is a legal issue, and the delineation of medical responsibilities falls to those licensed to perform such activities by the state of issuance.

108. B: Metabolic acidosis refers to a condition that occurs when the body produces too much acid. This condition in athletes is induced by intense bouts of exercise that causes a rapid decrease in blood pH due to increased H^+ ions in the blood. This response can be indicative of the current training capacities of an athlete or group of athletes, but can also be used to determine proper training intensity levels.

109. D: Repetition training. Repetition training is a training approach that requires an athlete to train above her VO_2 max using an interval approach, with each interval lasting between 30 and 90 seconds. Repetition training relies heavily on anaerobic metabolism, which will benefit the athlete's running economy, faster running speeds, and increased working capacity at higher intensity levels. Training in this manner will allow the athlete to finish races more effectively or with a better finishing kick.

110. A: The sinoatrial node generates the electrical signals that contract the heart and is commonly referred to as the pacemaker for this reason. The SA node is located in the right atrium. The sinoatrial node establishes the normal heart rhythm, which is referred to as the sinus rhythm.

111. A: Include horizontal and vertical pulling exercises in all three training sessions. For the strength and conditioning coach to achieve training balance when performing specific movement patterns, the opposite muscles must be trained at sufficient training volumes. This does not require a one-to-one ratio, but in the provided example performing upper- and middle-back exercises during each session will only serve as a positive for developing the strength and joint stability for the athlete to reach the primary resistance goal.

112. D: The sympathetic nervous system is responsible for the "fight or flight" response in humans, as this response causes a release of adrenaline and norepinephrine, which causes increased rate of respiration, elevates heart rate, raises mental focus, increases body temperature, etc. This system is of key importance in preparation for a competition, as a strength and conditioning coach must maintain a high level of activity, increase performance, and develop specific work capacities for competition without overworking the sympathetic and central nervous systems.

113. D: Complex training. Complex training is combining a reactive stretch-shortening cycle exercise, such as a depth jump for height, and a traditional strength exercise in a similar movement pattern, such as the squat. Utilizing a complex training method, the athlete will benefit from the manipulation of the stretch-shortening cycle by increasing power via elastic energy recovery, increased movement efficiency, and rate of neural signaling through feedback and impulse strength.

114. D: 150-meter sprint. The best test to assess an athlete's speed is the 150-meter sprint. When assessing an athlete's maximal speed, the testing procedure requires a straight line on a flat surface, with the final distance not surpassing the 200-meter mark. The reasoning behind limiting the distance of the testing procedure is because going beyond 200 meters becomes a test of anaerobic

Copyright © Mometrix Media. You have been licensed one copy of this document for personal use only. Any other reproduction or redistribution is strictly prohibited. All rights reserved.
This content is provided for test preparation purposes only and does not imply an endorsement by Mometrix of any particular political, scientific, or religious point of view.

capacity and not straight-line maximal velocity. The additional distance violates the purpose and focus of the testing procedure.

115. B: The type I fibers are slow oxidative fibers (i.e., slow-twitch) that are primarily engaged in long-duration activities, as these fibers produce low levels of force and are fatigue resistant. Type IIa fibers are considered fast oxidative and glycolytic, are "fast twitch," produce medium amounts of force, and are highly fatigue resistant. Type IIb are considered fast glycolytic, are "fast twitch," produce large amounts of force, and are rapidly fatigued.

116. B: Higher-intensity activities increase the surface area of the neuromuscular junction and the length of nerve terminal branching, and increase and disperse more widely the available synapse locations. These alterations in morphology indicate that with anaerobic training, neural transmission can be improved.

117. D: The sarcomere is the location of contractile proteins within a skeletal muscle. The sarcomere is the basic unit of a muscle fiber, containing the contractile proteins actin and myosin. The sarcomere occurs between two Z-lines and provides the striated appearance of skeletal and cardiac muscle. Sarcomeres occur throughout the entire length of a muscle fiber. All muscular contractions take place within the sarcomere.

118. B: Diastole is the phase of the cardiac cycle where relaxation of the ventricles and atria allows for the heart to fill with blood. Diastole is marked as the lowest measured pressure during measurement, as the ventricles and atria of the heart are collectively relaxed to allow for the chambers to fill with blood.

119. B: The parasympathetic nervous system is responsible for relaxation, or periods of decreased activity levels that govern various passive activities such as digestion. A high activity level in this division of the autonomic nervous system would be detrimental to competition because this system decreases mental acuity, focus, heart rate, and other physiological processes that need to be at heightened activity levels to respond to the competitive environment.

120. D: Myosin ATPase, like other enzymes, is involved in a specific chemical reaction. Myosin ATPase is responsible for catalyzing the actomyosin cross bridging response in muscular contraction.

121. C: Negative punishment. This is a form of reinforcement that removes something that is highly desirable, in this case playing time, to deter the negative behavior. Negative punishment is the antithesis of positive reinforcement, and is the most easily understood and applied method for behavior deterrence.

122. D: I, III, and IV only. Differentiating between open- and closed-chain movements is important when assigning exercises to injured individuals. This is because exercise selection should follow a natural development path as the athlete heals and can produce greater force through a joint. It should begin with an open-chain movement, which can typically be performed on a machine or with dumbbells to allow free joint movement but also control the amount of resistance being used to promote the desired training effect. Closed-chain movements tend to be big compound movements that allow for large forces to be produced using free weights, e.g., squats, deadlifts, or overhead presses. The key is understanding when to use a closed- or open-chain movement in an injured player's programming to the greatest benefit for the athlete.

123. A: Strength allows an athlete to overcome increased resistance generated on the body as acceleration occurs. The ability to overcome the force of gravity as movement velocity increases via

Copyright © Mometrix Media. You have been licensed one copy of this document for personal use only. Any other reproduction or redistribution is strictly prohibited. All rights reserved.
This content is provided for test preparation purposes only and does not imply an endorsement by Mometrix of any particular political, scientific, or religious point of view.

greater force production through increased muscular contraction is essential for developing maximal linear speed, but also significant for decelerating, changing directions, or leaping.

124. A: Maintain strength and endurance in adjacent muscles. Training during the inflammatory phase is not a forbidden activity, but the training should be limited to the healthy joints and muscles. This may require using a body part split to avoid excessive loading in the injured area, e.g., squatting with a leg or hip injury. The key is to work to maintain strength and endurance at sufficient levels such that once the athlete is cleared to return to training or competitive activities, the athlete will not be as far away from being in the required shape as he would be if he were not to engage in any training at all.

125. C: An EKG is used to assess the electrical signals generated during polarization and depolarization of cardiac tissue, which provides insight into the overall function and health of an athlete's heart. This test assesses the rate and frequency of the heartbeats while also determining the size and position of the heart's chambers. Assessing cardiovascular health in athletes is of extreme importance when considering issues like left ventricular hypertrophy, congenital heart defects, or other cardiac rhythm distortions that may cause health complications or even sudden death.

126. C: Human growth hormone levels significantly increase when utilizing higher loading intensity (10 RM) and brief rest periods (60 seconds or less). This increase is likely caused by a combination of the increase in oxygen utilization in muscle tissues from the reduced resting period as well as the increased rate of protein turnover from the training load intensity.

127. B: Elbow to Elbow. The preferred methods of assessing the correct grip width for the snatch lift is to measure from elbow-to-elbow or fist-to-opposite shoulder. Either approach is acceptable. Taller or longer-armed lifters benefitting from the fist-to-opposite shoulder method as this accounts for the longer ulnae that will cause the lifter to have a longer transition phase from second pull to overhead resulting in more energy and effort expended. Shorter stature and armed lifters will benefit from the elbow-to-elbow approach.

128. C: Plasticity. Muscular plasticity is the capacity of a muscle to be gradually stretched to achieve a new and greater length after a passive or static stretching action. This allows for the stiffness in the athlete's hamstring to be reduced to manageable levels to facilitate a high level of performance and reduce apprehensions of sustaining an injury. Elasticity is the ability to return to a specific resting length after a passive stretching action.

129. C: Muscular force is a mechanical reaction to biochemical stimuli or the response of an uncontrolled reaction in non-contractile tissues, e.g., excessive ligament or tendon stretching. Muscular force is the means of producing adequate forces required to produce a wide range of locomotion, which includes low-velocity activities such as walking or typing on a keyboard, as well as high-velocity movements such as sprinting or jumping. Resistive force refers to an external resistance acting on the body that is acting in opposition to the muscle forces.

130. D: Sarcopenia is a reduction of the skeletal muscle in older adults and results as part of the aging process and a sedentary lifestyle. The most pronounced reduction in muscular function in adults experiencing sarcopenia is found in the lower limb and trunk extensors.

131. C: Eccentric, amortization, concentric. After an athlete contacts the ground, the agonist muscles are preloaded, storing elastic energy, and stimulate the muscle spindle (eccentric). After the muscles are preloaded, and the energy has been stored, there is a momentary pause in muscle action (amortization). If the amortization phase is brief, then the greater the stored energy release

Copyright © Mometrix Media. You have been licensed one copy of this document for personal use only. Any other reproduction or redistribution is strictly prohibited. All rights reserved.
This content is provided for test preparation purposes only and does not imply an endorsement by Mometrix of any particular political, scientific, or religious point of view.

will be, but if this phase is too long, then the energy will be significantly less. The final phase (concentric) occurs when the stored energy is released at the same time as the contraction of the affected muscles, which increases the force of the movement or is dissipated as heat.

132. C: This recruitment pattern is established based on the relationship of the twitch force, size of the motor unit, and the recruitment threshold for each motor unit. This means that smaller, lower-force, fatigue-resistant units will contract first when movement is initiated; once the threshold for the larger units is reached, they will then contract.

133. B: The phosphagen system relies on the hydrolysis of ATP from local muscle stores, as well as on the breakdown of creatine phosphate. This system is active during bouts of intense, brief exercise that includes heavy resistance exercises and short, intense sprints. This system is active during all activities at the outset, but is active for a short time before other systems become the primary energy resource depending on the duration of exercise.

134. A: Stress fracture. Stress fractures are the most common type of fracture among athletes, due to the high forces generated repetitively during practices, training sessions, and competition. Stress fractures will also most often occur when training volume suddenly increases, or an athlete accumulates significant training stress on hard training or competitive surfaces.

135. A: Reaction time. Reaction time is specific to an athlete's ability to respond to external stimuli, e.g., visual or auditory, and to respond in an appropriate manner. This element of athletic competency is not easily trained because much of this response is governed by how quickly information is relayed to the CNS and then translated to a response, and this will vary from individual to individual. Reactive time can be altered via manipulation of the stretch-shortening cycle by performing reactive-explosive movements as part of a training program.

136. B: I and III. The process that should be undertaken when an athlete or member of the strength and conditioning facility violates a rule for the first time requires the staff member to provide a verbal warning to the member and an explanation of the rule. This verbal reprimand should also include a reminder of the disciplinary action that will be taken for a second offense.

137. B: Ballistic stretch. Ballistic stretching requires an athlete to be moving or producing muscular force/movement and requires a rhythmic bouncing action at the end position. This is a dangerous practice due to the activation of the stretch reflex generated by the bouncing action at the end position, as this extends the range of motion after each repetition and can result in damage to the connective and soft tissues of the joint and muscle. Activating the stretch reflex during stretching activities negates the purpose of stretching the tissues to facilitate increased range of motion, as the stretch reflex will increase muscular tension in response to the bouncing action.

138. B: Peptide hormone. Insulin is a peptide hormone that is secreted by the pancreas when blood and amino acid levels are elevated. Insulin's role is to facilitate the removal of amino acids and blood glucose; and to deposit them into the cell, e.g., muscle tissue, liver, or adipocytes.

139. B: Excess post-exercise consumption refers to the increased rate of oxygen above resting rates after an intense bout of exercise. This increased oxygen need post-training session causes an increased metabolic demand that causes a significant increase in the resting metabolic rate for six to twelve hours post training session.

140. C: In-season. Using a superset approach during the in-season training program is the best time of year to include this approach, as this increases the amount of work performed in a brief window of time. During the in-season training period, time is at a premium due to other obligations that

Copyright © Mometrix Media. You have been licensed one copy of this document for personal use only. Any other reproduction or redistribution is strictly prohibited. All rights reserved.
This content is provided for test preparation purposes only and does not imply an endorsement by Mometrix of any particular political, scientific, or religious point of view.

include practice, film study, position and team meetings, etc. Using a superset approach will allow the athlete to train with great focus and intensity for a brief period, and this will benefit the athlete during the season by maintaining strength, stamina, and other work capacities that may decrease during the season.

141. A: Skeletal adaptations. During childhood and adolescence, when undertaking resistance training exercises, protecting the diaphysis of the long bones and the growth cartilage is extremely important in preventing injury to these areas by emphasizing loading intensity over skill and technique acquisition. An adult will be able to handle higher training loads without risk to these areas, as these growth areas will cease growing and solidify between 17 and 22 years of age.

142. C: Prepare the athlete for demands of next training phase. An unloading week is intended to reduce overall training stress on the athlete before engaging in the next phase of the training period. This is generally intended to allow the athlete to recuperate sufficiently and begin to express some, if not all, of the trained capacities of the prior phase. This concept serves as a means for one phase to build on top of another and to avoid overreaching in the short term and overtraining in the long term. An unloading week can be very useful for athletes moving from a hypertrophy phase with significant volumes to a combination strength/hypertrophy phase with higher loading and increased training volumes or from a strength phase heading into a competition period.

143. D: In glycolysis, one molecule of glucose is reduced to two pyruvate molecules. The two pyruvate molecules can then be used through two separate mechanisms to produce energy. The first is via conversion into acetyl-coenzyme A, which is the primary means of entering the series of reactions known as the Krebs cycle. The second process for producing energy is via conversion to oxaloacetate to produce intermediaries involved in the Krebs cycle.

144. A: When training for strength and power, the neural adaptations will occur most quickly due to, in large part, the size principle. The nervous system will recruit all motor units to facilitate maximal force generation, from weakest and slowest firing to strongest and most rapidly firing. During strength and power training phases, the high-threshold units are depended on heavily to perform the required work but also become more easily recruited due to a lowered recruitment threshold. This change allows for these motor units to be recruited more effectively and with greater speed.

145. B: Anatomical and functional asymmetry of the leg. The distinction between the two patterns arises from the mechanical constraints on the two movements, due to the anatomical and functional asymmetry of the leg, and is evident in the kinetics and kinematics of each. Backpedal running is characterized by shorter stride length, increased stride frequency, greater support phase time, and smaller range of motion at the knee, hip, and ankle joints.

146. A: I, II, III, and IV. The principle of progressive overload refers to a gradual increase in the amount of external resistance an athlete must work against during training-related activities. Overload can be achieved by increasing the number of repetitions per set with a specific resistance, increasing the volume of work performed in a training session or set period (supersets, compound sets, etc.), increasing the total number of sets performed at a specific loading parameter, and reducing rest periods, which is another form of increasing work density. This is not an exhaustive list of possible applications of the overload principle other than simply adding resistance to the selected movements

Copyright © Mometrix Media. You have been licensed one copy of this document for personal use only. Any other reproduction or redistribution is strictly prohibited. All rights reserved.
This content is provided for test preparation purposes only and does not imply an endorsement by Mometrix of any particular political, scientific, or religious point of view.

147. B: 36 inches. Weight trees should be limited to a distance of 36 inches from the lifting area. This will allow space between the equipment area and the plate storage area so that the loading and unloading of plates will not be hindered by limited space, and will also help to expedite the loading and unloading process by having the necessary space to move the necessary tonnage to and from the training area. This will ensure the safety of the athletes when loading and unloading plates during training.

148. A: The concentration of a reactant or a product is wholly dependent on establishing equilibrium within the system. The law of mass action/mass action effect is specific to the concentrations of reactants or products in solution. Equilibrium is required to maintain a threshold of ATP to perform the necessary work that is being undertaken during energy production in human physiology during exercise generally and in enzyme-driven reactions specifically. Various enzymatic activities must continue throughout the exercise session to maintain threshold ATP levels, and once stimulus is reduced or ceased, these processes will discontinue.

149. B: Ensuring the primary joint involved in an exercise is aligned with the axis of resistance. The athlete must be in proper alignment for the desired joint to be loaded correctly with utmost safety and for optimal movement execution. To achieve this when using a machine or pulley system, a seat, ankle, arm, chest, or back pad may need to be adjusted.

150. A: Swimmer. Swimming is not considered a power sport, but the athlete will still need to be explosive in the pool at the starting position and will also need significant strength levels to move through the water as quickly as possible. This type of athlete would not need to train near maximal loading intensities and will not require large training volumes to be successful in his sport. The athlete will need moderate training intensity and volumes to develop the sufficient strength and resiliency needed to be successful in his sport.

151. C: The sagittal plane is the plane that passes through the posterior and anterior aspects of the body, and divides the body into left and right halves. Leg extensions and biceps curls are examples of movements that occur in the sagittal plane.

152. D: 20 seconds. The recommended rest period for athletes training to enhance muscular endurance is ≤30 seconds. This is intentional to perform large amounts of work in a brief period, which will enhance an athlete's ability to sustain effort over time. This is also a result of the percentage of 1RM that is recommended, as lighter training loads (<70 percent) can be lifted for a higher total number of repetitions per set than heavier training loads.

153. C: Post-high-intensity and high-volume training session. A high-intensity loading session coupled with high volume will require significant resources to facilitate recovery and tissue restoration because glycogen stores will be significantly depleted, along with neural and biochemical fatigue. This type of session must be supported with sufficient caloric intake post-training, with most calories being derived from carbohydrates and proteins and a minimal amount of fats.

154. D: 49-square-foot area. The suggested square footage allotment for each athlete in the stretching and warm-up area is 49 square feet. This is to allow for dynamic and static stretching exercises. Each athlete should have ample room to move in the space and to eliminate the possibility of injury due to being too close in proximity to one another. If partner stretching is an emphasis in the training program, a large stretching and warm-up area is necessary.

155. D: Selective attention. Selective attention refers to a person's ability to engage with the correct source of input, while ignoring other forms of input simultaneously. For an athlete, this means

Copyright © Mometrix Media. You have been licensed one copy of this document for personal use only. Any other reproduction or redistribution is strictly prohibited. All rights reserved.
This content is provided for test preparation purposes only and does not imply an endorsement by Mometrix of any particular political, scientific, or religious point of view.

focusing on the performance tasks required during a competitive event while ignoring other inputs such as fans, loud noises, cheerleaders, players from the opposing team, etc. An athlete who has a high capacity to focus on the important aspects of performance will perform at a higher level than an athlete who struggles to handle excessive sensory inputs.

156. A: 5 sets of 10 repetitions. When training for muscular hypertrophy, the outlined criteria call for as few repetitions as 6 per set and as many as 12. The suggested number of sets falls between 3 and 6 total sets. An athlete who performs 5 sets of 10 repetitions will perform 50 total repetitions of a given movement, which will result in the highest training volume of the options listed and will cause the greatest change in muscular hypertrophy over time.

157. D: Strength and conditioning director. The strength and conditioning director is responsible for the selection of the equipment for purchase. This is due to the strength and conditioning director's expertise and understanding of the athletic needs of the program participants. Of the options listed, he is the only one who will have this unique qualification and authority. This does not mean, however, that he has the final word on whether the equipment is purchased; budgetary constraints may limit the strength and conditioning director's options, but this is an area where communication between staff members is essential.

158. C: Lower-body plyometrics; horizontal bounding; single-leg jumps. Developing sprint speed, which is considered a form of horizontal single-leg bounding, can be achieved effectively using a combination of horizontal bounding and single-leg jumps. These exercises can also be included in a sprinting program before sprint technique and speed work.

159. D: Basic strength phase. The basic strength phase is the first phase when sport-specific and practice activities occur. This training phase is part of the preparation phase and occurs after the hypertrophy and endurance phase, and is highlighted by high-intensity training loads and moderate training volumes. The emphasis of this training phase is to improve muscular strength for the primary muscles involved in the sport-specific movements the athlete will need to perform at the highest level possible.

160. C: Acetaminophen. Ergogenic aids are pharmacological substances used to augment physiological processes to enhance athletic performance. These substances can be used to enhance muscular recovery and metabolism or to increase circulating anabolic hormones. While acetaminophen can reduce inflammation of joints and other tissues, this will not help recovery, and current research indicates that using non-steroidal anti-inflammatory drugs after a training session can hinder physiological recovery.

161. B: Strength/power phase. In the provided list, the strength/power phase is representative of one of the alterations that have been made to the Matveyev's model of periodization. The three alterations to the Matveyev model occur during the preparation phase, and they are the hypertrophy/endurance phase, the base strength phase, and the strength/power phase. Each training phase builds into the next phase, and is defined by specific training load intensities and training volumes, with intensity increasing and training volume decreasing, as the athlete moves from hypertrophy/endurance to strength/power.

162. C: Hemoglobin is a combination molecule of iron and protein, and is carried via red blood cells throughout the circulatory system of the human body. Hemoglobin serves as a transport system delivering oxygen to the body's tissues and is also responsible for buffering hydrogen ion concentrations in the blood.

Copyright © Mometrix Media. You have been licensed one copy of this document for personal use only. Any other reproduction or redistribution is strictly prohibited. All rights reserved.
This content is provided for test preparation purposes only and does not imply an endorsement by Mometrix of any particular political, scientific, or religious point of view.

163. B: 70-85 percent, 6-10 repetitions. The athlete's position on the volleyball court dictates that she will need sufficient strength and muscular resiliency in her pressing musculature as well as in her upper back. To meet this requirement, she will need to train at sufficient loading intensities to develop the strength in the targeted upper-body musculature, and this can effectively be achieved with 70-85 percent loading intensity. At that intensity level, she will develop over the entire off-season program. To develop muscular resiliency and work capacity, she will need to train with a sufficient number of repetitions per set, which should fall between 6 and10 repetitions.

164. A: A uniaxial joint is a joint that rotates about a single axis. An example of a uniaxial joint would be the elbow. Other joint arrangements consist of biaxial joints such as the ankle and wrist, or multiaxial joints that include the shoulder and hip.

165. A: Sticking point. The sticking point is the transition point between the eccentric and concentric movements. This point can occur exactly at this moment of transition or slightly above or below this transition depending on the movement pattern or an athlete's specific muscular weaknesses. It is important to note that the Valsalva maneuver can lead to a loss of consciousness and requires extreme caution.

166. A: III, I, II, IV. Best practice for competition warm-up begins with movements of a general or lower-intensity sport-specific activity, which include jogging, skipping, dribbling a basketball, or throwing a football. After the general warm-up period, the specific warm-up activities begin and will include dynamic stretching activities that mimic the movements of the sporting event, and can gradually increase in intensity up to jumping and bounding activities to prepare the nervous system for competition, but not sufficient to induce metabolic or neural fatigue.

167. D: The downregulation of insulin results in the type 2 diabetes. This is due to the resistance of the insulin receptors in the body's tissue to the secretion of insulin from the pancreas. This resistance is caused in large part by elevated, or uncontrolled, blood glucose levels over many years and is generally coupled with significant periods of inactivity.

168. C: The arterial system is broken down into two divisions, the pulmonary and systemic arteries. The pulmonary division is responsible for delivering deoxygenated blood from the heart to the lungs and returning oxygenated blood back to the heart. The systemic arteries are responsible for carrying oxygenated blood away from the heart and returning deoxygenated blood back to the heart.

169. A: Cartilaginous joints are joints between two bones via cartilage; they allow movement that is primarily intended to allow the body flexibility and elasticity, e.g., during growth or respiration.

170. A: Increased resting heart rate. Reduced resting heart rate is a primary chronic aerobic training adaptation. This occurs because of the stretching of the left-ventricle over time, which increases the volume of blood ejected per contraction of the heart but causes a reduction in the frequency of contraction. This can result in bradycardia, which is a resting heart rate of 40-60 beats per minute.

171. D: Improve strength ratios at the affected joints. Improving the strength ratio at the affected joint where frequent injuries occur is a basic step in programming to correct a structural weakness. Addressing the issue after proper rehabilitative steps have been completed would consist of addressing the underlying deficiency through properly programming the resistance training for the athlete. In this example, the athlete would be required to focus on developing posterior strength and resiliency, and this could be achieved through movement patterns that directly engage this area, e.g., deadlift, glute-ham raise, reverse hyperextension, step-ups, hip thrusts, etc., with a wide

Copyright © Mometrix Media. You have been licensed one copy of this document for personal use only. Any other reproduction or redistribution is strictly prohibited. All rights reserved.
This content is provided for test preparation purposes only and does not imply an endorsement by Mometrix of any particular political, scientific, or religious point of view.

range of repetitions from which to choose, including strength emphasis work, e.g., 4-12 repetitions per set. This phase would also see a maintenance level of quad-dominant training prescribed, and for a period of four to six weeks could be eliminated to allow all training energies to be directed to correcting the imbalance.

172. B: Power, 3-5 repetitions at 75-85 percent; structural, 4-6 repetitions at 80-90 percent. When considering using both power and structural movements in a training session, training block, or throughout a training program, the key consideration is neurological fatigue. Power movements are extremely demanding on the nervous and metabolic systems due to the technical and ballistic nature of these movements. This means programming the power movements in the program first is paramount. Limiting the athletes to a training intensity that will allow multiple repetitions per set will generate the greatest performance benefit without risking excessive fatigue accumulation in the long term. Programming the structural movements for moderate loading intensities and training volume will cause significant performance increases as well, due to improving technical skill and developing the muscular strength without pushing the boundaries of neural and metabolic recovery.

173. D: Cognitive and somatic techniques. Counterconditioning uses a combination of somatic and cognitive responses to reduce an athlete's performance-related anxiety. This is achieved through systematic desensitization that requires an athlete to engage in visualization of a stressful competitive situation; to counter the stress response, the athlete engages in progressive muscle relaxation to induce a relaxed mental and physical state.

174. D: Enhances memory. Caffeine is heavily studied and has been shown to increase fat mobilization in aerobic athletes, increase power output in anaerobically trained athletes, and enhance mental acuity and focus. Caffeine has not been shown to enhance memory or fine motor skills, as caffeine tends to excite the nervous system in a significant way that negatively affects fine motor skills and limits the capacity to focus on a singular task necessary to store subject material in long-term memory for usage on an exam or general recollection purposes.

175. B: Vertical jump. If equipment limitations are an issue when wanting to test maximal anaerobic power, the vertical jump is the most cost-effective method. To test the vertical jump, you need a wall, a measuring tape or stick, and chalk. To perform the test, the athlete will stand flat-footed next to the testing wall and reach to mark, in chalk, the highest point possible with the dominant arm. Once this has been completed, the athlete will set her feet and jump as high as possible and set her chalk mark. After the two marks have been set the measurement can be taken to assess the height of the jump.

176. D: Center of the barbell using an alternated grip. Spotting a barbell bench press in this fashion ensures that the spotter will not lose grip suddenly if the athlete is struggling to complete a set or has missed a maximum intensity load attempt. The alternated grip is the best approach to spotting the bench press.

177. D: Both affect multiple joints and muscle groups, but structural movements load the spine either directly or indirectly. Multi-joint movements are compound movements that affect multiple joints and affect large muscle areas across the body. Structural movements are also multiple joint exercises and affect large muscle areas, but are specifically movements that load the spine directly, e.g., a back squat, or indirectly, e.g., a power clean.

178. C: The electron transport chain is a component of the oxidative system that uses redox reactions that transfer electrons from donors to acceptors via an electrochemical gradient. This

Copyright © Mometrix Media. You have been licensed one copy of this document for personal use only. Any other reproduction or redistribution is strictly prohibited. All rights reserved.
This content is provided for test preparation purposes only and does not imply an endorsement by Mometrix of any particular political, scientific, or religious point of view.

system produces ATP via two different chemicals, NADH and $FADH_2$. NADH produces three molecules of ATP and $FADH_2$ produces two molecules of ATP. The ETC is extremely important for maintaining the necessary ATP stores available for energy utilization during aerobic exercise.

179. B: Decrease potential injury risks and improve performance. The primary focus of the strength and conditioning facility is to decrease potential injury risks and to improve athletic performance. The facility may offer a range of services, from restorative massages to blending smoothies, the objective of which is to decrease the risk of injury and improve performance.

180. D: 1.5 to 2.0 g/Kg of body weight. Athletes will have a higher protein need because of higher protein turnover rates, the need to maintain a positive nitrogen balance, and the need to facilitate recovery and restoration of working tissues. The general recommendation for daily protein intake for the average person is 0.8 g/Kg of body weight.

181. D: Proprioceptors are sensory receptors that can be found in joints, tendons, and muscles. These receptors are very sensitive to levels of muscular tension and changes in pressure, as well as to changes in the external environment. These receptors relay information on the moment-to-moment circumstances of the muscles to the central nervous system.

182. D: Practice specificity; closed movement skill. Athletic development for sports requires that general and specific tasks be performed to develop coordination, retain movement patterns, and transfer skills to the sport, along with the sensorimotor elements needed to perform in the athletic environment, which falls under the overarching principle of practice specificity. The athlete in the example needs to develop closed movement skills to enhance technique and execution of the required skills for his sport.

183. A: Leydig cells. The primary site of testosterone production is in the Leydig cells in the testes of males, with some testosterone being secreted from the adrenal glands. Testosterone is a steroid hormone that is derived from cholesterol, and its production is regulated via luteinizing hormone and follicle stimulating hormone.

184. D: Prevent muscle atrophy and joint deterioration. During the repair phase of tissue healing, the treatment focus is on preventing muscle atrophy and joint deterioration. This phase must be handled delicately, as the newly regenerated tissues, primarily collagen, are still vulnerable to stress, so a low-load stress process must be undertaken while still working to prevent the joint from losing range of motion. This process will allow the joint to stabilize and the tissues to heal sufficiently to begin the next phase of healing, the remodeling phase.

185. B: Combination training is a type of cross-training that requires an anaerobic athlete to train aerobically for a period to facilitate recovery from prior training sessions. There is some debate as to the overall effectiveness of this approach when considering the traits and characteristics of an anaerobic athlete's sport, as training aerobically may cause a reduction in muscle size, strength, and power.

186. C: Assistant strength and conditioning coach. The assistant strength and conditioning coach will possess many of the same responsibilities as the strength and conditioning director, but may not directly oversee the training and development of as many athletic teams. The assistant strength and conditioning coach should achieve and maintain the necessary certification credentials, as there is no differentiation from the facility or university professional standards and guidelines from those expected of the strength and conditioning director.

Copyright © Mometrix Media. You have been licensed one copy of this document for personal use only. Any other reproduction or redistribution is strictly prohibited. All rights reserved.
This content is provided for test preparation purposes only and does not imply an endorsement by Mometrix of any particular political, scientific, or religious point of view.

187. A: Meal timing, well-tolerated food choices, meal macronutrient content, and enjoyable food selection. This meal should occur three to four hours before competition to avoid gastric discomfort. Athletes should consume a meal that contains all three macronutrients, as this will allow for proper energy and blood glucose levels throughout the competition. Endurance athletes will require larger amounts of carbohydrate as a percentage of total calories consumed, because of energy demands of their selected sport. All pre-competition meals should be suited to the athlete's preferences and individual differences and responses to various food types and meal composition.

188. A: Free throw shooting; overhead press. A basketball player who is shooting a free throw must use the primary movers for the upper body, which include the triceps, the pectoral muscles, the deltoids, and the biceps, along with the forearm flexors and extensors. Using an overhead pressing movement for strength development in a basketball player meets the specific needs of the athlete's sport by targeting and training the specific muscle groups involved in this action.

189. B: Rectus abdominis and erector spinae. During spinal flexion, the rectus abdominis acts as the agonist and the erector spinae acts as the antagonist by stretching to accommodate the forward torso flexion. A muscle that is acting as an antagonist during a movement is performing a protective action, as the antagonist muscle groups are working to decelerate a force acting on the body, while also stabilizing the working joints.

190. B: Contusion. A contusion is a trauma that occurs in the muscles and the tendons of the affected muscle. A contusion occurs because of direct trauma, usually a heavy impact or sudden, excessive stretching of the muscle, and results in the accumulation of blood and fluid in the tissues surrounding the injured area. This injury occurs as a result of an external force and is not a result of overuse or overtraining.

191. D: Increased anabolic hormone activity. Older men who engage in high-intensity resistance training experience increased anabolic hormone activity. Research suggests high-intensity resistance training in older males causes similar mechanisms in younger males. The hormonal alterations are accompanied by higher nitrogen retention, increased resting metabolism, and reduced body fat.

192. B: Heart rate reserve. Heart rate reserve is the difference between an athlete's maximal heart rate, measured in a laboratory during exercise testing, and the resting heart rate. Because this process requires an athlete to undergo laboratory testing procedures to assess his actual maximal heart rate, this will allow the strength and conditioning coach to assign the training intensities for the athlete more accurately. This method is superior to age-predicted and Karvonen methods for estimating aerobic training intensities.

193. D: Recovering from an injury. Using a body part split in an athletic training program is usually not the most effective method for developing an athlete. Body part split training requires limiting training frequency and the movements used. Power and structural movements require large muscle groups to work together and are difficult to segment according to predominant muscle activity. An athlete who is returning from an injury, or is currently rehabilitating an injury, can benefit from training the body parts, as this will allow the athlete to train around an injured area and still train non-affected muscles and joints. This approach will result in better results than rehabilitation or avoiding training.

194. C: Evaluate the athlete's jumping technique. After evaluating an athlete's balance, strength, and speed, the coach should evaluate the athlete's jumping technique, as this is necessary to

Copyright © Mometrix Media. You have been licensed one copy of this document for personal use only. Any other reproduction or redistribution is strictly prohibited. All rights reserved.
This content is provided for test preparation purposes only and does not imply an endorsement by Mometrix of any particular political, scientific, or religious point of view.

develop a plyometric program. If the coach is not aware of movement errors in the athlete's jump, then the training program will not be successful.

195. A: The semilunar valves, the aortic and pulmonary valves, are responsible for preventing backflow into the ventricles during ventricular relaxation (diastole). This function is passive, as these valves open and close based on the directional pressures produced by the heart. Backward pressure causes the valves to close, while forward pressure opens the valves to allow movement of blood out of the ventricles.

196. C: Power is defined as the time rate of doing work, or power = work/time. Power can also be calculated as the product of an object's velocity and force on an object in the direction in which the object is moving.

197. B: Needs analysis. Performing a needs analysis is a two-step process that requires the strength and conditioning coach to evaluate the movements and physiological requirements for a specific sport as well as evaluating the specific needs of the individual athlete. This process ensures accuracy in addressing the essential needs of competition, while also considering the specific needs of an individual athlete based on her injury history, training status, and physiological status.

198. B: Complete health and movement screenings. Following the standard pre-screening practices –which include completing the health history questionnaire and implementing developmentally appropriate movements, loading intensities, training frequency, and volume for an older adult – will produce the desired effect on the trainee without engaging in any risky behaviors that may lead to injury due to thinning joints or falls. There are few, if any, limitations on an individual who has been diagnosed with osteopenia.

199. A: High intensity; low volume. The strength/power phase is the final stage in the preparation phase and is characterized by high-intensity, lower-volume training activities. Activities that take place in this training phase include high-intensity plyometric activity, sprinting against resistance, and resistance training that includes power/explosive exercises with heavy training loads and low training volumes.

200. A: Barbell row. The barbell row is the correct answer because this movement does not occur in a prone position, the bar does not move overhead, and the spine is not directly loaded by the barbell. The athlete can safely execute the lift on the platform and abandon the lift if necessary without fear of injury or being unable to complete the lift. It is important to note, that the trainer must always be alert, even if they are not technically spotting.

201. C: Type-I muscle fibers have the greatest capacity for morphological and physiological adaptations to aerobic training, due to their higher initial oxidative capacity and the effect that training has on the size and number of mitochondria in the muscle cells along with the volume of circulating myoglobin. Type I muscle fibers have a higher initial oxidative capacity than type II variants, which is increased significantly and much greater than other muscle fiber type. Type I fibers will also hypertrophy in response to aerobic training, though not to the same degree as the type II fiber types when undertaking anaerobic training programs, e.g., resistance training and sprint conditioning programs.

202. D: 30 seconds. The correct period for PNF stretching techniques is 30 seconds. This is primarily to allow for an increased range of motion to be sustained for a period long enough to increase the range of motion but not enough to elicit a negative response by increasing muscular tension due to stretching the muscle too far and for too long.

Copyright © Mometrix Media. You have been licensed one copy of this document for personal use only. Any other reproduction or redistribution is strictly prohibited. All rights reserved.
This content is provided for test preparation purposes only and does not imply an endorsement by Mometrix of any particular political, scientific, or religious point of view.

203. B: Decreased physical endurance. Ketosis can be detrimental for an athlete, as the body needs significantly higher levels of energy substrate to perform higher-intensity or long-duration activities, and the supply of energy from ketosis will not provide adequate energy substrate for optimal performance levels. Transitioning into this state due to a low-carbohydrate diet can affect performance by reducing physical endurance, mental focus, cognitive function, and the ability to produce maximal muscular contractions for absolute strength purposes or high-velocity muscle activities such as sprinting or jumping.

204. B: Swimming in the ocean. Swimming in the ocean is the best example of which activity exemplifies neuromuscular control. Of the options listed, this is the most significantly changing environment with which the individual's nervous system will interact. The changing of the tide will affect the individual's ability to stabilize the body in the water and maintain a set directional heading, while also requiring varying levels of force to move through the water.

205. C: Need for increased recovery time. Athletes who train with maximal or near-maximal lifting intensities will require longer recovery times between training sessions. This is necessary because of the neural and muscular fatigue that occurs when lifting at heavy training intensities.

206. A: The vertebral column in the human body can have between 32-34 vertebrae. There are 7 cervical vertebrae, 12 thoracic vertebrae, 5 lumbar vertebrae, 5 sacral vertebrae, and 3-5 coccygeal vertebrae.

207. C: Lower back is highly arched to increase spinal stability. The lower back is highly arched, which suggests there is no contact with the bench or back pad and is not considered to be part of the five points of body contact in the supine position. When performing supine resistance exercises, the body should contact the bench/ground at five points. The head should be firmly in place on the bench or back pad, the shoulders and upper back firmly in place and even on the bench or back pad, the buttocks placed evenly on the bench or seat and under the hips, with the right and left foot placed firmly and flatly on the floor.

208. D: Assistance. Assistance exercises are movements that recruit smaller muscle groups, involve one primary joint, and serve to balance out muscular imbalances. Exercises that fit into this category can be added to a training program without the strength and conditioning coach being concerned with overtraining or adding substantial training volume to an athlete's program, as these movements do not place significant demand on the neural system and do not require significant loading to elicit the desired training effect.

209. C: Stride frequency. Stride frequency is the primary determinant of an athlete's maximal velocity due to greater change in stride frequency as speed reaches maximal velocity, as stride length is relatively unchanged at maximal velocity.

210. D: Free swimming. An athlete who has completed his competitive season should engage in some light activity that is not related to his sport skill. This activity should be a low-intensity, non-baseball sport activity, and free swimming is the selected option as this best meets the core criteria of the second transition phase. The other activities listed are not excellent choices. Motocross is a dangerous activity for an athlete to engage in during the off-season. High-intensity intervals are too demanding and do not fit into the second transition paradigm. Lounging on the beach, while leisurely in nature, does not require any activity; while an athlete should rest, light-to-moderate general activity should be engaged in every day.

211. A: A shift in momentum because of force, (Impulse = Force x Time). An impulse changes the momentum of an object as a result of a force and is required to achieve a predetermined

Copyright © Mometrix Media. You have been licensed one copy of this document for personal use only. Any other reproduction or redistribution is strictly prohibited. All rights reserved.
This content is provided for test preparation purposes only and does not imply an endorsement by Mometrix of any particular political, scientific, or religious point of view.

momentum in less time or greater momentum in a set period. This essentially outlines the necessity of high rates of force production to generate the requisite momentum to move an object, e.g., an athlete sprinting down the track from a dead start in a set time.

212. C: Establishes total cost. The feasibility study is primarily intended to assess the costs of building and establishing the necessary components of a strength and conditioning facility. The feasibility study also serves to assess the conceptual strengths and weaknesses of a facility as a secondary focus to determine its practical viability and to make changes to the initial business plan and concept.

213. B: Exercise relief patterns. Properly administering exercise relief patterns during speed-endurance training sessions is very important because the work-to-rest ratio needs to be adequate to facilitate proper neurological patterns and to avoid premature fatigue, but also needs to challenge the athlete's metabolic responses to become fatigue resistant. To achieve proper work-to-rest ratios, the coach should monitor an athlete's technique when he engages in the training activity and track the training volume from session to session.

214. A: Goal repetitions. Setting goal repetitions for a training session, e.g., 3-5 repetitions for 3-6 sets, will allow an athlete to train slightly below her maximal capacities without the athlete fretting about a poor performance when she is not at her peak abilities. This approach serves as a form of auto-regulation, as training intensity and volume are modulated based on the athlete's day-to-day capacities instead of strict adherence to a rigid set and rep scheme that would force the athlete to attempt to work beyond her capacity, leading to poor performance and possibly compromising a training block or program.

215. B: IV, I, III, II. Lower-body plyometric intensity levels are established by assessing the metabolic and neural demands placed on the athlete's body. Jumps that require lower force levels to generate the movement are of lowest impact, while jumps that require higher force levels are of higher impact.

216. A: Strength. Rotating the sequenced training blocks for an athlete who has just completed an agility-focused training block to begin to develop strength qualities addresses the physical quality that was trained at maintenance levels and will necessarily need to be trained in the next training block. This will also allow the progress made during the agility training block to manifest and continue to improve via enhanced neural connections, but increases in strength from the current training block will also play a role. Sequenced training is intended to develop multiple characteristics separately while also relying on the relationships between characteristics to develop the athlete's capacities.

217. C: Deconditioned football player. In this example, the deconditioned football player would benefit the most from circuit training, as this will allow him to perform a high volume of work with minimum rest periods, which will contribute to improving muscular endurance and work capacity in the upper and lower body, while also enhancing cardiorespiratory fitness. If the athlete is overweight, this approach will also contribute to shedding the excess body fat.

218. C: Competition; peaking. When preparing an athlete for a single competitive event, the proper approach is to engage in a peaking strategy that will push the athlete's performance to the highest level possible for a three-week period. The peaking strategy differs from a maintenance approach of moderate intensity and moderate volumes, as this period calls for very high intensity and very low training volumes to maximize the necessary characteristics for competition.

Copyright © Mometrix Media. You have been licensed one copy of this document for personal use only. Any other reproduction or redistribution is strictly prohibited. All rights reserved.
This content is provided for test preparation purposes only and does not imply an endorsement by Mometrix of any particular political, scientific, or religious point of view.

219. A: Increased mitochondria density in muscle tissue. A physiological adaptation that allows for greater ATP production is the increased number of mitochondria in the muscle tissue. This alteration occurs because of the increased energy demands placed on the muscles due to the continuous aerobic endurance exercise or training; this change increases the availability of ATP in closest proximity to the working muscle tissues, which is a result of increased oxidation in the tissues.

220. B: Increased injury rate. Without proper programming balance, the body will alter movement patterns to produce the necessary force needed to perform the lifts and perform in competition. These alterations, over time, will lead to increased injury rates. To prevent this from occurring, the strength and conditioning coach must build a balance between the muscle groups at intersecting joints. This does not necessarily mean equalizing strength in antagonist muscle groups, but improving the strength ratios, e.g., hamstring to quadriceps strength at 3:4, which will prevent significant injuries and joint breakdown over time.

Copyright © Mometrix Media. You have been licensed one copy of this document for personal use only. Any other reproduction or redistribution is strictly prohibited. All rights reserved.
This content is provided for test preparation purposes only and does not imply an endorsement by Mometrix of any particular political, scientific, or religious point of view.

Thank You

We at Mometrix would like to extend our heartfelt thanks to you, our friend and patron, for allowing us to play a part in your journey. It is a privilege to serve people from all walks of life who are unified in their commitment to building the best future they can for themselves.

The preparation you devote to these important testing milestones may be the most valuable educational opportunity you have for making a real difference in your life. We encourage you to put your heart into it—that feeling of succeeding, overcoming, and yes, conquering will be well worth the hours you've invested.

We want to hear your story, your struggles and your successes, and if you see any opportunities for us to improve our materials so we can help others even more effectively in the future, please share that with us as well. **The team at Mometrix would be absolutely thrilled to hear from you!** So please, send us an email (support@mometrix.com) and let's stay in touch.

If you'd like some additional help, check out these other resources we offer for your exam:
http://mometrixflashcards.com/CSCS

Copyright © Mometrix Media. You have been licensed one copy of this document for personal use only. Any other reproduction or redistribution is strictly prohibited. All rights reserved.
This content is provided for test preparation purposes only and does not imply an endorsement by Mometrix of any particular political, scientific, or religious point of view.

Additional Bonus Material

Due to our efforts to try to keep this book to a manageable length, we've created a link that will give you access to all of your additional bonus material:

mometrix.com/bonus948/cscs

Copyright © Mometrix Media. You have been licensed one copy of this document for personal use only. Any other reproduction or redistribution is strictly prohibited. All rights reserved.
This content is provided for test preparation purposes only and does not imply an endorsement by Mometrix of any particular political, scientific, or religious point of view.

Made in the USA
Coppell, TX
23 November 2024